Scope of Public-Sector Bargaining

Scope of Public-Sector Bargaining

First George W. Taylor Memorial Conference on Public Sector Labor Relations

Walter J. Gershenfeld
J. Joseph Loewenberg
Center for Labor and Human
Resource Studies
Temple University

Bernard Ingster
Hay Associates

Lexington Books
D.C. Heath and Company
Lexington, Massachusetts
Toronto

Library of Congress Cataloging in Publication Data

Main entry under title:
    Scope of public-sector bargaining.

    Includes bibliographical references.
    1. Collective bargaining—Government employees—United States—
Addresses, essays, lectures. I. Gershenfeld, Walter J. II. Loewenberg, J.
Joseph. III. Ingster, Bernard.
HD8008.S37   331.89'041'353   76-53904
ISBN 0-669-01298-x

Published simultaneously in Canada.

Printed in the United States of America.

International Standard Book Number: 0-669-01298-x

Library of Congress Catalog Card Number: 76-53904

Contents

Foreword

George Taylor's extraordinary contributions to the shaping of industrial collective bargaining and labor-relations policies in the United States—recognized with the award of the Presidential Medal of Freedom by President Kennedy and its presentation by President Johnson—are increasingly becoming significant for public employers.

In many ways George Taylor was very close to Hay Associates. A number of Hay consultants were his students at Wharton, and two of my partners served with him during his chairmanship of the War Labor Board and the National Wage Stabilization Board. On many occasions we had discussions concerning his perception of the managerial insights and technical skills that would be needed by public administrators as they entered into collective-bargaining relationships.

From these discussions it was clear that our national economy will be substantially affected by this new form of employee participation in public-employment decision making, and the lesson of private-sector management experience in a changing role for public administrators is essential. Private-sector collective bargaining also might change as a result of a massive extension of bargaining in the public sector.

To the great sorrow of many, Dr. Taylor's death left the nation early in our experiences with public-sector collective bargaining. But that beginning has been a substantial one, and important evidence is developing about the forms and consequences of public-employee bargaining. The public-policy issues are becoming clear.

To help initiate a disciplined study of these policy questions, Hay Associates and Temple University sponsored a George W. Taylor Conference on Public Sector Labor Relations and commissioned the papers included in this volume. The influences of the events described here will be felt in the executive offices of every industrial and commercial organization in the United States, because these events are, in fact, affecting the basic character of our economy.

Milton L. Rock
Managing Partner
Hay Associates

Themes of George Taylor

Although I was never a formal student of Professor George Taylor, he was one of a handful of teachers in the best sense of the word from whom I learned the most. My association with him spanned almost 30 years and a vast variety of circumstances. They included the days of the War Labor Board in World War II and the Wage Stabilization Board in the difficult Korean period, our association in the Kaiser Long Range Sharing Plan in the 1960s and in a special mediation board with Judge Fahy appointed by President Johnson for a railroad dispute, and the association we had with David Cole and other colleagues on the New York Governor's Committee on Public Employee Relations. I worked with him on a variety of publications like the CED study of 1961, *The Public Interest in National Labor Policy*, and a volume entitled *New Concepts in Wage Determination* (1957). Also, on numerous occasions I visited the University of Pennsylvania for various industrial-relations seminars and meetings, just as George Taylor visited us in Cambridge. These experiences were always learning opportunities for me.

These contacts do small justice to the richness and the diversity of his career and ideas, because they neglect his role in a vast range of still other activities. Particular attention should be paid to his role in the development of the impartial umpireship in a number of labor-management situations, such as those involving hosiery, clothing, and General Motors. Indeed, he played a critical role in the development of the modern umpire institution itself as it has emerged after the Wagner Act in industrial settings. Arbitration has been changed from a broad-interest setting into the umpireships that are now conventional in our industrial world, limited to the interpretation and application of the agreement. He was mediator and arbitrator par excellence. He played a significant leadership role in the University of Pennsylvania. Perhaps most of all, to those of my generation he was the leader and teacher who nurtured and stimulated a whole generation, not so much of academic professors as practitioners in the arts and in the service of collective bargaining and arbitration.

There was another world—his consulting and counseling of management and unions and of government officers and even presidents. The thought I am trying to convey is that because of the diversity of roles and the wide range of activities associated with George Taylor, each of us may tend to remember him for only one activity and thereby neglect the whole.

There were certain central themes and convictions in his ideas and his views. The first theme is that industrial relations are very much the product of and are conditioned by the technology and the economic environment in which they take place. He was prone to emphasize that the change in technology and the change in competition in the economic setting becomes decisive to the problems of workers and managers, and to industrial relations and collective bargaining.

His first book was an elaboration of this theme, and the theme never left him. It served him well in each individual situation into which life subsequently took him. The first words of his first book *Significant Postwar Changes in the Full Fashioned Hosiery Industry*, a short volume of 118 pages published in 1929, are: "In recent years it has been increasingly plain that the normal state of American industry is one of change. Increasing mechanization, greater production, the introduction of style in many products, and the consequent obsolescence of others are but a few of the recent changes that have taken place in our dynamic industrial society."

He goes on in that book to explain a whole set of circumstances, not the least of which were the flapper era and the rise in the height of women's skirts, and the interest in silk, colors, and sheerness, which led the full-fashioned hosiery industry to expand to two and a half to three times its size. George Taylor fastened his eye on the fundamentals of changes in technology, the economic environment, price, style, sheerness, inventory, and skills that are decisive to industrial relations. He emphasized the decisive role of improved management. He always reminded us of these basic elements.

It is significant that his first book has a distinctive perspective. It was written primarily not as a scholarly volume but rather as that of a consultant in the trade: "This study has been made from the point of view of a consultant investigating the industry for the different branches of the trade" (p. 7). He regarded the trades as the hosiery manufacturers, the hosiery-machine manufacturers, and the knitters—the workers and their union officials.

The second theme recurrent in his work and his spirit is the emphasis that collective bargaining is a centerpiece of industrial relations, and his concern was how to make it work better for the workers, the managers, and the public.

The second book he wrote over his own name alone was *The Government Regulation of Industrial Relations*, published in 1948, which depicted in large part his World War II experience and his convictions developed from that period. At the outset of the preface to this volume are these words: "Ever since the right of employees to organize and to have representatives of their own choosing were given governmental protection by the Wagner Act, the great industrial relations challenge has been the effectuation of collective bargaining as a constructive, social institution" (p. vii). At the end of the volume he says:

There is no certainty at all that the ideal of industrial self-government through collective bargaining will be realized. It is virtually certain that the alternative is government regulation of industrial relations by a combination of rules affecting the balance of power and directly specifying the terms of employment. That prospect alone would seem to justify unusual efforts to create a stronger collective bargaining. (p. 372)

As he looked at that institution, he concentrated on certain features: the critical role of the duration of the agreement and its linkage to the no-strike provision;

management rights and union security; the critical role of grievance procedure and the arbitration process as centerpieces with varying styles and practices geared to the special problems of each and every relationship.

The third theme in his writing and in his life and teaching was to see industrial relations always as a part of the larger problem of making modern democracy work.

George Taylor and I used to exchange course outlines. From the first page of his 1964 course outline are these words:

Labor-management relations are an aspect of the broader problem of making democracy work. Ours is a meeting of minds society, and not one that is based on the arbitrary imposition of rules and regulations. A basic concept is reflected in our industrial relations in the proposition that voluntary agreement between the parties of direct interest is the democratic way of establishing the terms and conditions of employment. . . . In our kind of a democracy, differences are to be resolved by agreement, or at least acquiescence in the accommodation which is worked out.

There is no lesson more important for industrial relations and, in our time, for the larger society in which we live than the process of democratic accommodation or acquiescence under which one interest does not push its concerns to ultimate limits or "go all the way."

The last of the themes is central to an appreciation of George Taylor's thought and life: the need to reconcile private decision making with public interest, to reconcile collective bargaining on one hand with national concerns and national economic policy making on the other. He was highly distrustful of many of the superficial and formula-type ways of achieving that objective, which have been advanced in our time, not the least of which are guideposts and guidelines.

In the Termination Report of the War Labor Board, in 1946, he wrote the introduction that included this key sentence, "It soon became evident that the work of the Board centered about solving problems rather than determining arguments." How much of our time and effort is wasted in seeking to try to determine arguments rather than solving problems.

Again you find this sentence in a speech he gave in 1971. He said, "No simple imposed formula, and no clever gimmick can sublimate the need for an acceptable accommodation of diverse interests." That is the problem of reconciliation of private interests in the public good. Or take another quotation on this theme from the 1965 paper before the National Academy of Arbitrators.

One has to be notably unobservant to overlook the increasing public interest and concern over the possibility that the total effect of fragmented wage and price decisions in private power centers may impede or even prevent attainment of the national goals established as vital to the national well being and safety. . . . Fundamentally involved is a harmonizing of governmental and private policies, which to an unprecedented degree have substantially interacting effects. There is little or no evidence of a disposition in the United States to phrase this problem in such terms let alone to seek ways of dealing with it. (*Proceedings of 18th Annual Meeting, National Academy of Arbitrators*, Washington, D.C., 1965, p. 201)

He concluded: "The search for the answer is largely to be found ultimately, I believe, through a greater degree of cooperation between representatives of labor, management, and the government, than presently seems to be possible" (p. 202), and I concur totally.

These quotations on these four themes seem to pervade his life and experience. There is one further quality that deserves special mention—the quality of inventiveness. George Taylor was inventive, not in the sense of a person looking for a patent—he was not concerned about immediate practical applicability, but about inventing a workable set of precepts and policies from individual cases. His great strength was to take a case, or a group of cases, and to develop from them a set of precepts and policies that had much more general application. He was often inventive and thus able to accomplish something in a way that no one else who had looked at the problem could. He developed so clearly proposals in an institutional setting that produced practical and administrable results.

A couple of illustrations in the context of World War II may be helpful. The Little Steel Formula and its applications were developed to deal with a very complicated range of wage problems recognizing that wartime inflation had distorted wage relationships. The peg points in textiles and the order that led to the CWS wage structure of basic steel were illustrations of imaginative problem solving. The contributions to the institution of industrial umpireships, and the separating of grievance arbitration as we know it today from umpireships of the past are other illustrations.

I would like to call attention to development in my own work which I believe is in the spirit of George Taylor. My approach to problem solving certainly owes a great deal to our association over the years. I was recently able to announce that we were sending to Congress a bill seeking to review the collective-bargaining structure of the construction industry. The legislation is designed to improve the processes of collective bargaining in that troublesome industry, not by having the federal government lay out in detail the substantive answers about the scope of bargaining or the structure of bargaining or a host of other related difficult questions, but by setting a bargaining mechanism for the national leaders on both sides of that industry so the process of collective bargaining itself will improve the results of bargaining.

I emphasize that fundamental to all of George Taylor's work was a concern to enable collective bargaining to work better, and his keen recognition that modern industrial society does not have a viable or desirable alternative. You either make collective bargaining work or the government will do it through regulation. There is no other course. Today our country faces the question of how to deal in the employment area, in areas of pension and safety, and with reference to hundreds of laws on our books, in a way so regulation does not eventually stifle, overcome, or eventually displace collective bargaining. The Labor Department, in 1940, administered perhaps 16 major statutes. Today the department administers 134 major statutes. The Labor Department has been turned into one, if not the major, regulatory agency of the federal government. So the way in which one approaches the regulatory process is vital to the future of collective bargaining.

Let me indicate one illustration of an effort to try to make collective bargaining and the regulatory process compatible, so the virtues of the collective-bargaining process will permit different answers in different circumstances, different rules tailor-made—and rightly the term is used—to the special circumstances of each and every enterprise or union or sector of our economy. Some time ago I was confronted with the problem of dealing with the fact the federal government provides subsidies to local transit companies, and that legislation proscribes that the secretary of Labor shall determine certain protective provisions that shall apply to any employee adversely affected by the capital outlays or operating economies developed from government grants. The legislation is an invitation for secretaries of Labor to propose rules and regulations and issue them in the *Federal Register* for comment, getting conflicting comments from unions and from management; then not knowing what really should be done, the secretary goes his way, which exacerbates the situation, which leads to years in the courtrooms.

In this situation I was able to persuade the three major union groups involved and the Association of Transit Managements to engage in negotiations over what those rules ought to be. I was able to secure one of George Taylor's old War Labor Board students, Lew Gill, to work with me. In a few days we had a 13-page document, which was signed and ratified by all of the unions and the management, and I was happy to issue it. Moreover, it had a three-year term. That is the way in which the collective-bargaining process and the regulatory process can be made more compatible. Our present posture, otherwise, is on a course of mutual collision to the great detriment of the freedoms for which collective bargaining stands.

It is important to make collective bargaining work in our society in the ways George Taylor has spelled out for us, for if we cannot make it work by finding acceptable accommodation of diverse interests, we have no chance at all to make the larger purposes of our democratic society work well.

John T. Dunlop
Lamont University Professor
Harvard University

Scope of Public-Sector Bargaining

1

An Introduction to the Scope of Bargaining in the Public Sector

Walter J. Gershenfeld

The Scope of the Bargaining Issue

By *scope of bargaining* we mean "What subjects are bargainable?" That is, we are concerned with which aspects of the employment relationship shall be determined bilaterally or unilaterally by management in the public sector. Strong differences of opinion exist between public employers and public-employee unions as to what may be negotiated. Public-employee unions often seek an enlargement of the scope of bargaining. Public employers with a tradition of managerial control frequently attempt to limit topics subject to bilateral determination.

Guidelines provided by legislation and executive orders may raise as many questions as they resolve. The parties face complex problems not only about what may appear on the bargaining table, but also about the manner in which subjects may be discussed or bargained. For example, some legislation distinguishes between bargainable subjects, often defined generally, and "meet and confer" rights with regard to managerial policy affecting wages and conditions of work. At times, the impact of managerial policy on wages and conditions is deemed to be bargainable by reviewing authorities. It is understandable that debate arises as to the dividing lines among these categories.

The field of education illustrates the nature of the problem. Ralph Brown has considered bargaining in education and points out the intermingling of interests likely to affect the scope of bargaining:

First, the matter of salaries is linked to the matter of workload; workload is then related directly to class size; class size to range of offerings, and range of offerings to curricular policy. Dispute over class size may also lead to bargaining over admissions policies. This transmutation of academic policy into employment terms is not evitable, but it is quite likely to occur.[1]

The scope-of-bargaining issue is important because it goes to the heart of the collective-bargaining relationship. The public employer is understandably uneasy when he believes that union demands affect the core of the agency mission. Employees and their organizations are equally distressed when they believe legislation, executive orders, and/or employers unreasonably seek to limit their legitimate concerns involving income and security.

In this chapter, we first consider the nature of the scope question in the private sector. Private-sector scope doctrines have had an important effect on

1

scope in public-employee bargaining. Next, we indicate some of the special aspects of public-employee bargaining that impinge on the scope of bargaining and identify the spectrum of scope-of-bargaining approaches. Finally, the basis for selection of the jurisdictions covered in this volume is discussed.

Background and Perspective

The Private Sector

Ever since the National Labor Relations Act in 1935 defined the scope of bargaining as "wages, hours and other terms and conditions of employment," heated controversy has existed over what can, may, and should be discussed or negotiated by the parties. In fact, in 1945 a presidential commission foundered over management rights and the determination of what was bargainable. Over the years, scope-of-bargaining questions have come to the National Labor Relations Board (NLRB) under the aegis of Section 8(d) of the National Labor Relations Act:

For the purposes of this section, to bargain collectively is the performance of the mutual obligation of the employer and the representative of the employee to meet at reasonable times and confer in good faith with respect to wages, hours, and other terms and conditions of employment, or the negotiation of an agreement, or any question arising thereunder, and the execution of a written contract incorporating any agreement reached if requested by either party, but such obligation does not compel either party to agree to a proposal or require the making of a concession. . . .

The NLRB has created a trichotomy of bargaining topics. In the first category are those subjects that are patently illegal. These subjects, for example, closed shop or hot-cargo clauses, may legitimately be denied discussion at the bargaining table when they appear. There can, of course, be topics that only one party believes to be illegal. The admissibility of a topic to bargaining then depends upon an administrative and/or court determination that the topic falls within the legitimate scope of bargaining. The remaining two categories used by the NLRB are mandatory and nonmandatory bargaining topics.

Mandatory topics are those judged to be within the purview of "wages, hours, and other terms and conditions of employment." The definition has continually stretched to accommodate a wider variety of topics. Students today are astonished to learn that the subject of pensions became a mandatory subject of collective bargaining only after a Supreme Court decision.[2] Until 1949 there was no legal compulsion to bargain over pensions. Similarly, for years companies held that subcontracting was a matter for unilateral managerial determination. In the Fibreboard case the Supreme Court ruled that replacement of employees in a bargaining unit with employees of an outside contractor to do the same work was subject to an obligation to bargain.[3] Although the U.S. Supreme Court limited its consideration to the specific facts of Fibreboard, a spate of cases having to do with other aspects of subcontracting and location of operations came to the fore.

As noted and illustrated above, the general trend in the private sector has been toward a growing scope of bargaining. More topics are found to be within the mandatory bounds of bargaining. When bargaining subjects are mandatory, there must be good-faith bargaining. Importantly, the party seeking the benefit or gain may insist upon its position to the point of impasse. The right to strike or take a strike is present and may only be enjoined in the interstate private sector for reasons of national emergency, and even then, the result can only be to delay but not eliminate a strike. Some students of labor relations believe we are on the verge of a major expansion of private-sector scope as unions begin to consider seriously the question of employee participation in management.[4]

When a subject is not illegal and also not mandatory, the parties are free to bargain about it at their joint pleasure. Either party may refuse with impunity to consider a nonmandatory bargaining topic. Nor may it be taken to the point of impasse and strike by a party without risking unfair labor-practice sanctions. The rub, of course, is the grey area between mandatory and nonmandatory topics.

Thus, although questions remain and issues emerge, the scope of bargaining is relatively well established in the private sector. The public sector, on the other hand, is in an evolutionary phase with regard to the scope of bargaining.

The Public Sector

For many years, the public employer relied on the Tenth Amendment to the Constitution as the source of the sovereign power that precluded public-employee organization and bargaining. Additionally, the public employee, although not well paid, was presumably satisfied with the security of his lot in a manifestly insecure world. As distance from the depression grew, as aspirations rose, and as public employees recognized disparity in rewards with other segments of society, public employees became restive. Surprisingly, with a minimum of opposition, the doctrine of public-employer sovereignty was set aside and the public employer and public employee both approached the bargaining table, albeit as novices. Almost inevitably, much of the early debate focused on what was bargainable.

Here, the public sector derived much from private-sector experience. Many of the laws affecting public employees mirror the National Labor Relations Act by providing for bargaining over "wages, hours, and other terms and conditions of employment" or similar language. The effect is substantial when we consider that more than 30 states now have comprehensive public-employee bargaining laws or laws covering certain classes of public employees. It is not unusual in public-sector jurisdictions to find the distinction among mandatory, nonmandatory, and illegal topics. Often, nonmandatory topics are labeled "meet-and-discuss" items. There is consensus, too, that the scope of bargaining has tended to widen in the public sector as it has in the private sector.

At this point the analogy stops. The commonplace NLRA language has received varying but often more limited interpretation with regard to scope for public employees than it has for private employees. Interpretations have in fact differed sharply among states with the same language covering scope. Some states and the federal sector have inserted a management-rights proviso in their legislation or executive order. In the federal sector the management-rights requirement must be part of each agreement negotiated. At times, distinctions are made in legislation among classes of employees as to which subjects may be negotiated.

Public-sector scope of bargaining is also affected by factors that distinguish the public employee from the private employee. In most cases the public employee does not have the legal right to strike. The lack of a right to strike, has, of course, not always inhibited strikes. Interestingly, the scope of bargaining has, at times, widened to a greater degree among public employees without a statutory right to strike. The public is increasingly disaffected by public-employee strikes. When key underlying issues involve scope differences, the general public is not likely to be sympathetic to the inability of the bargainers to settle on what should be bargained.

The definition of the public employer, that troublesome split frequently present between financial control and administrative control, has created scope problems. The governing board of a school system, public college, or prison may be responsible for the operation of the entity but may receive a significant portion of its income from city, county, and/or state sources. The employer groups party to the relationship may simply differ in their views as to what should properly be included in the bargain.

The broad coverage of many public-sector labor laws raises scope dilemmas. On the one hand, we may find professionals organized who have had a customary voice in determining the nature of the service provided. On the other hand, some public employees may be closer to the industrial model. Indeed, some transit employees have been transferred from the private sector to the public sector overnight. Unitary-scope legislation may not fit these disparate cases.

The public sector is also subject to multilateral bargaining pressures from individuals not privileged to sit at the bargaining table. End runs to and by legislators and organized positions by community groups have to be considered in terms of their impact on public-employee scope of bargaining. The important role of related law is a constant in the public sector. At the least, there is a civil-service statute and concomitant procedural regulations. To what extent do these pronouncements supersede or are themselves superseded by collective bargaining? Other laws, frequently in important fringe-benefit areas such as pensions and insurance, must be considered. In short, although the form and format of public-sector bargaining parallels much of the private sector, care must be taken to examine differences within apparent similarities and the effect on scope of bargaining of those factors that are unique to public employees qua public employees.

Approaches to Scope

The debate over scope of bargaining began in the private sector and has carried over to public-sector bargaining. In 1919 President Woodrow Wilson convened an industrial-relations conference. After 17 days of discussion, the conference closed when the management and labor participants were unable to agree on the appropriateness of union security as a bargaining issue. President Harry S. Truman called a successor conference, chaired by Dr. George W. Taylor in 1945. Although this conference was more successful in achieving agreement on some subjects, it too found the scope question intractable. Management representatives at the conference noted:

Labor members of the Committee on Management's Right to Manage have been unwilling to any listing of specific management functions. Management members of the Committee conclude, therefore, that the labor members are convinced that the field of collective bargaining will, in all probability, continue to expand into the field of management.

The only possible end of such a philosophy would be joint management of the enterprise. To this, the management members naturally cannot agree. Management has functions that must not and cannot be compromised to the public interest. If labor disputes are to be minimized by "the genuine acceptance by organized labor of the functions and responsibilities of management to direct the operation of the enterprise," labor must agree that certain specific functions and responsibilities of management are not subject to collective bargaining.[5]

Labor members of the committee responded:

Because of the complexities of these relationships, the labor members of the Committee think it unwise to specify and classify the functions and responsibilities for such specification, the Committee was unable to agree upon a joint report. To do so might well restrict the flexibility so necessary to efficient operation.

It would be extremely unwise to build a fence around the rights and responsibilities of management on the one hand and the unions on the other. The experience of many years shows that with the growth of mutual understanding the responsibilities of one of the parties today may well become the joint responsibilities of both parties tomorrow.[6]

The debate was thus joined and the management-rights clause emerged as a significant battleground in many negotiations. A fillip-of-scope consequence involved living under the agreement. Management frequently took the position that those rights not granted by an agreement were residual in management. Labor opposed this view and tried to substitute a broader problem-solving approach to contractual rights. Management often sought a "zipper clause," which purported to seal the agreement as to coverage. Unions countered by arguing that certain items not explicitly mentioned in the agreement were grievable and arbitrable by virtue of the implications of a clause. An illustration is the use of the recognition clause by unions to support a charge that subcontracting is improper.

The debate continued but, at least among sophisticated practitioners, moved to new ground. Labor argued that it was not seeking to usurp the management right to direct the enterprise, but was properly concerned with the impact of management policy on the worker. This impact notion has had important carry-over results in the public sector.

As public-sector bargaining has grown, the scope debate has achieved new levels of complexity. The public employer frequently seeks to exclude from bargaining determinations over the quality and extent of the service to be performed. Typically, the public employer does not wish to negotiate over basic policy determinations affecting the inherent mission of the organization. These positions, however, may vary somewhat between the public employer, per se, and the legislative body providing funding for the activity. One group may be more willing than the other to compromise over such issues as class size, case loads, work standards, and the like. Overall, however, there is a general, public-employer stance that seeks to limit the bargainable items to those matters not directly affecting the management determination of the thrust of the agency. Illustrative of this position is the following comment.

It is critically important for the municipal employer to stake out firmly those areas of decision-making which it regards as essential for running the public enterprise in order to preserve its flexibility of operation.[7]

Unions and professional associations, on the other hand, argue that they should be free to bargain over any and all items affecting compensation and security except when explicitly prohibited by legislation. The dilemma is illustrated by the following positions in a case involving police officers:

Patrolman's Association argues that a one-man car is basically poor police procedure and unsafe because it exposes the patrolman to an inordinate degree of risk. Safety is a condition of employment which is a legitimate subject of collective negotiations. The city argues that it has the exclusive right and duty to determine the assignment of patrolmen and to balance priorities of assignment against public safety needs. The city further argues that the question of whether to put on an additional number of patrolmen affects the tax rate on which subject the city has an exclusive mandate.[8]

The broad mandate sought by public-sector unions may result in challenge to apparently limiting language in enabling legislation. Similarly, public-employee unions often seek to establish the primary role of collective bargaining vis-à-vis civil service and other legislation affecting public employees. Unresolved bargaining-table debates over scope often bring the parties to labor boards and the courts.

In addition, legislative dispute-settlement procedures calling for interest arbitration bring the scope question to the attention of neutrals. In some of these cases, the neutral is faced with the propriety of the process itself. One of our analysts, Dr. Charles M. Rehmus, reports elsewhere on the dissent of a city arbitrator in Michigan:

Who elected the arbitration panel of which I am a part? To whom is this panel responsive? What pressures can the citizens . . . bring to bear on the panel? How do they express their satisfaction or dissatisfaction with the decision?[9]

As indicated earlier, specific challenges about negotiability normally go to labor boards and the courts. Some jurisdictions have sought, however, to answer the questions posed above by placing the cognizant legislative body as the appropriate final determinant of impasse issues. A related approach in some cities has taken the form of requiring electorate approval of negotiated items via referendum. Thus, even agreed-upon items may be rejected by voters concerned with issues covered or settlement amounts.

In some cases, interest arbitrators have considerable authority with regard to scope. In Pennsylvania, for example, the police and fire fighters arbitration statute requires that legislation required to implement an award shall be passed forthwith. However, the Pennsylvania courts have, nevertheless, found that some arbitral decisions have exceeded permissive scope.

Management-union debate over scope extends visibly into the public-sector grievance area. Arbitrability as a threshold issue is not unknown in private-sector grievance arbitration. It is in public-sector grievance arbitration, however, that matters of arbitrability reach their peak. No count is available but arbitrators are acutely conscious of the large numbers of public-sector grievance cases where the arbitrability of the item must be analyzed before the merits of the case may be considered. Scope determinations by public-sector grievance arbitrators have frequently been the subject of litigation.

Of all public-employee jurisdictions, the federal sector has been the most limiting in its approach to scope. As prestigious a group as the Labor Relations Law Committee of the American Bar Association has noted:

The most important aspect of the federal employee labor relations program, or any other labor relations program, is the scope of bargaining. The broader the scope, the greater the employee involvement and satisfaction; conversely, the greater is management's concern for its ability to manage and to operate efficiently. In fact, a major criticism of the entire federal employee labor relations program has been the extremely narrow scope of bargaining; the major items, wages and fringes are controlled by statute or regulations. . . .We full believe that the purpose of the Executive Order . . . can only be satisfied by broadening the scope of collective bargaining.[10]

Other observers have commented that widening the scope of federal-sector bargaining creates the spectre of massive expenditures of public funds essentially uncontrolled by Congress and having a substantial impact on the country. Further, the large and disparate groups involved in federal bargaining might involve themselves in whipsaw arrangements with serious strike and other potential.

In Sum

The scope of bargaining has clearly expanded in the private sector. Similarly, it is expanding in the public sector but under a blanket of far more complex concerns. Lines are being drawn and are daily being adjudicated. These lines underscore the essential scope dilemma of public employment. In the private sector, for example, automobile workers are likely to show little interest over the number of models an automobile company chooses to introduce. The automobile workers will seek to achieve appropriate remuneration and work loading in connection with these assignments. The public employer views the provision of the type of service as fundamentally a policy consideration outside the scope of bargaining. The public employee finds the nature of the service to be offered a direct determinant of his working conditions. Hence, the school board perceives the matter of class size to be an unwarranted intrusion on fundamental educational policy. The teacher unions view class size as one of the most important aspects of the teacher-performance role.

Scope-of-bargaining issues in the public arena are likely to remain with us as real concerns and not straw issues. Both sides struggle realistically because they share fundamental concern over the outcome of the scope issue.

Jurisdictions Covered

Given the primacy of the scope-of-bargaining issue, it is surprising that relatively little has been done in the way of organized analysis in the public sector. There is no shortage of arbitration, court, and labor-board decisions on the subject. The need for careful data collection and analysis of these decisions as well as practices of the parties is clear. Accordingly, the organizers of the first George W. Taylor Memorial Conference on Public Sector Labor Relations determined that a manageable and meaningful sample for our purposes would consist of six states with varying experience and the federal sector.

Wisconsin was an easy selection for inclusion in the study. Wisconsin pioneered with a public-employee bargaining law for municipal employees in 1959. The law was basically a declaration of principle but was given administrative implementation in 1961. Additional legislation affecting public-employee bargaining was passed later. Wisconsin, too, is the home of the public-employee labor-relations board with the longest period of experience.

New York and Michigan have also had extensive exposure under public-employee labor-relations statutes. In the case of New York, the statute bears the name of Dr. George W. Taylor, the honoree of this volume. New York's experience also represents a breadth flowing naturally from the size of the jurisdiction. The Michigan experience is particularly worthy of note. Court decisions have produced the anomaly of a public-sector scope of bargaining perhaps wider than the scope of bargaining in the well-organized industrial sector in that state.

Pennsylvania was, of course, the home of Dr. George W. Taylor, and the locale of this project. In its own right, however, Pennsylvania deserves reporting because of its wide and differential experience under both a general public-employee labor-relations statute and a compulsory-arbitration law for policemen and firemen. New Jersey provides a valuable comparison with its neighbors, Pennsylvania and New York. Additionally, its statute has been one of the most litigated in existence. The reason for selecting Texas was altogether different. Although it is one of the two states ostensibly outlawing public-employee bargaining, nevertheless legislation there has been interpreted to permit a form of de-facto bargaining for public employees. Although new, a separate statute permitting police and fire-fighter bargaining in Texas has come into being and warrants study.

Finally, the federal government has been a leading impetus to public-employee unionization. Executive Order 10988, issued by President John F. Kennedy in 1962, touched off widespread federal-employee unionization and served as a spur to many states in the enactment of their own legislation. It is well known that there are severe limitations on the scope of bargaining for federal employees, but the traffic in scope issues among the remaining topics has been nothing short of prodigious.

Thus, we have seven jurisdictions that have, for varying reasons, been included in this volume. In each case we have examined what the parties have done and the consequent case load for supervising labor boards or other agencies, arbitrators, and the courts. We believe the data and analysis are valuable for two principal purposes. First, the jurisdictions directly affected require this type of presentation for orderly consideration of their own experience. Second, comparison of the findings permits these jurisdictions, as well as others with or without employee labor-relations legislation, to examine comparative data as a guide to appropriate public policy in their own situation. Consequences flowing from particular approaches can be evaluated. It has often been said that the states are an experimental laboratory for public-sector labor-relations legislation. However, it is only when the results of experimentation and experience are known and understood that they provide us with a basis for useful application. It is our belief that the following chapters will provide valuable data and analysis vital to informed discussion of the scope-of-bargaining issue.

Notes

1. Ralph S. Brown, Jr., "Collective Bargaining in Higher Education," *Michigan Law Review* February 1969, p. 1075.

2. Inland Steel Company vs. United Steelworkers of America, 336 U.S. 960 (1949).

3. Fibreboard Paper Products vs. NLRB, 379 U.S. 203 (1964).

4. Charlotte Gold, *Employer-Employee Committees and Worker Participation*, Key Issues No. 20 (New York State School of Industrial and Labor Relations, Cornell University, Ithaca, N.Y., 1976).

5. *President's National Labor Management Conference*, Vol. III, Doc. 125 II/13, Washington, D.C., 1945, p. 47.

6. *President's National Labor Management Conference*, Vol. III, Doc. 120II/11, Washington, D.C., 1945, p. 45.

7. Allan W. Drachman, *Municipal Negotiations: From Differences to Agreement* (Labor Management Relations Service, Washington, D.C., 1970), p. 18.

8. Ibid.

9. Charles M. Rehmus, "Legislated Interest Arbitration," *Proceedings of the Twenty-Seventh Annual Winter Meeting*, Industrial Relations Research Association, 1974, p. 308.

10. Report of the Committee on the Law of Federal Government Employee Relations, *Section on Labor Relations Law*, American Bar Association, 1972, p. 151.

2 The Scope of Bargaining in the Public Sector in Michigan

Charles M. Rehmus

In 1965 the Michigan Legislature enacted Public Act 379, which amended an earlier Public Employment Relations Act (PERA) to allow public employees in Michigan, other than those in the constitutionally autonomous state civil service, to select a bargaining representative and to enter into collective-bargaining negotiations with their employers.[1] The legislative parameters of the duty to bargain under PERA are found in section 15, which reads, in pertinent part:

> For the purposes of this section, to bargain collectively is the performance of the mutual obligation of the employer and the representative of the employees to meet at reasonable times and confer in good faith with respect to wages, hours, and other terms and conditions of employment, or the negotiation of an agreement, or any question arising thereunder, and the execution of a written contract, . . . but such obligation does not compel either party to agree to a proposal or require the making of a concession.

Michigan does not record and publish a legislative history of its enactments, but this section is stated by those involved to have been adopted by the legislature without debate or controversy.

It is obvious that this language was patterned after section 8(d) of the National Labor Relations Act (NLRA).[2] Both statutes use almost identical language in describing the duty to bargain. The fact that there was no disagreement in the Michigan legislature over the definition of the duty to bargain in public employment suggests general approbation or at least acceptance of private-sector concepts concerning the scope of the obligation. A number of years later the Supreme Court of Michigan, in commenting on this language, concluded:

> Although we cannot state with certainty, it is probably safe to assume that the Michigan Legislature intentionally adopted §15 PERA in the form that it did with the expectation that MERC [the Michigan Employment Relations Commission] and the Michigan courts would rely on the legal precedents developed under NLRA, §8(d) to the extent that they apply to public sector bargaining.[3]

Similarly, the Michigan Court of Appeals completely followed private-sector labor law—specifically the U.S. Supreme Court's decision in *Fibreboard Paper Products* vs. *NLRB*—in a recent holding that a Michigan school district must bargain with the union of bus drivers over its decision to subcontract school bus-driving services. The Court concluded it should:

11

. . . look for guidance to federal case law construing section 8(d) of the National Labor Relations Act, since the language of the two sections is identical and the Michigan Legislature apparently sought to pattern section 15 of PERA after section 8(d) of the NLRA.[4]

In Michigan, as in the other states that have adopted statutory language on the scope of public-sector bargaining similar to that found in the NLRA, it is hardly surprising that the Michigan Employment Relations Commission (MERC, the administrative agency for PERA) and the courts have followed private-sector precepts in cases delineating the specific nature of the scope of the duty to bargain. Somewhat more remarkable is that in Michigan the evolution of decisions in recent years has had the result that the scope of bargaining is today probably *broader* in the public sector than it is in the private sector.

Scope of the Duty to Bargain

The group of public employees in Michigan that has been most active in testing the scope of bargaining before MERC has been the public school teachers. One of the first cases that moved in the direction of expanding the subject areas of bargaining beyond the traditional scope of private-sector bargaining was a Michigan administrative law judge's decision in *North Dearborn Heights School District*.[5] He delineated a list of proper subjects of collective bargaining for teachers and caused considerable furor in Michigan education circles by holding all 14 of the issues submitted to him to be bargainable, including such matters as curriculum, classroom schedules, class sizes, selection of textbooks, planning of facilities, and establishment of summer-school programs. Most of these subjects had previously been assumed by educational administrators to be within their exclusive discretion and not bargainable. Exceptions were filed to the decision, but the dispute was settled and ruled moot before it was heard on appeal. Since that time, no decision has gone quite as far, but neither has the holding there been specifically repudiated.

It is clear that matters such as those involved in *North Dearborn Heights* do relate in some way to wages, hours, and other terms and conditions of employment. Teachers' educational backgrounds, their psychological role orientation and traditional responsibilities endow the profession with a strong interest in the totality of the educational enterprise. Hence they seek to bargain over subjects of "professional" concern. Yet these same subjects about which they wish to bargain to a binding decision are undeniably matters of educational policy and sometimes are social issues as well. This overlap of bargainable subjects with public interest and management functions has led to some delicate case-by-case decision making as administrative agency and courts attempt to strike a proper balance between the several legitimate but occasionally conflicting interests.

In Michigan MERC has not accepted the standard private-sector distinction between mandatory and permissible subjects of bargaining. Instead, in the landmark opinion in *Westwood Community Schools,*[6] a majority of MERC, over the dissent of its chairman, adopted a two-part balancing test to determine whether a given subject is a management prerogative over which bargaining is voluntary with the employer or whether it is a term or condition of employment and therefore a subject over which bargaining must take place upon employee demand. The two elements of the test are these: "(1) Is the subject of such vital concern to both labor and management that it is likely to lead to controversy and industrial conflict? And, (2) is collective bargaining appropriate for resolving such issues?"[7] MERC observed that this:

. . . balancing approach to bargaining may be more suited to the realities of the public sector than the dichotomized scheme—mandatory and non-mandatory—used in the private sector. . . . Economic force is illegal in the public sector in Michigan as PERA prohibits strikes by public employees. In Michigan, in the public sector, economic battle is to be replaced by invocation of the impasse resolution procedures of mediation and fact finding.

An expansion of the subjects about which the public employer ought to bargain, unlike the private sector, should not result in a corresponding increase in the use of economic force to resolve impasses. In the absence of legal public sector strikes, our only proper concern in the area of subjects of bargaining is whether the employer's management functions are being unduly restrained. All bargaining has some limiting effect on an employer.

Therefore, we will not order bargaining in those cases where the subjects are demonstrably within the core of entrepreneurial control. Although such subjects may affect interests of employees, we do not believe that such interests outweigh the right to manage.

In reversing the Trial Examiner on this issue, we hold that the opening and terminating days of the school term are subjects about which the employer must bargain.[8]

This decision is the basis for my earlier comment that the scope of bargaining in Michigan is broader in the public than in the private sector. According to *Westwood*, since public employees in Michigan are prevented from using the strike or the threat of a strike at the collective-bargaining table, there is no reason to restrict severely the subjects that may be brought up in negotiations. The rationale is that the public employer cannot be coerced by threatened or actual work stoppages to agree with its organized employees and is under no compulsion to accept any employee proposal that unduly restricts managerial rights or is thought contrary to the broader public interest. This combination by MERC of the duty to bargain with the legal ban on strikes suggests that the list of subjects appropriate for collective bargaining has no readily apparent limit, since we have no further elucidation of what subjects might be at the nonbargainable "core" of sole managerial control.

I believe, and I am not alone in this opinion,[9] that *Westwood* is a "shining palace built upon the sand." In the first place, if the scope of bargaining may include any subject that "is likely to lead to controversy and industrial conflict," such interpretation probably includes a number of subjects not within the conventional definition of "terms and conditions of employment." In the second place, and more importantly, the fallacy of the *Westwood* test is that it relies on the effectiveness of the strike proscription contained in Michigan law. In fact, this proscription has been largely ineffective. In 1973 Michigan had more public-employee strikes—73—than any other state in the Union, and 20 percent of the nation's total.[10] This same pattern of high public-sector strike frequency has held firm for a number of years. As a result, the *Westwood* rationale is an illusion. It merely creates the possibility that some groups of public employees may force employers to bargain to impasse on subjects that in the private sector might not be mandatory subjects of bargaining.

As Professor Harry Edwards has noted, this is indeed anomalous.[11] He cites the teachers' strike in Detroit during 1973 as an example. Although the strike was unlawful from its inception and was enjoined after several weeks by court order, the injunction was not an effective sanction to bring the stoppage to an end. The teachers ignored the injunction, the board in the strike settlement agreed to withdraw its claim against the union for damages, and the union has not yet and may never have to pay the fines imposed for contempt of court. Moreover, under the terms of the strike settlement, the parties submitted the issues of salaries and classroom size to binding arbitration. The arbitrator then decided the appropriate size of classes at different educational levels, a subject that may well not have been considered a mandatory subject of bargaining in the first place if public-employee strikes in Michigan were legal and if the NLRA mandatory or permissive test defined the scope of bargaining. As Edwards puts it, "Thus, the teachers arguably gained more by virtue of a de facto right to strike than they would have gained with the traditional private sector scope of bargaining model and a lawful right to strike."[12]

Despite such criticism, in the last several years both the Michigan Court of Appeals and the state Supreme Court have adopted an expansive view of the duty to bargain, seemingly based upon rationale similar to *Westwood*.[13] For example, in *Van Buren* the court of appeals stated:

... section 15 of PERA must be even more expansively construed than its NLRA counterpart. Only by requiring mandatory bargaining on a wide range of subjects are public employees' rights protected, since pursuant to section 2 public employees are forbidden to strike. (citing *Westwood*)[14]

Yet in these same decisions basing a broad view of the bargaining obligation on the strike ban, the courts specifically continue to discuss the issue using the words mandatory and permissive, as in the quotation above. This combination of mandatory-permissive language on the one hand with the ban-on-strikes rationale on the other, although seeming illogical, in fact makes sense. If the union is strong and a subject is of real employee concern, then labeling the subject "permissive" as a legal matter may operate as small, practical restraint on union pressure to achieve some accommodation in the area. Yet there are some issues that should ultimately be left to public management to decide. Hence the combination of the broad *Westwood* rationale with the limiting concept of permissive subjects reflects the actual power realities of many bargaining relationships and yet retains the possibility of future assertion that some subjects are appropriate for discussion but not for impasse.

The Obligation to Bargain

As a conceptual matter, the scope of bargainable subject matters and the nature of the obligation to bargain in good faith are two different issues. In practice, however, at least from the employer's point of view, the two often seem alike. For Michigan public employers, the problem of knowing when they are free to take unilateral action in areas of management prerogatives, whatever they may be, is further complicated by the fact that their duty to bargain continues seemingly indefinitely. It certainly goes beyond an impasse. The city of Dearborn negotiated to impasse. It then used mediation and, failing agreement, went to fact finding. After obtaining the fact finder's recommendations, it continued to meet and discuss the recommendations with the union. The parties still were unable to agree. The city nevertheless violated its obligation to bargain when it finally acted unilaterally, not because it was in bad faith, but because it had not made "a serious attempt to reconcile its differences with the union."[15] Although Dearborn's often rigid bargaining posture is well known, it is presumably entitled under *Westwood* ultimately to be its own judge of its citizens' best interests.

Even more significantly, public employers are not relieved from the duty to bargain even when faced with an unlawful work stoppage. In *Saginaw Township Board of Education*,[16] MERC ruled that despite the fact that the union has engaged in illegal strike activity, the board nevertheless had the obligation to continue "good-faith" bargaining. This ruling perhaps reflects the fact that MERC has both enforcement and mediation obligations. From a mediator's point of view, no matter what the union's course of conduct the dispute could not be settled if the employer could not be forced to meet with the union.

Finally, as the ultimate irony, the union's use of illegal strike tactics is not a violation of *its* duty to bargain responsibly and in good faith.[17] This treatment of the obligation to bargain in good faith on the one hand and the common use of illegal strike tactics on the other as two wholly separate and unrelated issues seems almost determinedly obtuse. This muddle may have been clarified to a degree by the Michigan Supreme Court's recent decision in *Crestwood*, however.[18] There it was held that striking teachers, even those with tenure, were legally terminated by the board without a prior hearing. Once there were no longer any union adherents in the bargaining unit, as a practical matter the board's obligation to bargain may well have ended, at least for the time being.

Conflict between Scope of Bargaining and Other Laws

A number of state public-employee bargaining statutes give precedence to civil-service specifications regarding employment terms over collective-bargaining agreements. Several mandate the opposite. In Michigan the public-employee bargaining statute is silent on the subject of whether bargaining or civil service is to be given precedence. The Michigan Supreme Court, however, has consistently construed PERA as the dominant law regulating public-employee labor relations. It has based this on the state constitution's grant of power to the state legislature to resolve disputes involving local-government employees and what the court believes is an apparent legislative intent that the PERA should be the governing law for *all* public-employee labor relations.

In 1971 the court held that the original authority and duty of the Wayne County Civil Service Commission "was diminished *pro tanto*" by the PERA "to the extent of free administration of the latter."[19] For the uninitiated, this means that the court held that the commission's powers were reduced to the extent necessary to allow meaningful collective bargaining to take place.

In 1973 the court "harmonized" the authority given by the constitution to the Regents of the University of Michigan to supervise the university with that of the constitutional authority given the legislature to provide for the resolution of public-employee disputes. The court held that interns and residents of the University of Michigan Hospital were employees as well as students, and therefore entitled under PERA to engage in collective bargaining.[20] The court did limit the scope of bargaining to subjects other than those within the educational sphere, however. It gave as an example the fact that although employees normally could negotiate to discontinue a certain aspect of a job they found distasteful, ". . . interns could not negotiate working in the pathology department because they found such work distasteful." The number of hours to be devoted to training in pathology is a nonbargainable faculty-administrator decision.

In 1974 the court finally resolved a long standing tug-of-war between MERC and the inferior state courts over the question of whether residency requirements for police and fire fighters and their retirement benefits are mandatory subjects of collective bargaining under PERA. The court held that they are, even though such residence requirements and retirement benefits had been promulgated by voter-adopted city ordinance or charter, and under the State Home Rule Act.[21]

In 1975 the Michigan Supreme Court resolved a conflict between the

Teacher Tenure Act, which requires hearing *before* discharge, and PERA, which only permits an employee discharged for participating in an illegal strike to request a hearing within ten days *after* termination. As noted previously, the court held that 180 striking teachers in the Crestwood School District could be terminated regardless of tenure status without a prior hearing, in accordance with PERA.[22]

In summary, the Michigan Supreme Court has interpreted PERA and collective bargaining thereunder to take precedence in setting the terms of public-employment relationships over the powers of home-rule cities, the constitutional grant of autonomy to three of Michigan's public universities, the traditional teachers' bulwark of tenure, and the powers of local civil-service boards and commissions. I find no suggestion in any of these cases that the court is likely to back away from this general interpretation unless it is specifically instructed to do so by the legislature. Given the political power of organized labor in Michigan such a legislative change appears unlikely. Hence, Michigan public employees, other than state civil servants, may today, if they so desire, use collective bargaining as the means of establishing virtually all of the terms and conditions that affect their employment. In practice, however, the range of subjects upon which most public unions and managements in Michigan have written-contract clauses is up to the present time largely traditional and unremarkable.

Scope of Bargaining in Municipal Government

Based upon the evidence available, it appears that unionized blue-collar public employees in Michigan, like those in the private sector, have found their collective-bargaining concerns to be closely related to compensation and job security. This conclusion is based upon a 1975 study of municipal-labor agreements conducted for the Michigan Municipal League.[23] Unions have, of course, negotiated higher wage scales. Until recent years most had stabilized their contract language sufficiently so that before the contemporary round of rapid inflation over 80 percent of Michigan's municipal unions were negotiating two-year and three-year contracts. Beginning in 1974, when long-term contracts failed to anticipate rapid inflation and resulted in reduced real earnings for some municipal workers, Michigan cities saw their unions pressing once again for one-year contracts. If inflation slows, this trend will almost undoubtedly reverse again.

Interest in cost-of-living provisions in union contracts in Michigan has followed the same cycle that it has in the private sector in America during the last three decades. The higher the inflation rate the greater the unions' interest in obtaining such clauses. Data from early 1975 suggest that slightly over one-third of all municipal contracts in Michigan now contain a cost-of-living adjustment

(COLA) clause, a substantial increase over five years ago. Because of delays in data collection this figure probably does not reflect adequately the number of COLA clauses that have been negotiated during 1975. In all probability cost-of-living provisions could be found in closer to one-half of all municipal contracts in Michigan by the late summer of 1975. Interestingly, however, the cities that did introduce COLA clauses in their agreements between 1970 and 1975 were primarily in the medium-sized group, with populations ranging between 15,000 and 50,000. Both the larger and the smaller cities in Michigan seem to have resisted introduction of COLA clauses more successfully. The reasons for this are unclear. It may result from the tremendous financial and budgetary pressures on the largest cities, making them extremely resistant to new and unpredictable wage-cost increases, and, in the case of smaller towns and cities, either greater union weakness and/or the possibility that inflation has a somewhat less-serious impact upon employees in rural areas than upon those in metropolitan areas.

Finally, in the area of compensation, longevity pay based upon years of service is very characteristic of Michigan municipal-labor agreements. Over 83 percent of agreements in 1975 provide for longevity pay—a growth of 20 percent in the last five years. It appears that in the not-too-distant future longevity pay will be a nearly universal benefit for municipal employees. Should cities continue their traditional practice of employing a substantial part of their work force throughout their entire careers, longevity pay could become an increasing fiscal burden.

Seventy percent of all municipal contracts now contain agency-shop clauses. This form of union security was specifically approved by legislative amendment to PERA in 1974. The only major surprise in the area of union security is that 16 percent of all municipal-government labor agreements in Michigan have some form of union shop or modified union shop, which is presumably illegal under the present law.

Despite almost universal acceptance of grievance arbitration in the private sector, its introduction in the public sector in Michigan has not been smooth and untroubled. Municipal employers have been skeptical about this institution with which they have had little direct experience. They have worried about possible infringement upon their traditional prerogatives, and, at least in the early 1960s, many had a number of doubts about its legal propriety in the setting of local government. Originally these same concerns were common in the private sector. They have long since been allayed there and they are also being put to rest in the public sector in Michigan as well. Binding neutral arbitration is now the final step in the grievance procedure in 82 percent of all municipal contracts in Michigan, a growth of 21 percent in the last five years. Alternative forms of final resolution of grievances, such as a hearing before a commission, city council, or civil-service board, exist only in a small number of cities, almost all of them under 25,000 in population.

Municipal unions generally have been effective in obtaining desired working conditions in the narrow sense of such benefits as coffee breaks, clothing allowances, and provision of safety equipment. They have been somewhat less effective in obtaining bans against the contracting out of work that their members are qualified to perform. The degree of specificity or particularity in guaranteeing that union members will not lose time due to the contracting out of work varies significantly from contract to contract and one-half of municipal collective-bargaining agreements still make no provision in this area.

Municipal unions have been least successful in Michigan in assuring their members that assignments to desirable shifts or work locations will be made on a seniority basis. With scattered exceptions, they have also been uninterested or unsuccessful in controlling work loads and manning schedules.

A majority of contracts cover promotions within the bargaining unit. Management has traditionally asserted that it has the right to select employees for promotion and to set the relevant criteria for such selections. But unions are of course concerned with the right of the worker to request and receive fair consideration for better job opportunities. In bargaining, the issue usually centers around the relative weight to be given ability versus seniority. By 1975, 35 percent of all municipal contracts in Michigan provide that the senior, qualified applicant is entitled to promotion. Another 35 percent of agreements specify that when other criteria are equal, or are generally equal, then seniority will be a factor considered. The remaining contracts—nearly one-third in all—still do not specify the criteria for promotion to better positions within the bargaining unit.

In addition to the area of promotions, four out of five municipal labor agreements in Michigan specify or limit management rights in the area of demotions and layoffs. But the retention areas to be used in the event of layoff as well as the extent of retreat and bumping rights given displaced employees varies widely among labor agreements. Some limit such rights to the classification, others to the division or department, and a few make bumping-rights bargaining unit-wide. In all cases, of course, some present or early ability to perform the new job is required.

The major exception to these generalizations regarding the traditional nature of municipal-union bargaining goals is among the public-safety officers who have sometimes attempted, with varying degrees of success, to set manning requirements and minimum-shift levels, to control the nature of their assignments, and the like. They cannot strike to enforce their demands, however, even on a de-facto basis. Instead, impasses in collective bargaining between police and fire fighters and their employers are subject to binding arbitration, by final offer selection for individual economic issues, and conventional arbitration for noneconomic issues. Some of the neutral chairmen of arbitration panels have been willing to render awards on issues such as those described above. For example, one arbitration panel recently decided that command police officers of the city of Inkster no longer have to reside within the city's boundaries, but the panel then created a wholly new set of somewhat arbitrary boundaries within which they do have to live.[24] Another arbitration panel decided the number of firemen the city of Alpena has to have on duty at particular times, basing this award on the assumption that this issue affects "the firemens' safety." The right of this panel to render such a binding decision was upheld by the court of appeals.[25] In another situation, unreported because as often happens all issues were settled during the hearing, I refused to grant the request of a combined unit of public-safety officers that the "bargaining-unit work" clause be more tightly drawn to prevent command officers from assigning citizens or other public employees to perform "their work," even in emergencies. My refusal to grant such an award was based on the conclusion that it was contrary to public policy as stated in other Michigan laws rather than because I thought the matter beyond my statutory jurisdiction. A number of other Michigan arbitrators have stated similar reluctance to render binding awards granting union requests in novel areas such as these. Their qualms, whether or not valid, seem based on the belief that it is an improper use of arbitral power—that only the parties themselves should break new ground in the terms of collective-bargaining agreements—rather than any doubt that the subject matters were within the legal scope of collective bargaining and hence of arbitration. Very recently the Michigan Supreme Court seems to have confirmed this view. With regard to arbitral authority in interest disputes, half of an evenly divided court stated, without objection from its colleagues, "Michigan has adopted a broad view of conditions of employment, making most issues mandatory subjects of collective bargaining and, presumably, subject to arbitration under Act 312."[26]

In general, however, and with the exceptions noted in the previous paragraph, the scope of municipal bargaining by public employees in Michigan appears to parallel closely the conclusions of David Stanley in *Managing Local Government Under Union Pressure*.[27] Although municipal unions have thrown up temporary roadblocks to management, and have certainly forced increased time to be spent on personnel and labor-relations matters, as in the private sector the resulting accommodations cannot be shown to have made substantial inroads on essential management freedom to accomplish the public work. The municipal unions in general have not wanted to undertake basic responsibility for attempting to make fundamental policy changes in their communities. This kind of responsibility with its multiple pressures for setting priorities, innovation, compromise, and maximum use of inadequate resources has not been appropriate to the needs or taste of most municipal unions. Instead, as Stanley characterized it, "They need someone else to be 'management,' so that they can be 'labor.' "[28]

Scope of Bargaining in Education

Although the phrase "wages, hours, and working conditions" has generally been interpreted by blue-collar employees to exclude basic managerial decisions, as previously noted this has not been the case with teachers and perhaps to some lesser extent with police and fire fighters. Charles Perry and Wesley Wildman suggested in 1970[29] that over time teacher concerns would expand from an initial interest in wage and salary matters to interest in matters affecting organizational security. After this first expansion would come a second: increased concern with working conditions such as the length of the work day and year, the length and frequency of before- and after-school meetings, the scope of extracurricular activities, and relief from certain nonteaching duties. Finally, and even later, teachers would increasingly be concerned, Perry and Wildman believed, with policy issues such as racial integration, pupil discipline, grading policies, promotions, and choice of curricula and textbooks.

At least to a degree the present scope of collectively bargained teacher contracts in Michigan appears to bear out this prediction. Teacher-bargaining agreements in Michigan are collected each year by the Michigan Education Association and it publishes an annual summary tabulating the percentage of about 500 teacher-bargaining agreements in the state that contain certain types of clauses.[30] It should be emphasized that the following comments, which are based upon this summary, reflect percentages of total collective-bargaining agreements rather than numbers of teachers covered by particular clauses. If one accepts the reasonable assumption that teacher-bargaining strength is greatest in medium-sized and larger cities, and that this strength reflects itself in a greater likelihood of contractual language reflecting at least some encroachment on traditional management prerogatives in the educational field, then most of the percentages that follow should be upgraded appreciably if one is interested in estimating the percentage of all Michigan teachers who have obtained collective-bargaining clauses of each type.

The Michigan Education Association analyzes teacher-bargaining agreements in terms of four clauses it characterizes as being of "instructional concern." These four areas are the presence of an instructional, curriculum, or policies council; whether there is a negotiated clause requiring instructional materials that treat racial-minority contributions fairly; whether class size is limited; and whether class size is grievable.

Forty-two percent of all K-12 collective-bargaining agreements in Michigan provide for an instructional, curriculum, or policies council. No reliable data are available on the influence of such councils. Eighteen percent of all collective-bargaining agreements do require the board of education to act in one way or another with regard to recommendations emanating from such a council. I assume that at least in these one-fifth of all school systems the recommendations of teacher-administrator councils receive fairly serious and public consideration by appropriate policy-making bodies.

Only 6 percent of all collective-bargaining agreements covering K-12 education in Michigan require the board of education to obtain instructional materials that treat equally the contributions of racial and other minorities. But since the 29 school districts that have such clauses are almost all in the largest cities, including Detroit, it is a fair inference that something over one-half of all teachers in Michigan share with their school boards the responsibility for attempting to obtain instructional materials that treat minority contributions fairly.

Class size is limited in almost one-half of the teacher contracts in Michigan. Only one-half of these require that the school board hire additional teachers or teacher aides, or make supplemental payments to teachers when the size of classes goes above the negotiated norm. The other half of such agreements simply require that when or before class sizes go above the negotiated level the administration consult with the teachers' organization. No empirical data are available on the results of such consultation. It is my opinion, however, that average class size across the state may actually be increasing slightly at the present time. Finally, class size is grievable in slightly over one-half of all teacher collective-bargaining agreements in Michigan. This means that in some cases neutral grievance arbitrators as well as fact finders and interest arbitrators are making decisions as to appropriate class sizes in public education.

The Michigan Education Association also analyzes teacher-bargaining agreements in terms of some ten other areas, which it characterizes as being of "professional concern." Among these, 39 percent of all agreements permit a dismissed probationary teacher to grieve and go to arbitration over a refusal to grant tenure. Teacher-evaluation procedures are specified in four out of five teacher-bargaining agreements, but in only 15 percent of all agreements is peer evaluation provided for.

Student disciplinary procedures are regulated in 41 percent of all teacher collective-bargaining agreements in Michigan. Over half of all collective-bargaining agreements provide for in-service education, in a quarter of which the agreement specifies that teachers participate in planning such training. Teachers are often allowed to attend educational conferences or make professional visits to other education institutions at school-board expense. Twenty-seven percent of the contracts provide for teacher aides to relieve teachers of nonprofessional duties, although only a small minority of them make supervision of these aides a responsibility of the teachers to whom they are assigned.

Finally, and perhaps most strikingly, 44 percent of all teacher contracts in Michigan permit the teachers' organization to grieve a violation of school policies. School policies and a policy manual are ordinarily unilaterally adopted by school boards, and, in many cases, unilaterally ignored if the circumstances seem to the board to warrant it. Collective-bargaining agreements, which allow the teacher organization to bring a grievance and, if need be, go to arbitration over management's failure to follow its own enunciated policies, represents a not-insignificant means by which Michigan teachers can attempt to control school-board actions.

Scope of Bargaining in Higher Education

Collective bargaining has been selected by faculties as their desired method of academic governance at most Michigan community colleges. In fact, the first collective-bargaining agreement in higher education in the United States was negotiated in Michigan—at Henry Ford Community College in 1966. The first representation election won at a four-year college was at Central Michigan, and the first strike at a four-year institution was at Oakland University in Michigan. Many conditions of faculty employment and institutional policy are negotiated and included in these new, written bargaining agreements. In general, however, it cannot be said with any real justification that collective bargaining has fundamentally changed the nature of institutional decision making at the community-college level.[31] Faculties obviously have a far larger voice than formerly in the setting of salaries, and to a degree in establishing work loads and normalized working conditions. To some degree, they may also have achieved a greater voice in faculty personnel practices, such as increased rights through peer evaluation to share in the decision to grant or withhold tenure. But in areas such as adaptation and change in curricula and instructional methods, or in selecting their own chairmen and administrators, no fundamental change seems to have occurred as a result of collective bargaining. This lack of fundamental change reflects the fact that faculties in higher education always did share in such decisions to some degree, and thus their bargaining agreements, when they deal with such issues, simply restate existing policies and practices.

It is interesting that community-college faculties now seem to feel more secure in the possession of these traditional rights than formerly. Presumably this results from their statement in a jointly negotiated agreement rather than an administratively promulgated policy manual, and hence they cannot be changed or withdrawn without faculty acquiescence. But the scope of bargaining at the community-college level in general seems unremarkable.

Collective bargaining has come only recently to the four-year colleges and universities in Michigan, and several have shown no interest at all. Three quarters of the 11 state-supported four-year institutions bargain; the large majority of private colleges do not. Even in those institutions where faculty bargaining exists, only one or two rounds of negotiations have occurred. Thus the scope of bargaining has not moved greatly beyond the traditional concept of "wages, hours, and working conditions" as such ideas would be understood in a university setting. One major exception to such short bargaining histories exists at Oakland University, where five successive faculty agreements have been negotiated over an even greater number of years. The agreement there contains several unusual achievements, such as a complex factored system for salary setting that includes all of the elements traditionally thought appropriate for consideration in higher education—academic rank, length of service in rank, merit evaluation by peers, and relative demand for academic disciplines established by the labor market. Moreover, the negotiated procedures for the granting or withholding of the crucial tenure decision are developed in great detail in the Oakland University agreement, as are many limits on administrator discretion in the determination of class scheduling, time of teaching, and the like. Such clauses may be a headache for administrators, but they represent no new breakthroughs in the scope of collective bargaining.

Summary and Conclusions

The state of Michigan adopted for its public sector the private sector NLRA formulation of the obligation of employers and the representatives of employees to bargain collectively regarding "wages, hours, and other terms and conditions of employment." The Michigan Employment Relations Commission has nevertheless rejected the standard private-sector dichotomy between mandatory and permissible subjects of bargaining. Instead, it has concluded that since public employers are not legally subject to coercive tactics, and therefore are under no compulsion to accept union proposals, there is no reason unduly to limit to traditional areas the subjects over which public managers are obligated to bargain.

In practice, notwithstanding this rule and despite the fact that illegal strikes by public employees are common and take place for the most part without sanction or punishment in Michigan, in many relationships it is clear that the scope of public-sector bargaining has not thus far gone greatly beyond those subjects that would be deemed appropriate for bargaining under either test. Municipal-employee unions, particularly those composed in part or in whole of blue-collar workers, seem largely content to bargain within traditional boundaries, for the most part leaving decisions over policy areas to management. The same has been true for the most part in faculty collective-bargaining in higher education, although this fact may reflect the relative novelty of bargaining at this level. Attempts to expand the scope of bargaining and to encroach upon areas traditionally thought to be management prerogatives have been most characteristic of several groups of professional and quasi-professional employees, particularly K-12 teachers, police, and fire fighters. Both groups have had some success in this area. They have done it either through persuasion of their employers that shared decision making is appropriate in areas where it formerly did not exist or, very occasionally, through the threat or actuality of strikes. Finally, in the case of public-safety officers, some encroachment on traditional management prerogatives has occurred through the results of legislated binding arbitration.

I confess to considerable doubt regarding a legal structure that permits them to do so. Collective bargaining as a procedure for allowing employees—public or private—to improve their wages, hours, and fringe benefits can hardly be challenged, certainly not in Michigan. But collective bargaining is not an ideal process for effectuating social change. When teachers want to bargain about the school curriculum, class sizes, or the kinds of instructional materials they will use; when hospital interns want to bargain about the quality of services offered and nurses about the number of duty stations; when firemen want to bargain contractual levels of fire protection their communities will receive; or policemen want to regulate the number of men on patrol duty as opposed to the number riding in squad cars; they are not concerned solely with conditions of work.

They are also attempting to use the collective-bargaining process to resolve a number of significant public-policy questions.[32]

As noted, I have reservations about whether collective bargaining is the ideal process for such a purpose. First, it seems that the second element of the test proposed by MERC in *Westwood* over whether such subjects are bargainable—"Is collective bargaining appropriate for resolving such issues?"—does nothing to resolve the question posed. Arguably, all questions *may* be resolved by the Hegelian decision-making model of synthesis resulting from conflict. But this does not answer the issue of whether some questions *might better* be resolved by the Lockean model of deference and consensus based upon rational decisions resulting from joint analysis of common data. In sum, I think there are some policy issues better resolved in a calmer and more dispassionate forum than the negotiating room, particularly when negotiations take place against a strike deadline.

The second reason for my reservations regarding a mandatory, expanded scope for bargaining into policy areas is that very frequently the new classes of issues are matters of social and public policy of fundamental concern to a broader constituency than organized public employees and their public managers. The whole community has an interest in many of these issues, both in regard to the quality of public services and the amount of certain kinds of services it wants and is willing to pay for. In the long run, the view of "professionals" that certain kinds and levels of services are essential is bound to fall of its own weight if the public is not equally well persuaded of the merits of the issue. Just as issues of war and peace are too important to be left to generals, so are issues of this kind too important to be left solely to professional employees and their supervisors.

The foregoing is not to suggest that issues of a policy nature are always inappropriate for discussion between the representatives of organized public employees and public managers. To such issues I would apply the traditional distinction—that they are permissible, but not mandatory subjects of bargaining. As noted earlier, labeling an issue as only a permissible subject of bargaining may have not complete practical effect where the union is strong and the membership militant. But the label is of some effect, as private-sector experience shows. As to permissible subjects, of course, the strike weapon may not be used to force agreement and subterfuges to avoid the ban are not too common. During the summer of 1975, the Michigan Legislature legalized strikes of limited duration in public education although the enactment failed to survive the governor's veto.[33] The issue is not dead, however, and a formula may yet be found that will obtain legislative and executive agreement. If this occurs, similar legalization may in time take place for other groups of employees. Such a development would certainly be more congruent with the present situation where most public-employee strikes in Michigan are legitimate in fact, if not in law.[34] The legalization of public-employee strikes might encourage MERC to return to a more careful consideration of the kinds of issues that should be permissible but not mandatory subjects of bargaining.

Finally, I believe that in some Michigan collective-bargaining relationships this distinction is already being accepted to a degree by the parties themselves. Such developments are akin to the distinction between the "real" and the "formal" scope of bargaining.[35] One is not always reflective of the other. Formal items are those appearing in a collective-bargaining agreement; real items are those that have been subjected to joint discussions and joint decision making. My impression, based upon personal experience, is that in many public-sector bargaining relationships in Michigan, particularly at all levels of education, the real scope of bargaining is considerably wider than the formally bargained agreement would suggest. In some cases, of course, the parties have simply bargained the procedural mechanism by which certain policy issues will be jointly discussed during the life of the contract. In other relationships the discussions occur, but without contractual requirement for them. In either case, discussions take place between faculty representatives and educational adminis-trators that result in joint agreement that certain kinds of quasi-policy decisions are in the public as well as the educational institution's interest. Such discussions are largely voluntary and seem to take place on a rational consensus basis without threat of conflict or sanction if agreement cannot be reached. If so, I deem these developments wholly appropriate in that they conform to the mandatory-permissible scope of bargaining test. Such developments in part reflect a maturation of rather new bargaining relationships. More importantly, they represent a major achievement for those public employees who are attempting to make their professional authority commensurate with their conception of professional responsibility.

Notes

1. Mich Comp. Laws Ann. §423.215 (1967).

2. 61 Stat. 142 (1947), 29 USC 158(d).

3. *Detroit Police Officers Ass'n* vs. *City of Detroit*, 391 Mich. 44, 214 NW 2d 803 (1974).

4. *Van Buren Public School District* vs. *Wayne County Circuit Judge*, 61 Mich. App. 6, 232 NW2d 278 (Nos. 15473-4, 18493, released May 27, 1975). In the same fashion and for similar reasons, the Court of Appeals ruled that promotions based on seniority to positions outside the bargaining unit were a term and condition of employment and therefore a "mandatory subject of bargaining," citing *NLRB* vs. *Century Cement Co.*, 208F2d 84 (1953), in support of this conclusion. *City of Detroit* vs. *Detroit Police Officers Ass'n*, 61 Mich. App. 487, 233 NW2d 49 (No. 20926, released May 30, 1975); appeal denied September 17, 1975.

5. 1 Michigan Employment Relations Commission Labor Opinions 434 (1966), [hereinafter MERC Lab. Op].

6. 7 MERC Lab. Op. 313 (1972).

7. *Id.*, at 318-319.

8. *Id.* at 320-321.

9. For example, see Harry T. Edwards, "The Emerging Duty to Bargain in the Public Sector," 71 *Mich. L. Rev.*, 885 at 922-923 (1973).

10. "Work Stoppages in Government, 1973" Report 437, Bureau of Labor Statistics, 1975, pp. 7-12.

11. "The Impact of Private Sector Principles in the Public Sector," Chapter III in *Union Power and Public Policy*, (New York State School of Industrial and Labor Relations, 1975), pp. 51-74.

12. *Id.* at 74.

13. *Detroit Police Officers Ass'n*, note 3, *supra*; *Van Buren Public School District*, note 4, *supra*; *City of Detroit*, note 4, *supra*.

14. *Van Buren Public School District*, note 4, *supra*, at 16-17; quoted with approval in *City of Detroit* at 3.

15. *City of Dearborn*, 7 MERC Lab. Op. 749 (1972).

16. 5 MERC Lab. Op. 127 (1970).

17. *Montrose Community Schools*, MERC Case Nos. C73 J-235 and CU73 K-24, Government Employee Relations Report [hereinafter GERR], February 10, 1975, pp. B12-13. Interestingly enough, there is no exact private-sector counterpart to this decision. The closest analogy is *NLRB* vs. *Insurance Agents International Union*, 361 U.S. 477 (1960), in which it was held that union members engaging in unprotected (but not, as in *Montrose*, illegal) activities for which they might have been terminated, e.g., work slowdowns, did not end the employer's obligation to bargain in good faith.

18. *Board of Education of the School District of Crestwood*, vs. *Crestwood Education Association,* 393 Mich. 616, 227 NW 2d 736 (1975), GERR, April 28, 1975, pp. F1-11.

19. *Wayne County Civil Service Commission* vs. *Board of Supervisors*, 384 Mich. 363, 184 NW 2d 201 (1971).

20. *Regents of the University of Michigan,* vs. *Employment Relations Commission*, 389 Mich. 96, 204 NW 2d 218 (1973). Subsequently, the university followed this opinion by voluntarily recognizing its graduate students who also act as teaching and research assistants for collective bargaining purposes. It did so knowing that the NLRB had found similar graduate assistants not to be employees with the meaning of NLRA. *Leland Stanford Junior University*, 214 NLRB 82 (1974).

21. *Detroit Police Officers Association* vs. *City of Detroit*, 391 Mich. 44, 214 NW 2d 803 (1974).

22. Note 18 *supra.*

23. The data on municipal agreements contained in this section are based primarily upon John C. Chambers, "1975 Labor Contract Analysis" (May, 1975), mimeograph, Michigan Municipal League.

24. In the Matter of Arbitration between the city of Inkster and Teamster Local 214 Police Command Unit, March 4, 1975. This decision was reversed by the Wayne County Circuit Court on June 24, 1975. Nevertheless, a subsequent arbitration panel then made a similar ruling on expanding the residential privileges of Inkster patrolmen. GERR, September 8, 1975, pp. B9-11.

25. *Alpena* vs. *Alpena Firefighters Ass'n*, 56 Mich. App. 568, 224 NW 2d 672 (1974).

26. *Dearborn Firefighters Local Union 214* vs. *City of Dearborn*, 394 Mich. 229, 231 NW 2d 226 (June 24, 1975).

27. The Brookings Institution, 1972.

28. *Id.* at 145.

29. *The Impact of Negotiations in Public Education*, Worthington, Ohio: Charles A. Jones Publishing Co., 1970, pp. 129-30.

30. *Summary of Selected Contract Provisions, 1973-74*, Research Office Michigan Education Association, East Lansing, Michigan.

31. The comments on community-college bargaining that follow are drawn in part from Jack R. McDonald, "The Impact of Collective Bargaining on Decision Making in the Michigan Community College Instructional Program," doctoral dissertation, Center for the Study of Higher Education, The University of Michigan, 1975.

32. I fully agree with the similar comments on this same subject by Arvid Anderson, "Address delivered to the United States Conference of Mayors," Denver, Colorado, June 14, 1970, mimeograph.

33. House Bill 5181 was passed in June, 1975, permitting a legal teachers' strike to take place during approximately the month of September. Failing agreement, the dispute could then be sent to binding arbitration. The Senate concurred, although it shortened the period during which the strike could continue before arbitration could be ordered. The governor still thought the strike period too long, particularly as the legislature contemplated a reduction in mandatory pupil attendance days in struck districts.

34. *Holland School District* vs. *Holland Education Ass'n* 380 Mich. 314, 157 NW 2d 206 (1968).

35. This distinction was developed in detail by Paul F. Gerhart, "The Scope of Bargaining in Local Negotiations," *Proceedings*, 1969 Annual Spring Meeting, Industrial Relations Research Association, published in XX *Labor Law Journal*, 545-52 (August, 1969).

3

The Scope of Bargaining in the Public Sector in New Jersey

Ernest Gross

New Jersey has one public-sector collective-negotiation statute for all public employees. It is written in broad and sometimes ambiguous terms. The law is administered by an appointed and statutorily mandated tripartite commission. Up to January 20, 1975 the commission's functions were limited to resolving representation questions, conducting elections, and administering the voluntary-impasse procedures of mediation and nonbinding fact finding in the act. Perhaps because it had so little power, there has been surprisingly little critical comment about the statutorily mandated partisan nature of the commission. The 1974 amendments to the law established administrative procedures to remedy "unfair practices," including refusals to bargain in good faith, and administrative procedures to determine scope-of-negotiations questions. The jurisdiction for both was placed in the commission. As a definitive statement of scope of negotiations, this chapter is about three years premature. With only six months' experience with the amended law to draw on, and only one commission decision, conclusions of necessity are somewhat tentative. Three points of interest can, however, be drawn:

1. The court has defined terms and conditions of employment from two approaches in construing the original law. In one, inherent limitations on negotiability arise out of the concept of government carrying out the public's business. In that view the governmental prerogative and duty to govern informs the subjects which may be negotiated. The other view arises from a construction of the Employer-Employee Relations Act and concludes that there is a dichotomy between policy matters and those matters that have a direct impact on working conditions. In January 1975 an amendment to the statutes, which ostensibly broadened the scope of negotiations, became effective. At a guess, but based on the reasoning in the cases taken as a whole, when the amended statute is construed the court will still find a dichotomy between policy and day-to-day impact on working conditions. If in fact there are inherent limitations on negotiability arising out of the nature of government the conclusion seems inescapable. The Public Employment Relation Commission in its only decision on scope so far has reached the conclusion that even when a matter is not manditorily negotiable, the impact of the action must be negotiated.

2. The second point of interest is the conclusion that different employees have different rights depending on the chance of their employment. Although the statute speaks of all public employees in the same general language, it fails to identify who negotiates for the public employer. The civil-service rights of

29

employees are saved but there is no statutory mention of statutory rights of other employees.

3. The third point of interest arises from the public-school cases. Although the cases speak of questions of negotiability, most of the cases do not arise during contract negotiations. By and large they arise as questions of contract administration. The courts have been called upon to enjoin arbitration and the issues discussed have been whether the matters in question were within the scope of negotiations. No court has yet discussed or voiced the question of whether good-faith, bilateral negotiations are even possible if the application of contract language may be tested by a standard of management prerogative, reserved policy areas, or management discretion.

In this chapter I have concluded that scope-of-negotiations questions have not had any substantial impact on the process of negotiations. It simply means that there were insufficient measurable data to support any other conclusions. It is probably safe to conclude that the tensions arising from court decisions and public-employer positions taken on scope matters certainly exacerbated situations where the ostensible issues in dispute have been reported as "economics."

Legislative Definition of Scope

The New Jersey Employer-Employee Relations Act became effective July 1, 1968. It was amended in 1974, effective January 20, 1975.[1] For convenience the original law will be referred to as C.303 and the amendment as C.123. The scope of negotiations is not defined in C.303 or in C.123. The public employers must negotiate proposed new rules or modifications of existing rules governing working conditions before they are established.[2] Public employers are required to negotiate written policies setting forth grievance procedures that may provide for binding arbitration.[3] The majority representative of employees in an appropriate unit and representatives of the public employer shall meet at reasonable times and negotiate in good faith with respect to grievances and conditions of employment.[4] The statute also provides that "nothing herein shall be construed to deny to any individual employee his rights under Civil Service laws or regulations."[5] C.303 was not intended to repeal other statutes and stated ". . . nor shall any provision hereof annul or modify any statute or statutes of this state."[6]

C.123 made what may be a very significant change by adding the word "pension" before "statute" so the language now reads: ". . . nor shall any provision hereof annul or modify any pension statute or statutes of this state."[7]

The Public Employment Relations Commission (PERC) was created to administer C.303. PERC adopted rules and a statement of procedure covering representation, impasses, and violations of the act.

The New Jersey Supreme Court held that PERC did not have the power to remedy unfair labor practices. The courts, however, were open to fashion remedies for violations of statutory rights of public employees and violations of the act.[8]

C.123 established unfair practices for public employers and employees including refusals to negotiate in good faith and established in PERC exclusive jurisdiction, subject to appeal, to investigate and hear unfair practice charges. In addition, PERC was given jurisdiction, subject to appeal, to determine whether a matter in dispute is within the scope of collective negotiations.[9]

Decision Affecting Scope

Courts (the New Jersey Supreme Court)

In *Lullo* vs. *Fire Fighters*[10] the New Jersey Supreme Court construed C.303 for the first time. No specific issue that required an exposition of the meaning of collective negotiations was before the court. In a wide ranging opinion the court distinguished between the term "collective bargaining" and the term "collective negotiations as used in the statute":

It is crystal clear that in using the term "collective negotiations" the legislature intended to recognize inherent limitations on the bargaining power of public employer and employee. The reservation in Section 7 of the Civil Service rights of the individual employee is a specific indication of that fact. The lawmakers were sensitive that Civil Service statutes in many areas provide for competitive employment examinations, eligible lists, fixed salary lists, for promotion, transfer, reinstatement and removal, and require all employees to be dealt with on the same basis. And undoubtedly they were conscious also that public agencies, departments, etc., cannot abdicate or bargain away their continuing legislative or executive obligations or discretion. Consequently, absent some further charges in pertinent statutes public employers may not be able to make binding contractual com nitments relating to certain subjects.[11]

Significantly, although the court saw limitations on the scope of bargaining, it was in the context of an inherent difference between the private sector and the public sector rather than on the proviso that C.303 was not intended to annul or modify any other statutes. In fact section 10 of C.303 was not mentioned at all in the opinion.

In Re Salaries for Probation Officers of Bergen County[12] upheld the validity of negotiating meal allowance; reimbursement for use of accrued vacation credit for sick leave; insured vacation, sick leave, and improved medical benefits given other employees to be automatically made available to probation officers; union-steward leave to attend union convention, and residence out of the county. The court said that the employment relationship is more than fixing wages. The normal fringe benefits commonly incidental in the private sector applied in the public sector.

In 1973 the New Jersey Supreme Court considered the meaning of "terms and conditions of employment" and negotiability in three cases argued, reargued, and decided at the same time. *Dunellen Board of Education* vs. *Dunellen Education Association*[13] upheld the right of a school board to consolidate department chairmanships in the high school as a matter of educational policy and as nonnegotiable. *The Board of Education of the City of Englewood* vs. *Englewood Teachers Association*[14] held that working hours for special-education teachers and compensation for graduate tuition were issues that intimately and directly affected teacher work and welfare and thus were negotiable as terms and conditions of employment. *Burlington County College Faculty Association* vs. *Board of Trustees, Burlington County College*[15] held that the board of trustees of a county college were not required to negotiate with the college faculty on the college calendar. In *Dunellen*, the main case, the court distinguished between matters that were educational policy and thus nonnegotiable and those matters that intimately and directly affected the work and welfare of employees and thus were terms and conditions of employment and mandatively negotiable. In both *Dunellen* and *Burlington*[16] the court suggested that even though nonnegotiable, the matters should have been voluntarily discussed with the associations. It would follow therefore that there are mandatory subjects for negotiations and nonnegotiable matters but not permissive subjects. Discussing a nonnegotiable matter is not the same as negotiating. *Burlington* was a true scope of negotiations case. The issue arose in the trial court as a refusal to bargain by the college. At the time, PERC was without authority to adjudicate alleged violations of rights granted by C.303. All parties and the trial court agreed that it had jurisdiction to hear the case.[17] Although the thrust of *Dunellen* and *Englewood* went to the question of negotiability, the issue before the court really was whether arbitration should be enjoined. The issues did not arise out of negotiations but from contract administration.

In *Dunellen*, since the matter was one of educational policy, arbitration was enjoined. The court did say that the issue should have gone to the commissioner of education as a school law problem. In *Englewood*, since the problems were not policy but working hours and compensation, no substantive school law question was raised and the matter could proceed to arbitration. As will be seen later, in the other school cases the education cases do not arise as problems of scope of negotiations. In fact, the matters are negotiated and the problem arises whether the interpretation should be left to an arbitrator pursuant to a negotiated grievance procedure, or to the commissioner of education who would not necessarily interpret the contract but would test the disputed language by the school laws of New Jersey as found in Title 18A of the statutes.

Although the court said nothing in either *Dunellen* or *Burlington* to whittle away the language in *Lullo*[18] that public employers are prohibited from negotiating certain subjects, it did not rely on *Lullo* but did rely on the language in C.303 that it was not to modify or annul other statutes to uphold the proposition that the legislature had intended a narrow scope of collective negotiations. The change in C.123, which inserts the word pension before statute,[19] may conceivably mean that now the legislature intends a very broad interpretation of scope of negotiations.

The supreme court construed *Dunellen* and *Burlington* in 1974 in *Association of New Jersey State College Faculties, Inc. et al.* vs. *Ralph A. Dungan as Chancellor.*[20] The Board of Higher Education unilaterally adopted tenure rules for college faculty. Among other arguments a direct challenge was made that the unilateral adoption of tenure rules violated the statutory requirement to negotiate in good faith with respect to grievance and terms and conditions of employment, or to propose new rules or working conditions without prior negotiations. The court once more repeated as in *Dunellen* that, although the legislature failed to define "working conditions" or "terms and conditions of employment," and also failed to specify what subjects were exclusively within management's prerogative, section 10 of C.303 explicitly provided that nothing in the act should "annul or modify any statute or statutes"; therefore the legislature did not intend to negate the Board of Higher Education's overall statutory responsibility as set forth in the education law. The court held that, although granting of tenure entails individual consequence, the tenure guidelines represented major educational policy and were not mandatorily negotiable. The court then said that although it held the tenure guidelines not to be mandatorily negotiable it did not mean such guidelines or alterations should be adopted without full and timely prior consultation with accredited faculty representatives and other interested persons. In *Dunellen*, in urging voluntary discussion of matters of policy not mandatorily negotiable, the court referred to teachers as "trained professionals who may have much to contribute towards the Board's adoption of sound and suitable educational policies." In *Association of New Jersey State Colleges* the court quoted with approval from *Faculty Tenure, A Report and Recommendation by the Commission on Academic Tenure in Higher Education* (the Jossey Bass Service in Higher Education 1973) that issues of freedom and tenure be referred to academic procedure outside the collective-bargaining process.

It appears therefore that the concept, although not specifically referred to, in *Lullo* that private-sector experience cannot be translated wholly to the public sector is still high in the court's consciousness as it tries to rationalize the imprecision of the statute.

In summary the statute does not define "terms and conditions" of employment nor specify what subjects were within and without the sphere of negotiations. It did specify at the time that none of its provisions were intended to modify any statutes of the state. The court thus attempted to balance the continuing effect of various statutes such as the education laws on a case-by-case basis without frustrating the objectives of the Employer-Employee Relations Act.

Consolidation of two high school department chairmanships into a new single department was a matter of predominantly educational policy and not mandatorily negotiable even though it had an incidental effect on terms and conditions of employment.[21] College calendars were held to be nonnegotiable as a matter of policy.[22] Faculty tenure policies for state colleges were nonnegotiable.[23] Issues that bore directly on the hours and compensation of individual teachers were proper subjects of mandatory negotiations.[24]

In *Association of New Jersey State College Faculties et al.* vs. *New Jersey Board of Higher Education,*[25] guidelines that restricted outside employment of state-college faculty were held to be mandatorily negotiable. The Board of Higher Education had authority to promulgate rules. It had a statutory mandate to promulgate a code of ethics but nevertheless the guidelines on outside employment intimately and directly affected the work and welfare of college employees and thus were terms and conditions of employment within the meaning of the employer-employee law and did not affect major educational policy. The court recognized that C.123 had been signed by the governor a month before its decision in the case, but declined to construe the new amendments. As pointed out previously, the limitation on annuling other statutes in the state in C.303 has been narrowed to pension statutes only in C.123. What the change in statutory language means is not clear at the present time.

The following is a consideration of decisions by the lower courts:

Higher Education. Aside from tenure and the college calendar held to be nonnegotiable and outside employment that was negotiable, there was one other significant case. The State Board of Higher Education unilaterally adopted a student-faculty ratio funding formula. The budget was held to be nonnegotiable. The suggestion was made by the court that the allocation of funds by the university once the budget was adopted could be negotiated or at least that portion of the budget that dealt with hours of work, work load, and individual compensation.[26]

Probation Officers. One of the blanks in C.303 and C.123 is the failure to identify who negotiates for the public employer. The governor has been held to be the employer for state employees.[27] Probation officers are part of the judicial system. County court judges appoint probation officers, regulate their duties, and fix salaries and expenses.[28]

An attorney general's opinion in 1969 held that for purposes of C.303 the county judges, not the Board of Freeholders, were the employers of probation officers and could negotiate. The supreme court in a decision that held that the fringe benefits negotiated in the private sector were appropriate in the public sector[29] approved the practice where the court negotiated and the Freeholders provided the money. In practice the chief probation officer or the court administrator of the county actually negotiates under the general supervision of a designated county judge.

The administrative director of the courts has suggested to the county judges that they should not permit negotiating in areas where they exercise no control. That is, areas regulated by statute, court rules, civil-service rules, or contrary to judicial policy, or recognized as management prerogative. He suggested[30] the following as nonnegotiable matters:

1. Pensions—statutory R.S. 43:1-15A
2. Holding other compensable employment court rule 1:17-1c and 4
3. Appointments and promotions in the Probation Service. Civil Service Rules 8, 12, and 14
4. Staff assignment, and location of office facilities, management prerogative

Some matters were considered negotiable:

1. Wages, and longevity pay as part of annual salary
2. Mileage
3. Meal allowance
4. Payment for educational leave
5. Location of residence
6. Payment for time spent processing grievances
7. Limited binding arbitration (interpretation of the contract)
8. Grievance procedures and implementation of meetings to solve grievance
9. Use of sick leave, vacation credit

As mentioned previously, the recognized negotiable matters in fact have been generally approved in reported cases.[31]

The question of fixed hours of work came before a trial court when the court day was lengthened. The court held that there was no need to negotiate the change because fixed hours or work and overtime were not negotiable for employees under control of the judiciary.

County Detectives, Prosecutors, and Sheriff's Employees. Fixed hours of work and overtime have been held to be nonnegotiable for probation officers as employees of the judiciary.[32] Detectives and investigators employed by the county prosecutor, clerical and stenographic employees of the county prosecutor, and the county clerk's employees are all funded through the county freeholders. Their work is also associated with the courts. When the judiciary lengthened the court day, all of the associated personnel were required to work a longer day. They were not given additional compensation. The Civil Service Commission determined that an extension of the workday was a reduction of pay without good cause and a violation of civil-service law. The court in reversing the Civil Service Commission[33] held compensation to be a mandatorily negotiable term and condition of employment. The organized employees' remedy for an extension of the workday was negotiations over compensation. The statutory language that saves employees' civil-service rights in the collective-negotiations process was not an impediment to negotiations or a remedy for the employees. The court reasoned that an extension in hours was generally to be treated the same as discharges and reductions in force, which are permitted if done in good faith for reasons of economy or the public interest and without discrimination. The distinction between the right of various judicially related employees to negotiate over the same subject varies simply because some are under the control of the court, which can exclude areas from negotiations by rule.[34]

Merit increments for county employees as a subject for negotiations has been indirectly approved. In an unreported decision, the county freeholders were restrained from adopting a salary resolution for 1975 that deprived any member of the bargaining unit of a merit increase in contravention of the negotiated agreement.[35] Job titles of sheriff's employees are subjects for negotiations and cannot be unilaterally changed.[36]

Welfare Board. Employees of county welfare boards negotiate in various counties where they are organized. They are individually employees of the county welfare boards, which are corporate entities authorized to appoint employees and determine their compensation within authorized funds.[37] They have the right to fix salaries for officers and employees within the limits of appropriations by the Board of Chosen Freeholders of the county.[38]

The various county welfare boards negotiated for salary raises, incremental steps, and cost-of-living adjustments. The State Department of Institutions and Agencies approved the terms of the agreements except for the salary provisions. The welfare boards were told that their salaries must comply with the state salary range for the same or comparable titles. In a suit in which the county welfare boards took the same position as the unions against the state of New Jersey, Department of Institutions and Agencies, and the Governor's Office of Employee Relations, the issue presented was the right to negotiate salaries as against the state's position that the Social Security Act requires it to maintain a statewide salary plan.

The state could have chosen to administer the federally assisted welfare programs at the state level. Having elected to permit administration by local boards, could it deprive welfare board employees of the right to negotiate salaries? The Department of Institutions and Agencies was not the public employer and had no legislative mandate to negotiate wages in any county. While the appeal was pending, the department implemented the social-security mandate by adopting a statewide compensation schedule fixing mandatory guidelines for salaries of all County Welfare Board employees. The court ordered that the commissioner of the Department of Institutions and Agencies hold a hearing and make appropriate findings and determinations before the compensation schedules contained in the state plan became effective. The employee organization would have the opportunity at the hearing to raise issues about work differences on counties, cost-of-living differences, monetary resources available in different counties, and recruitment problems.[39] Of course, as a practical matter, salaries have been effectively removed as a subject for negotiations for County Welfare Board employees at least on the classic bilateral model of negotiations.

Police, Fire Fighters, and Municipal Employees. A municipality argued that the work scheduling for police was nonnegotiable. The court held that a work schedule for a group of employees was a "term or condition of employment" and as such a mandatory subject for bargaining. A New Jersey statute limits police to a six-day week except in an emergency.[40] Another statute sets overtime pay for emergency duty for police at one and a half times the prevailing hourly wage rate.[41] The court reasoned that a demand by a municipality for a seven-day week would be illegal. The demand by police for double time for overtime would be illegal, but a demand to negotiate for a four days' on and two days' off shift was legal. The court relied on the lower court decision reversed in *Burlington County College Faculty*,[42] which held that a college calendar is a mandatory subject for bargaining. Whether this decision would still be good law is questionable. The work schedule might be a "policy" matter after *Dunellen, Englewood and Burlington*.[43]

A different aspect of negotiability was raised by "group dental care." The question was whether it was "ultra vires" for a municipality to negotiate for group dental care without a specific authorizing statute. A statute authorizes group life, hospitalization, and major medical benefits.[44] A dental-care statute was once proposed but did not pass. The courts have held in two opinions that municipalities could negotiate group dental-care programs with unions.[45]

As might be expected, the number of fire fighters required to man equipment has surfaced in the courts. In an unreported decision that is on appeal[46] the trial court held that the size of the work crew was a management decision and not negotiable.

Although wages are always accepted as a term or condition of employment, there may be a limitation for municipal employees. In 1971 the legislature reenacted the 1947 statute that permitted municipal-salary ordinances to be put to the voters in a public referendum.[47] It gave the municipal employees an alternative method of securing a wage increase if the municipal officials were reluctant. However, in a very recent case, after a salary schedule was negotiated, a group of citizens petitioned for a referendum, and the Police Benevolent Association (PBA) asked the court to enjoin the referendum. The question posed to the court was whether a negotiated wage could be set aside. The 1974 amendment to the employer-employee law specifically stated as a change from the previous law that it would not modify or annul pension statutes that seemed to broaden the scope of negotiations. The court did not construe section 10 of C.123 at all. In an unpublished oral opinion the court simply held that in C.303 the right to bargain was established in 1968. The legislature adopted the referendum statute in 1947 and amended it in 1971. It must have been cognizant of the effect of C.303. Since the legislature did not mention the right to negotiate, it must have intended the 1971 referendum law to be what it was.[48] The injunction was denied and the case is on appeal.

Public Schools. The general case law is quite clear. Educational policy matters are not negotiable. The application of the generalization has its problems. Not the least of the problems lies in the genesis of most of the cases—the substantial questions do not seem to arise from negotiation sessions—they arise as problems of contract administration.

Even the two leading cases that defined the dichotomy of educational policy and the direct effect of policy on working conditions, *Dunellen* and *Englewood*,[49] were started as attempts by school boards to restrain arbitration of specific grievances by teacher organizations. Could a school board agree to hours or compensation that violated specific school laws or specific departmental rules or negotiations? It could not go below any of the minimums expressed in statute but it could go above. A statute on hours or compensation does not preempt negotiations, it simply sets a floor.

Thus when the question of payment of unused sick leave or retirement by a teacher came before the court, it was held to be a proper subject for negotiations as additional compensation.[50] The board had actually adopted a policy to pay for a portion of unused sick leave on retirement and had negotiated with the teachers. It then decided it was not legal to pay.

In *Teaneck*[51] the board refused to arbitrate whether assignment of teachers to perform corridor, lavatory, outside, and tutorial duties were violations of the contract. The court enjoined arbitration in that none of the assignments involved additional time commitments beyond those in the normal school day and did not affect terms and conditions of employment and did not have an intimate and direct effect on the work load or working hours of teachers.

In *Hillsborough*[52] teachers were assigned to lunchroom duty, which took away some of the teachers' "free" time. The court enjoined arbitration as a matter of predominantly educational policy for the benefit of students. There was no change in work load or hours of employment, so the specific assignments of individual teachers were a matter of managerial discretion.

The Appellate Division of the Superior Court of New Jersey, which is the intermediate appellate court below the New Jersey Supreme Court, is developing a doctrine of "managerial prerogatives," which does not depend on *Dunellen*[53] as much as on *Lullo*.[54] *Lullo* defined certain inherent limitations on the right of public employers to bargain.

In *Hillside*[55] it was held that where the requirements of the School Board have only a minimal effect on working conditions they form a separate category of "managerial prerogatives" that are not arbitrable; nor apparently are they determinable by the commissioner of education as a question of school law. The matters considered by the court as managerial prerogatives were the establishment of "quiet-study" duty, a reduction in teacher aides to assist teachers, a change in the method of assigning home rooms, and a change in the method of weighing the proportion of teaching and nonteaching duties.

In *Chabak*[56] the court enjoined arbitration over a requirement for teachers to sign in and out each day, giving their full names and the time. Previously the teachers only signed in by initialing a sheet. High school teachers were required to sign in at the "new" building even if they worked in the "old" building. The trial court had restrained arbitration and referred the matter to the commissioner of education for decision. The appellate court held that the commissioner of education did not have primary jurisdiction to determine whether a dispute between the board of education and a teacher organization was arbitrable—the proper forum in the view of the court was the courts to determine threshold questions of arbitrability. Matters such as whether and how teachers sign in are not matters of major educational policy but do fall into the category of "managerial prerogatives," which have at most a minimal effect on terms and conditions of employment. Nowhere in either *Hillside* or *Chabak* does the court mention the clear mandate of C.123, which grants to the Public Employment Relations Commission jurisdiction subject to appeal to determine scope of negotiations.[57] The appellate division has created a managerial prerogative within the discretion of school boards. However, the supreme court held in several cases that there was a category of mandatorily negotiable and nonnegotiable matter. On other matters consultation was urged. In *Lullo*[58] the court has suggested that managerial prerogatives were discretionary. The inherent statutory limitations on negotiations if they exist are in fact nondiscretionary.

There may very well be managerial prerogatives, but the present standards are murky indeed. However, PERC is beginning to illuminate them.

Public Employment Relations Commission

Prior to January 20, 1974 PERC did not have the opportunity for a significant role in scope-of-negotiations problems. C.123 has given to PERC jurisdiction over unfair labor practices and scope-of-negotiations problems. As of this writing (July 1975) there have been about 135 unfair-practice cases and 17 scope cases. There have been four decisions to date, two dealing with PERC's jurisdiction to enjoin unfair practices to preserve the status quo and to enjoin arbitration until PERC determines a scope question. The two other significant decisions were orders to bargain in good faith.

One scope question has been decided so far and several have been disposed of by withdrawal after mediation effort by PERC. Some of the matters pending are:

1. Validity of dental and prescription plan.[59] The dental plan was upheld in court in *Dover and Camden*[60] so one imagines the petition is either moot or that PERC will follow the court.

The public school cases are:

2. Petition to enjoin arbitration on the school calendar.[61]
3. Petition to enjoin arbitration on nontenure teacher evaluation and rehire.[62]
4. Change of 12 months' position to 10 months held to be mandatorily negotiable, but the impact is negotiable.[63]
5. Petition to order arbitration.[64]
6. Extended sick leave.[65]
7. Petition to enjoin arbitration of sick leave and work schedule.[66]
8. Arbitrability of layoff of ten nontenure teachers due to closing of a school.[67]
9. Petition to enjoin arbitration of assigning teachers to early morning supervision.[68]
10. Teachers-aide employment, teachers to be available as substitutes, nonteaching duties to be done by nonteachers, and establishment of instructional councils.[69]
11. Development of curriculum, duty-free lunch periods, class size.[70]

What is significant about the listing of the public-school petitions pending before PERC is how few are really scope-of-negotiations cases. Out of the ten petitions from the public schools, six concerned arbitrability and arose from contract-administration problems rather than negotiations. Of the four petitions on scope only one raised a question as to instructional councils, curriculum, or class room size. Six of the petitions came from school districts with a history of some form of previous litigation one way or the other.

Not surprisingly, there is a petition from municipal-police negotiations concerning the table of organization of the police department.[71]

There are two fire-fighter cases—one in the manning of equipment.[72] The same matter is pending in the courts and the petition was filed to protect the parties' procedural rights. The other fire-fighter petition covers three issues.

1. Agency shop if the statute should be amended to permit it. (There are several petitions raising the question of agency shop. At present by case law agency shops are not permitted. A statute is pending that if passed will legalize agency shops. It has strong support.)
2. Binding arbitration for any disciplinary action where a fireman has not exercised his civil-service remedy.

3. Terminal leave pay of five days per year of service, which in case of death should be paid to a designated beneficiary.[73]

Except for class-size questions in one school petition, table of organization in a municipal-police case, and the crew size in the fire-fighter matter, most of the problems posed to PERC in the list recited so far do not pose the difficult questions that could really affect the scope of negotiations. The higher education petitions go to genuine questions of scope of negotiations. To say that does not mean there is nothing wrong in the public schools. Perhaps that puts the matter too strongly: out of 134 unfair-practice charges some 57 arise from school-district negotiations. However, there are some 500 school districts that negotiate with employees and most have more than one negotiating unit. Out of 17 scope petitions, 10 arose from public-school negotiations, but 6 of the 10 are problems of contract administration, not negotiations at all.

The pending petition by the American Association of University Professors (AAUP)[74] could affect higher education and even the public schools because they will force a close examination of the nature of educational policy:

1. AAUP to be consulted on those items of budget that have an impact on terms and conditions of employment
2. AAUP to have representation on all promotion-review committees
3. AAUP to appoint one member to every ad hoc committee appointed by the administration that contains a bargaining-unit member
4. Proposals for expansion, reduction, or reallocation of the physical plant that affect the terms and conditions of employment of bargaining-unit member to be submitted for consultation and review prior to implementation
5. No productivity studies to be made without participation of the AAUP
6. Calendar to be negotiated
7. No diminution of positions in the bargaining unit
8. Teaching assistants and graduate assistants fractional lines to be expanded to full lines
9. Faculty to be on the search committees for provosts and academic administrative officers
10. No policy on cancellation of classes or combination of sections on the basis of class size without AAUP approval

State-college bargaining has raised two questions:[75] increase of minimum number of minutes per week for faculty teaching-load contact time as a managerial prerogative and the proportion of tenured to nontenured faculty as a subject for bargaining.[76]

Commissioner of Education

The commissioner of education is instructed by the education law to hear causes and controversies arising out of school law. With the advent of C.303 in 1968 school boards and teachers turned to the commissioner for guidance and advice in determining the parameters of negotiations. The commissioner took a narrow view of his jurisdiction and refused to give any guidance as to the scope of negotiations but held himself ready to strike down agreements that in his view contravened school laws.[77] Drawing authority from section 10 of C.303, which held that nothing therein was intended to annul or modify any other statute, he generally took the position that any provisions of the education law were paramount to any provision of a negotiated agreement. Indeed, his position was not without support in the courts.[78]

He held, for example, that since the education laws created a tenure system, that subject was not negotiable. Any issue going to the bar regarding employment of nontenured teachers was a controversy under the school laws and not subject to negotiations or grievance procedures.[79]

Much of the support of C.123 separate and apart from a perceived need for an administrative procedure to remedy unfair negotiating practices was the feeling of teachers that section 10 of C.303 and its interpretation by the commissioner and the courts was a deterrent to the collective relationship—not perhaps so much to the process of contract negotiations as to contract administration.

Legislature

The supreme court made it quite clear in *Dunellen*[80] that it would have been desirable for the legislature to clarify "terms and conditions" of employment. In the first drafts of C.123 attempts were made. The ultimate legislative compromise was to change section 10 by inserting the word pension so the limitation in the act reads "nothing is intended to modify or annul pension statutes of the State." Its supporters thus hoped that the scope of negotiations was broadened. The legislature in a companion statute, C.124, created a study commission to recommend changes if desirable in impasse procedures and, among other things, whether scope of negotiations should be defined.

The study commission has been laboring for seven or eight months and the end is not yet in sight. Otherwise the statute's language is still as imprecise as in the original act. There has been precise action in response to precise needs; that is, multilateral or alternate bargaining has supplemented the bilateral relationship in certain areas. Thus, responding to the line of decisions that preempted negotiations over tenure in the public schools, a law was passed effective 1972 that requires school boards which do not intend to rehire a nontenured teacher to give written notice on or before April 30 of the school year; otherwise it will have been deemed to have made an offer of reemployment.[81] This year a law has been adopted that requires three evaluations each year for all nontenure teachers, which, among other things, are to be used as guides to reemployment.

In addition, teachers whose contracts are not renewed can ask for and receive written statements of reasons.[82]

School nurses have had a fair amount of difficulty in negotiating parity with teachers. A law effective 1974 requires the same salary guide for nurses and teachers.[83]

The statute that establishes tenure for state and county college faculty specifically states that it is not subject to negotiations pursuant to the Employer-Employee Relations Act.[84]

A question that has often surfaced has been the legality of negotiating for welfare-plan benefits not specifically authorized by statute. On the municipal level there has been litigation. On the state level, the Health Benefits Statute has been amended to permit drug-prescription plans to be purchased by the State Health Benefits Commission to implement duly executed collective-negotiations agreements.[85] The lack of the statute did not impede negotiations, only the implementation.

The other legislative action affecting scope of negotiations is probably in the category of inadvertent acts. As discussed previously, a 1971 revision of the Municipal Laws title of a 1947 act authorizing a referendum on petitions by 5 percent of the voters within 20 days after adopting a salary ordinance in principalities is presently in the courts.[86] The trial court held that the legislature must have intended the procedure with full knowledge of its 1968 law authorizing collective negotiations. The appeal will be interesting. At the risk of heresy, one suggests that it probably never even occurred to the legislature, neither in 1968 when the negotiations act was adopted nor in 1971 when the 1947 referendum law was reenacted. However, an argument can be made that in 1974 when the legislature amended the Employer-Employee Relations Act and specifically mentioned saving all civil-service rights of employees, it may actually have intended not to save noncivil-service rights of employees such as the referendum law. However, the referendum law is broad as it gives rights to "voters" in general, not only to employees. In any case, as with other provisions of the statutes, it will give the Legislative Study Commission another problem to study and the supreme court the ultimate responsibility to rationalize and harmonize the laws.

The Scope Question and Its Effect on Collective Bargaining

Impact on the Process of Bargaining

Except for higher education, there is no empirical study as yet in this state that will support a conclusion either way. With that caveat out of the way, it can be safely said that scope of negotiations problems have had no genuine impact on the process of negotiations in New Jersey. Although strikes are illegal, they occur from time to time. There has probably been only one strike in a school district in which scope of negotiations was a substantial issue.

In that one known instance, a school board allegedly violated a negotiated provision relating to notice to be given nontenure teachers and lost in arbitration. In subsequent negotiations the school board wanted to remove the language from the contract. It was an important issue in a subsequent strike. There may indeed be other situations where the impasse issue seemed to be salary, but in fact scope questions caused underlying tensions. In the public schools, scope of negotiations seems substantially to be a problem of contract administration. The conclusion is drawn not only from the court cases but the fact that since the locus of decision making about scope has been shifted to PERC by C.123, the same sort of petitions to enjoin arbitration are surfacing as prior to C.123. For every decision to date by the commissioner of education or the courts classifying something or other as nonnegotiable, one can find a school district where the board and the teachers have negotiated language on the subject. In a study of provisions in 1972-73 school agreements by the New Jersey State Education Association (NNJSEA),[87] 20 agreements or 6 percent of those studied, contained rights to reasons for nonretention to be given to nontenure teachers, an increase from the 20 agreements, or 5 percent, in the 1970-71 study. One hundred and thirteen agreements, or 24 percent, contained limits on use of teachers as substitutes and 156 agreements, or 33 percent, contained limits on nonteaching duties.

In a study of provisions in some 300 agreements for 1974-75 by the New Jersey School Boards Association,[88] 37 agreements, or 12 percent, contained provisions limiting class-room size, and 77 agreements, or 25 percent, had provisions to make an effort to reduce class size. More interesting and clearer, out of 300 contracts 25, or 8 percent, still had provisions on school calendar, notwithstanding decisions saying it was not negotiable.

At the college level there has been one strike by the state colleges' faculties that was over salary. Although the state colleges' faculties and the AAUP at Rutgers—The State University have been quick to litigate over scope questions, it has not prevented or apparently interfered with settlements. On the state level, negotiations so far have been concerned with economics. On the municipal and county level, there has been no discernible impact on the process of bargaining. It is possible that the settlements were not so much negotiated by employee organizations as accepted. The fact that from January 20, 1975 to January 23, 1975, 134 unfair-practice charges have been filed substantially by employee organizations indicates that something may have been percolating below the surface. Nevertheless, none of the informed observers interviewed for the purpose of this chapter in fact felt that from 1968 to date scope-of-negotiations problems have had any substantial impact on the process of negotiations.

Whether the contract-administration problems that seem to be real in the school districts because of the number of attempts to enjoin arbitration have any impact on governance is beyond this chapter. One rather doubts that in fact there has been any genuine change in the governance and operation of the public schools as a result of negotiations. There has been an observed polarization and a developing awareness that school administrators may have managerial interests.

There is little evidence that employment standards have been affected by negotiations. There has been standardization and increased participation by teachers, but the changes as in curriculum matters, too, are more in degree rather than kind. School boards may have spent more money on support services than they might have unilaterally, but it is difficult to identify a school district that put an addition on a building solely because of negotiations over class size for example.

Jack Chernick's[89] data indicates that out of some 340 impasse situations from July 1970 to June 1971 only 67 could be identified as resulting from noneconomic matters. From July 1971 to June 1972 only 41 out of 332 cases were concerned with nonsalary issues.

Impact on Substantive Results of Bargaining

There is no solid data to indicate that scope-of-negotiations questions have had an impact on the substantive results of bargaining. That statement should be narrowed to recognize that court decisions and statutes have withdrawn some subjects from bargaining and in other areas the legislature has helped employees achieve goals they could not reach through bargaining. There is no solid evidence to support a conclusion that public-sector bargaining is making a real change in the structure and operation of government in New Jersey. James Begin's[90] study of higher education bargaining seems to indicate that no change in structure has resulted as yet.

Of course it is perhaps too early to measure what is happening in New Jersey. The amendments to the law setting up a clear and simple administrative procedure for determining scope-of-bargaining questions coupled with an administrative remedy for refusing to bargain in good faith may have substantial impact.

Civil Service

The Civil Service System affects the scope of negotiations simply by being. C.303 and C.123 expressly preserve individual employees' rights. The Civil Service Commission has adopted as part of its personnel manual for both state service and for local jurisdiction the following language:

23:1.101C Limitations

This law expressly states that nothing therein shall be construed to deny any individual his rights under Civil Service Law and regulations. Therefore, no agreement shall be consummated which shall in any way alter or contravene the provisions of Title II (the Civil Service Statute or the Civil Service Rules).

What does it mean? New Jersey's civil-service laws and regulations are a complete personnel system. In addition to merit-system standards for hiring and promotion, sick leave, leave of absence, hours of work, assignments and transfer classifications, and compensation plans are covered.

The civil-service laws also contain an appeal system for individual, aggrieved employees. Does the statutory protection for individual employees' civil-service rights simply mean that the statutory-appeal procedure cannot be bargained away for, say, a binding-arbitration clause? Or is a right a benefit so that, say, a compensation plan promulgated by the Civil Service Commission cannot be the subject for bargaining.

The Civil Service Commission seems to think that protected rights means everything in the civil-service laws and regulations. On January 16, 1975 the commission adopted a procedure in the State Personnel Manual Sub-Part 702.101 setting out the procedure to be followed when an individual, an appointing authority, or an employee organization requests a salary reevaluation for a title included in a recognized negotiation unit. The employee organization is granted a right of appeal in the event of an adverse ruling. As of this writing in late July 1975 no employee organization has used the procedure and neither has the Office of Employee Relations, which negotiates for the state. For reasons that are beyond the scope of this chapter, up to this year there has been no serious negotiations demand in state negotiations to contravene or modify any of the benefits in the civil-service laws. Negotiations have centered on wage increases and fringe-benefit improvements that were not of any great substance. However, in this time of budget crunch and cutback, one can sense that the merit system itself may be on the table at least for discussion. If so, it seems certain that the Public Employment Relations Commission and the courts will decide questions of negotiability. It seems questionable whether the Civil Service Commission has jurisdiction to determine questions of scope of negotiations. Then again it could. C.123 expressly gives PERC exclusive jurisdiction in the field of unfair practices. The grant to PERC to determine whether a matter in dispute is within the scope of collective negotiation does not use the word exclusive—the statute simply says the commission shall at all times have the power and duty, and so on. Can one read into it the word "exclusive," or did the legislature deliberately omit the word exclusive to leave room for the Civil Service Commission to discharge its statutory role? This, too, will be resolved in time by the New Jersey Supreme Court.

Summary and Conclusion

Trends in Scope of Bargaining

What one sees in New Jersey is a developing relationship that is breaking out of the bilateral model. There has been a tendency for sound reasons to use private-sector models of bargaining as a starting place for thinking about the public sector. However, it just does not work. There are too many other and diverse interests involved in the public sector.

For example, in the field of higher education the increasing cost and the expansion of services has created a tendency in the Department of Higher Education (DHE) towards centralization of control—striving for centralization of control by DHE was neither a reaction to collective negotiations nor a result of it. The tenure case,[91] the budget case,[92] and the outside employment case[93] were not refusals to bargain by the state colleges or Rutgers administration nor by the governor's office of collective negotiations—in essence they were suits by faculty associations saying to the courts that an administrative agency carrying out its mission as it sees it is narrowing the area in which we can negotiate with our employer.

The New Jersey Supreme Court has sensed that the bilateral model is not sufficient. In the very cases where it held that there were mandatory subjects for bargaining and prohibited subjects, the court made the strong point that although certain subjects were nonnegotiable there should have been consultation and discussion with the employees' organization and also with other interested groups.

The public-school area will see the same trend. The New Jersey constitution and the courts require that the state establish and maintain a "thorough and efficient" system of education. What indeed does it mean and how is it obtained? There are over 500 school districts in the state. Each one negotiates with organized employees. The commissioner of education and the State Department of Education have promulgated guidelines for statewide standards. Community groups and even students are to be involved in the development of objectives and educational plans in each school district, which must then be approved by the commissioner's office and filed with him. This does not mean that organized teachers will not be involved. On the contrary, one expects a high degree of involvement but not at the bargaining table. The subjects with which they will deal of necessity will be removed from the bilateral table to some other forum. On the other hand, the alternate bargaining in which teachers have always been involved, that is, lobbying for beneficial legislation, will continue. It is in fact another way of establishing statewide standards in a fiercely independent "home-rule" state. Organized teachers secured minimum starting salaries through statutes that antedate formal negotiations. The statute that protects nontenure teachers and broadens their job security was a way of circumventing the frustrations of not being able to achieve the same result through bargaining. The analogy must be drawn here with the higher education situation. It is not that school boards were refusing to negotiate over nontenure teachers' rights. On the contrary, many were but an administrative agency hostile to the concept of negotiations intervened. As a result all school districts now are bound by a statutory procedure that may or may not be salutatory depending on ones viewpoint and how it works. When it was colorably negotiable, most school districts held their own in negotiations on the subject. The ones that did not found it a useful trade-off.

On the state, county, and municipal levels there has been no visible impact on the Civil Service System. There are two apparent reasons. One is that the focus of most bargaining on the state, county, and municipal level has been over salaries, increments, and fringe benefits. The other reason is the statutory protection afforded the Civil Service System. On the state level the Civil Service Association in conjunction with the State Employees Association has been certified to represent the large, state, white-collar and supervisory units. Under the pressure of reality, it has changed its opposition to the agency shop and is actively lobbying a bill through the legislature. The agency shop stands a good chance of being legalized.

The layoffs threatened by the fiscal crisis is causing interest in the merit system as a subject for bargaining but not yet to the extent of any real importance.

Prospects for Change in Scope of Bargaining

The major change in the amendment to the law that became effective January 29, 1974 has been to shift the locus of decision making at the first instance to the Public Employment Relations Commission. It has been held in enough authoritative cases that the rights guaranteed to employees in the act have been, except for the right to strike, substantially modelled on the National Labor Relations Act. One would expect, therefore, that PERC should tend to favor broader rather than narrower bargaining. The legislative mandate is to negotiate terms and conditions of employment and grievance procedures with or without binding arbitration and, negatively, civil-service rights of employees are not to be impaired and pension statutes are not to be annulled or repealed by negotiations. One doubts that the legislature will ever accept the invitation of the court to define the scope of bargaining. One even doubts that the legislature will accept its own invitation to its own study commission to do anything substantial in the area. What will the courts do and what will be the reaction?

The court will ultimately go back to its first major decision[94] and find that the legislature did not intend to broaden the inherent limitations in the public-service sector on the bargaining power of public employers and employees. Whether the court starts with its own previous statements as to the similarity of New Jersey's public policy on labor and the National Labor Relations Act (NLRA) and finds that terms and conditions of employment divide into negotiable and nonnegotiable subjects or simply rests on *Lullo*,[95] that there are sovereign obligations that cannot be bargained away, the result will be about the same. The other expected "given" is that the various powerful employee groups will go to the legislature with specific statutory changes to patch up where bargaining fails.

PERC in fact by rule and case decision divided the area of scope into required, permissive, and illegal subjects for collective negotiations. In its only decision to date it held that a school board could reduce a principal's work year from 12 months to 10 months but had to negotiate over the impact of its decision. It explained without particularly illuminating the matter that "items which are terms and conditions of employment are not subject to the duty to negotiate. Similarly, matters of inherent managerial authority and/or educational policy are outside the scope of collective negotiations."[96] Apparently there are inherent managerial rights separate and apart from the right to set educational policy. PERC also pointed out that it was permissible, in the absence of a statutory prohibition for a school board, to negotiate a matter not mandatorily negotiable.[97]

Implicitly PERC may be clarifying the amendment to section 10 of chapter 123 laws of 1974 without direct reference. The statutory change inserted the word "pension" before "statute" in the phrase "nothing herein is intended to annul or modify any other statute of this state." Proponents of the change have argued that now everything except pensions are negotiable. Without referring to section 10, PERC has held that there are areas not mandatorily negotiable such as "inherent managerial authority and/or educational policy," but permissibly negotiable nonetheless. Perhaps ultimately all that the change in section 10 will mean is that previously a matter that was outside the scope of collective negotiations because of the effect of the educational laws, for example, could not be a permissible subject for negotiations. Under the new language of section 10, pensions cannot be permissible subjects for negotiations. Other matters prohibited by a statute from the subject for negotiation cannot be negotiated. All other nonmandatory subjects a public employer may not be required to negotiate may be permissible subjects for negotiations.

Final Note

Many of the questions pending in September 1975 are now clear. PERC has held that matters of inherent managerial authority or educational policy are not required subjects for negotiations. The impact of such unilateral decisions are negotiable. Unless there is a specific statutory bar, a nonrequired subject may be permissively negotiable.[98]

The language may be a little different but the end result in scope cases in New Jersey is probably about the same as Michigan, Wisconsin, Pennsylvania and New York.

Notes

1. Ch. 303, Laws of 1968; R.S. 34:13A-1 et seq.; Ch. 123, Laws of 1974; R.S. 34:13A-1 et seq.

2. R.S. 34:13A-5.3; Sec. 7, Ch. 303, Laws of 1968.

3. Footnote 2 *supra.*

4. Footnote 2 *supra.*

5. Footnote 2 *supra.*

6. Sec. 10, Ch. 303, Laws of 1968; R.S. 34:13A-8.1.

7. Sec. 10, Ch. 123, Laws of 1974; R.S. 34:13A-8.1.

8. Burlington County Evergreen Park Mental Hospital vs. Dorothy Cooper and PERC, 56 N.J. 579 (1970).

9. Sec. 1 (d), Ch. 123, Laws of 1974; R.S. 34:13A-5.4(d).

10. Lullo vs. Fire Fighters, Local 1066, 55 N.J. 409 (1970).

11. Lullo at 440; see footnote 10.

12. In Re Salaries for Probation Officers of Bergen County, 58 N.J. 422 (1971).

13. Dunellen Board of Education vs. Dunellen Education Association, 64 N.J. 17 (1973).

14. The Board of Education of the City of Englewood vs. Englewood Teachers Association, 64 N.J. 1 (1973).

15. Burlington County College Faculty Association vs. Board of Trustees, Burlington County College, 64 N.J. 10 (1973).

16. Footnotes 13 and 15 *supra.*

17. Footnote 8 *supra.*

18. Footnote 10 *supra.*

19. Footnote 7 *supra.*

20. Association of New Jersey State Colleges Faculties Inc. et al. vs. Dungan, 64 N.J. 338 (1974).

21. Footnote 13 *supra.*

22. Footnote 15 *supra.*

23. Footnote 20 *supra.*

24. Footnote 14 *supra.*

25. Association of New Jersey State College Faculties et al. vs. New Jersey Board of Higher Education, 65 N.J. 290 (1974).

26. Rutgers Council of American Association of University Professors vs. New Jersey Board of Higher Education et al., 126 N.J. 53 (App. Div. 1973).

27. Association of State College Faculties vs. the Board of Higher Education et al., 112 N.J. super 237 (Law Div. 1970).

28. R.S. 2A:168-5, 7 and 8.

29. Footnote 12 *supra.*

30. Memorandum of Administrative Director, August 28, 1972.

31. Footnote 12 *upra.*

32. Passaic County Probation Officers Association vs. the County of Passaic et al., N.J. super (Ch. Div. 1975).

33. Prosecutor's Detectives and Investigators et al. vs. The Hudson County Board of Chosen Freeholders et al., 130 N.J. Super 30 (App. Div. 1974).

34. Whether a ruling by the administrative director of the courts can change the clear language of C.123, which gives PERC jurisdiction over scope-of-negotiations questions subject to appeal, remains to be seen.

35. Burlington County Council #16, N.J. Civil Service Association vs. The Board of Chosen Freeholders of the County of Burlington (Sup. Ct. Law Div. #P.W. L-25883-74 1975).

36. P.B.A. Local 208 vs. Camden County, N.J. Super (Law Div. 1973).

37. R.S. 44:7-7 and 7-9.

38. R.S. 44:1-27 and 44:4-35.

39. Communication Workers of America, AFL-CIO et al. vs. Union County Welfare Board et al, 126 N.J. Super 517 (App. Div. 1974).

40. R.S. 40A:14-133.

41. R.S. 40A:14-134.

42. 119 N.J. Super 276 (Law Div. 1972) reversed. See footnote 15 *supra.*

43. Footnote 13, 14, and 15 *supra.*

44. R.S. 40A:9-13.

45. Township of Dover vs. Teamsters Local 97 et al. (Sup. Ct. Ch. Div. 1975) unreported; N.J. Civil Service Association Camden Council #10 vs. Mayor & Council of Camden, 135 NJ Super 308 (Law. Div. 1975).

46. Newark Firemans Union of New Jersey vs. City of Newark.

47. R.S. 40A:9-165.

48. P.B.A. vs. Bergenfield (Sub. Ct. Law Div. 1975) unreported.

49. Footnotes 13 and 14 *supra.*

50. Maywood Education Association vs. Maywood Board of Education 131 NJ Super 551 NJ.L.J. 13 (Ch. Div. C-87-74, 1975).

51. Board of Education of Teaneck vs. Teaneck Teachers Association (App. Div. Docket No. A 910-72, Oct. 9, 1974), not officially reported, Cert. denied Jan. 29, 1975.

52. Hillsborough Township Board of Education vs. Hillsborough Education Association (Ch. Div. Docket #C-2277-73, Oct. 16, 1974) not officially reported.

53. Footnote 13 *supra*.

54. Footnote 10 *supra*.

55. Board of Education of Township of Hillside vs. Hillside Education Association (App. Div., Docket #A-2144-72, 1974), Cert. denied 66 N.J. 324 (1974).

56. Richard Chabak et al. vs. Board of Education of City of Plainfield et al. (App. Div. 1974), Cert. denied 66 N.J. 327 (1974). See also: Galloway Twsp. Board of Education vs. the Galloway Twsp. Education Association (C-4211-74) N.J. Super (Ch. Div. 1975).

57. Footnotes 13 and 14 *supra*.

58. Footnote 10 *supra*.

59. Passaic Valley Water Commission, SN-1, Jan. 22, 1975.

60. Footnote 45 *supra*.

61. Board of Education of Ridgefield Park, SN-76-1.

62. Board of Education, Ocean City, SN-18.

63. Fairlawn Board of Education and Fairlawn Administrative and Supervisory Association, Local 34, SASOC, AFL-CIO, P.E.R.C. No. 76-7, recorded Sept. 11, 1975.

64. Piscataway Education Association, SN-15.

65. Teaneck Board of Education, SN-14.

66. Hillside Board of Education, SN-10.

67. Board of Education, City of Englewood, SN-9.

68. Board of Education of Tenafly, SN-7.

69. Board of Education of Randolph Township, SN-6.

70. Board of Education of Bryan Township, SN-4 PERC, which was reported as 2NJPER 143, 1976.

71. Borough of Roselle & PBA #99, SN-3 PERC, which was reported as 2NJPER 142, 1976.

72. City of Newark & Newark Firemens Union of New Jersey, SN-5.

73. City of Trenton & F.M.B.A. Local 6, SN-2.

74. Rutgers—The State University & A.A.U.P. SN-12 and 13 reported as 2NJPER 13, 1976.

75. Stockton State College & Council of New Jersey State College Locals, NJSFT/AFT-AFL-CIO, SN-16.

76. State of New Jersey & Council of New Jersey State College Locals, NJSFT/AFT-ALF-CIO.

77. Board of Education, Newton vs. Newton Teachers Association, 1970 S.L.D. 444. See: Gross, Ernest, *Public School Law and Collective Negotiations:*

Problems in Interpretation, New Brunswick, N.J., Rutgers University I.M.L.R., 1973.

78. Porcelli vs. Titus, 108 N.J. Super 301 (App. Div. 1969), Cert. denied 55NJ 310 (1970); Board of Education, Township of Rockaway vs. Rockaway Township Education Association, 120 Super 564 (Ch. Div. 1972); Board of Education of Township of Ocean vs. Township of Ocean Teachers Association (Ch. Div. 1972) not officially reported, 70 L.C. 52, 968, GERR No. 481, 12-4-72.

79. Board of Education of Township of Lakewood vs. Lakewood Education Association, 1973 S.L.D.; Board of Education of the Township of Madison vs. Madison Township Education Association, 1974 S.L.D. See also North Bergen Federation of Teachers, Local 1060, AFT vs. Board of Education of Township of North Bergen, 1975 S.L.D. where even after C.123 the commissioner still holds nontenure teacher reemployment questions are his to decide and not grievable.

80. Footnote 13 *supra*.

81. R.S. 18A:27-10.

82. A-1668 laws of 1975.

83. R.S. 18A:29-4.2.

84. R.S. 18A:60-9.

85. C.12 laws of 1975.

86. R.S. 40A:9-165.

87. Analysis of provisions in selected articles of 1972-73 agreements, Bulletin A72-10, Feb. 1973, New Jersey Education Association.

88. Dr. Jack Chernick, Research Professor, Institute of Management and Labor Relations, Rutgers—The State University of New Jersey, has been gathering data on impasse resolution in public-sector collective negotiations in New Jersey.

89. Ibid.

90. State Institutional Relations under Collective Bargaining in New Jersey AERA Symposium, April 1, 1975, Washington, D.C., received April 8, 1975, Dr. James P. Begin, Research Professor, Institute of Management & Labor Relations, Rutgers—The State University of New Jersey. Begin, James P., *Faculty Governance and Collective Bargaining* Journal of Higher Education, XLV, No. 8, November 1974.

91. Footnote 20 *supra*.

92. Footnote 26 *supra*.

93. Footnote 25 *supra*.

94. Footnote 10 *supra*.

95. Footnote 10 *supra*.

96. N.J.A.C. 19:13-3.7 and footnote 63 *supra*.

97. Footnote 63 *supra*–footnote 9 therein.

98. NJAC 19:13-3.7, *Fairlawn Board of Education* PERC 76-7, 1 NJ PER 47 (1975); *City of Trenton* PERC 76-10 1 NJ PER 68 (1975); *Rutgers, the State University, AAUP* PERC 76-13 2 NJ PER 13 (1976); Byram Township Board of Education PERC 76-27 2 NJ PER 143 (1976).

4

The Scope of Bargaining under New York's Taylor Law

Robert D. Helsby

The subject of this book, the scope of public-sector bargaining, is most important. No subject has been more controversial. Neither has any subject been treated in a greater variety of approaches. Some have required negotiations over all terms and conditions of employment as that phrase has been interpreted under the National Labor Relations Act (NLRA); some have adopted various types of management-rights clauses; some have defined mandatory subjects of bargaining with varying degrees of specificity.

This chapter describes the New York State experience under the Taylor law. I am not including the New York City experience under its Office of Collective Bargaining. That experience is unique in many ways. The "tiered" system of bargaining used in New York City establishes different units for negotiating different conditions of employment.

The Taylor Committee and the Original Law

The Taylor law does not contain a management-rights provision. As originally enacted, it simply provided that:[1]

Public employees shall have the right to be represented by employee organizations to negotiate collectively with their public employers in the determination of their terms and conditions of employment.

The report authored by the Governor's Committee on Public Employee Relations, of which George Taylor was chairman, discussed the problem in the context of rejecting the strike as inappropriate in the public sector. The Taylor Committee observed:[2]

The issue of the "retained rights" of the employer (related in public service to the proper performance of both the legislative and executive functions) is more difficult to deal with in the public sector than in the private sector. In the private sector, certain subjects are dealt with unilaterally by the employer on the assumption that this is essential to the proper performance of the managerial function. There are limitations to the scope of collective bargaining in the private sector which unions recognize. To a greater extent, moreover, the governmental employing agency lacks the power directly to negotiate with its employees or to have effective means for securing necessary consent to an agreement from higher levels of authority (from the executive officers of government and ultimately from the appropriate law-making body). As compared to the private sector, the authority to negotiate is less likely either to be granted in advance or to be promptly obtained when desired. Such restraints are a concomitant of operations in a democratic political context. Unlike the private business organization, government is more directly responsive to the demands of its constituency.

The committee concluded:[3]

Governmental employing agencies secure their authority from legislative bodies representing the various public interests and they may have to secure a validation of agreed-upon terms from that body. In other words, the retained rights of government are defined, in the last analysis, by actions of the legislative body and executive officials who are subject to the restraints of the electorate. Employees may dis-elect their representatives and the public may dis-elect theirs. Collective negotiations in the public sector is obviously undertaken in an environment which is quite different, in important respects, from the private sector.

The impasse scheme proposed by the Taylor Committee obviated the need for a more precise statement or definition of the scope of bargaining. Since the final step in the impasse procedure was the legislative hearing, the committee proposed—by implication—that disputes over questions of negotiability be resolved at the legislative level if the parties could not successfully negotiate the issue. Thus, the committee report did not recommend and the law as originally enacted did not grant PERB improper-practice jurisdiction and the authority to resolve questions of bargainability.

The committee recognized the potential problem:[4]

There is the possibility that some public employing agency will improperly refuse to negotiate with a duly recognized employee organization on the ground that the subjects under consideration are within the exclusive control of the legislative body and hence not negotiable. To discourage this practice, it is suggested that there be clarification by statute as to which subjects are open to negotiations in whole or in part, which require legislative approval of modifications agreed upon by the parties, and which are for determination solely by the legislative body.

However, the resulting legislative enactment, as noted, did not follow this suggestion by the committee but instead adopted the language already quoted, and authorized PERB "[to] conduct studies . . . those subjects which are open to negotiation in whole or in part, . . . those subjects which require administrative or legislative approval of modifications agreed upon by the parties, and . . . those subjects which are for determination solely by the appropriate legislative body. . . ."[5]

The committee recognized that certain conflicts might arise between laws creating systems for the establishment of employee wages and fringe benefits and a new approach changing such benefits through collective negotiations. The committee thought this problem could be minimized by legislation imposing an obligation to negotiate and by including among the unit criteria the requirement that there be a match between "the terms over which employees in the employee unit wish to negotiate with those terms concerning which the executives of the corresponding employer unit can negotiate. . . ."[6]

Subsequent Legislation

Improper Practices

In the aftermath of the New York City sanitation-workers strike in the winter of 1968, Governor Rockefeller reconvened the Taylor Committee to evaluate the short experience of the law that had gone into effect the previous September. The committee filed two reports, one in June 1968 and one in January 1969.[7] In neither report did the committee address itself to scope-of-bargaining questions except to include the subject in its list of matters deserving study.

Although it was not included in the recommendations of the reconvened Taylor Committee, Governor Rockefeller proposed and the legislature adopted in 1969 an amendment providing improper-practice (unfair-labor practice) jurisdiction for PERB.[8] Among prohibited improper practices for both public employers and employee organizations was refusal to "negotiate collectively in good faith."

A joint legislative committee reported on the 1969 amendments and observed:[9]

PERB has also been given the power to require the parties to negotiate in good faith. The most significant aspect of this authority is in the determination of the proper scope of bargaining.

If an employee organization feels that a certain topic is a proper subject of mandatory bargaining and the public employer disagrees, the organization may seek a bargaining order from PERB. The administrative agency then would determine whether the issue involves a subject about which the public employer can be required to bargain. It can be expected that this authority may have far reaching effects.

In making improper-practice determinations, including those dealing with questions of bargainability, PERB was directed to recognize "fundamental distinctions between private and public employment . . . , and no body of federal or state law applicable wholly or in part to private employment, shall be regarded as binding or controlling precedent."[10]

Commenting on this provision, the 1969 legislative committee report observed:[11]

The amendment codified improper employer and employee organization practices. Most practitioners feel that these concepts, although not specifically stated in the original bill, were implied nevertheless, in order to protect the rights granted in the original law. (footnote omitted)

The concepts are similar to the National Labor Relations Act in seeking to prevent improper influence, coercion or other overreaching conduct by both employers and employee groups. The statute recognizes, however, that private sector precedents may not be controlling in the public sector. This is not an indication that public sector improper practices differ qualitatively or quantitatively from unfair labor practices in the private sector. Rather, in each instance, PERB should consider whether elements unique to public employment require a different interpretation or application of improper practices from those applied in the private sector.

Other Amendments

With three exceptions, attempts to limit the scope of bargaining by legislation have been unsuccessful. The most comprehensive effort to restrict the scope of bargaining occurred during the 1971 session. The following amendment, primarily applicable to teacher bargaining, was introduced as part of an omnibus bill:[12]

The term "terms and conditions of employment" means salaries, wages, hours and other terms and conditions of employment[.] , *provided however, such term shall not include, and the public employer shall have the sole right to determine, its mission, purposes, objectives and policies, including but not limited to the standards of admission to its facilities and the nature and content of curriculum or programs offered; the facilities, methods, means and number of personnel required for conduct of its programs, including but not limited to the ratios and standards of staffing of its facilities; the standards of examination, selection, recruitment, hiring, appraisal, training, retention, discipline, promotion, assignment, and transfer of its employees; the direction, deployment and utilization of its work force; the establishment of specifications for each class of positions; and the classification and reclassification and allocation and reallocation of new or existing positions.* (Note: The proposed new language is italicized.)

This provision was withdrawn because substantial union opposition developed and little management support could be found. Subsequently, another joint legislative committee observed:[13]

Definition of the scope of negotiations and the setting forth of management rights or responsibilities relate to substantially the same basic issue but not from the same point of view. Theoretically, the scope of negotiation could be defined by affirmatively listing the issues which are negotiable with all other issues considered as not negotiable. But in the absence of uniformity in terminology and in definition, and with the infinite interrelationships involving legislation other than the Taylor law, it is impossible to provide a detailed listing of all issues which are negotiable.

It is theoretically possible to approach the problem by listing in detail all the issues which are not bargainable but this is not practical for the same reasons. Furthermore such approaches run the danger of being too inflexible and restrictive as changes occur over a period of time which may make it desirable to change the dividing line between issues which are mandatory subjects of negotiation, those which are permissible for negotiation and those which are non-negotiable.

The 1971 effort represented the last serious legislative attempt to redefine the scope of bargaining on a comprehensive basis, but an attempt at a narrower restriction has been successful. In 1973 as part of a controversy over the escalating costs of public-pension systems, the definition of terms and conditions of employment was amended:[14]

... such term shall not include any benefits provided by or to be provided by a public retirement system, or payments to a fund or insurer to provide an income for retirees, or payment to retirees or their beneficiaries. No such retirement benefits shall be negotiated pursuant to this article, and any benefits so negotiated shall be void.

This legislation provided for a system of coalition negotiations on pensions, which would take place outside of the Taylor-law framework. However, the machinery for coalition bargaining has never been effected or implemented. Local governments, with the exception of New York City and school districts, have been permitted to negotiate pensions in the traditional manner with respect to options provided by existing legislation.[15] Such legislation has been enacted annually. School districts never did negotiate pensions because there is a uniform pension system for teachers outside of New York City. The pension options available to local governments other than New York City were never available to New York City. However, prior to July 1, 1973, when a new pension scheme was negotiated in New York City, it could not be implemented except by state legislation. Thus, since July 1, 1973 pension negotiations have been confined to local governments other than school districts and New York City.

A third legislative action is worthy of mention. In reacting to the report and recommendations of a fact-finding panel involving a dispute over the reallocation of correction officers, the legislature determined such matters to be beyond the scope of bargaining for state employees:[16]

... the legislature finds and declares the allocations and reallocations to salary grades of positions in the classified service of the state are not terms and conditions of employment under article fourteen of the civil service law. The legislature further finds and declares that such allocations and reallocations are not within the scope of a fact-finding board but are to be accomplished exclusively pursuant to the provisions of article eight of the civil service law.

Thus, in eight years there has been only one attempt by legislative leaders to enact a comprehensive legislative limitation upon the scope of bargaining and that attempt failed. The one statutory amendment that was adopted removed pensions from the normal bargaining arena but the new scheme for pension negotiations has yet to be effectuated. The other limitation was a statement of legislative intent regarding civil-service allocations and reallocations. It may be that an attempt at comprehensive, legislative modification stirs up so much controversy that legislation is virtually impossible, and that legislative modification of the scope of bargaining is more likely if it is directed to a single issue as in the pension controversy of two years ago.

*

Improper-Practice Determinations

The improper-practice amendment provided a forum for the resolution of questions concerning the scope of bargaining. Early in the process of making such determinations, the board faced the problem of adopting private-sector precedents to the public sector:[17]

The extent of such obligation has been defined to a degree in judicial decisions, which decisions do provide some guide lines in considering . . . [such issues]. In this regard we are mindful of the statutory provision that, in dealing with improper practices, fundamental distinctions between private and public employment shall be recognized and that no body of federal law applicable to private employment shall be regarded as binding or controlling precedent. Nevertheless, the wealth of experience in the private sector should not be completely disregarded.

In construing the bargaining obligation under the National Labor Relations Act, the Supreme Court has held that the duty is limited to wages, hours and other terms and conditions of employment. As to other matters, each party to the collective bargaining relationship is free to bargain or not to bargain. Thus, the National Labor Relations Act does not mandate that employers and labor organizations must bargain upon every subject which interests either one of them; rather, the specification of wages, hours and other terms and conditions of employment defines a limited category of subjects that are mandatory subjects of bargaining. This construction of the bargaining obligation under the National Labor Relations Act would appear to be equally applicable to the negotiating obligation under the Public Employees' Fair Employment Act because the terms used in each Act, while not identical, are quite similar. (Footnotes omitted)

The board's chief legal officer, Jerome Lefkowitz, has summarized the conditions precedent for a matter to be a mandatory subject of bargaining.[18] His analysis indicates that three conditions must be met:

1. The matter must be a term and condition of employment.
2. It must be within the discretion of the employer.
3. It may not go to the mission of the employer.

Public employers must negotiate and enter into written agreements in determining terms and conditions of employment, which the Taylor law redundantly defines as meaning "salaries, wages, and hours and other terms and conditions of employment." Although broad, this language is not all encompassing. In the private sector the words "terms and conditions of employment" have been recognized as expressing a limitation.[19]

When an employer has no discretion, it cannot bargain. For example, if the civil-service law provides for promotion on the basis of one's standing in competitive examinations, there is no duty to bargain on a demand for promotion based on seniority. Public-sector collective bargaining is a process by which employers share some of their discretionary authority with unions.

The third condition is related to the first. In the private sector the employer decides what product or service he will produce. Such decisions are normally not viewed as invoking terms and conditions of employment although there may be a clear impact. In the public sector, it is a governmental decision whether refuse should be collected once or twice a week, or whether a school system should offer certain courses.

The board has followed private-sector thinking and determined that bargaining on demands relating to nonmandatory subjects may be either prohibited or permitted. For example, the Taylor law prohibits the agency shop. The board has held that a school board was not required to negotiate with respect to agency shop on the grounds that it violates the Taylor law and other state laws.[20] On the other hand, the board has stated that some nonmandatory matters are permissive subjects of negotiation. For example, the board has held that class size is not a mandatory subject of negotiations.[21] The board, however, stressed that it was not prohibiting negotiations on class size:[22]

... neither does it preclude a public employer, such as a school board, from consulting with teacher organizations as to educational policies; rather this should be encouraged so as to take advantage of the teachers' professional expertise.

A union may seek to bargain over a nonmandatory subject and the public employer may legally enter into a contract granting the demand, but the union cannot compel the employer to negotiate about it. A party requesting negotiations on a nonmandatory, but permissive, subject of negotiations may continue to press for an argument on the matter during bilateral negotiations and through the mediation stage, but it may not persist in the demand once the dispute is submitted to a fact finder. On the question of whether a faculty organization pressed its demand for contract language barring student participation on committees considering faculty tenure and related matters, the board commented:[23]

The U.S. Supreme Court in *NLRB v. Borg Warner Corp.*, 356 U.S. 342 (1958), has declared that under the National Labor Relations Act a party may propose for agreement matters that are not mandatory subjects of negotiations, but it may not press such a proposal to the point of insistence. We determine that the test applied by the Supreme Court is the appropriate one to be applied to the duty to negotiate under the Taylor law. . . . We determine that the insistence on the demand in the instant case went too far when . . . it was carried into fact-finding and even beyond fact-finding.

This posture concerning nonmandatory but permissive subjects of negotiations has been challenged. The Supreme Court, Nassau County has recently held that it is beyond the authority of a municipality to agree to surrender governmental powers through the vehicle of a collective-labor contract unless the power involves a term and condition of employment and, thus, is a mandatory subject of negotiations.[24] The theory underlying that decision was that, in the absence of authority deriving from the Taylor law or some other state statute, a government could not compromise the interests of its electorate by withdrawing areas of decision from the political process. This decision was reversed. The court of appeals upheld an appellate division decision directing a school district to arbitrate the issue of staff size under a collective-bargaining agreement that covered this item and provided for the submission of disputes to arbitration.[25] The court pointed out that the school board, which could not be compelled to negotiate about staff size, "was always free to bargain voluntarily about staff size and was also, therefore, free to agree to submit to arbitration disputes about staff size."

Under the decisions of PERB where the mission of the public employer is involved it cannot be compelled to negotiate. For example, a superintendent of schools recommended budgetary cuts that would, if implemented, result in reduction in professional staff of about 20 percent, without negotiating the matter with the teacher union. The federation took the position that an employer must negotiate before making a decision to reduce its work force. The school district contended that such a decision was not a mandatory subject of negotiations. Because of the importance of the case and because it arose during the course of negotiations, the board bypassed the intermediate step of a hearing officer. (This expedited procedure was incorporated into PERB's Rules of Procedure later in 1971.) The board determined that "[d]ecisions of a public employer with respect to the carrying out of its mission, such as a decision to eliminate or curtail a service, are matters that a public employer should not be compelled to negotiate with its employees.[26]

The board concluded:[27]

. . . that the decision of the School Superintendent involving budgetary cuts with concomitant job elimination is not a mandatory subject of negotiations. . . . We conclude further, however, that the employer is obligated to negotiate with the Federation on the impact of such decisions on the terms and conditions of employment of the employees affected.

The 1974 legislative amendments providing for compulsory arbitration as the terminal step in the impasse procedure for disputes involving firemen and policemen required further considerations as to the process for resolving scope-of-bargaining questions. The board had previously held that pressing a nonmandatory issue before a fact finder constituted an improper practice.[28] In amending its Rules of Procedure with respect to the compulsory arbitration amendments, the board retained jurisdiction over such matters.[29]

(a) A charge filed by either party . . . which raises questions of arbitrability will be accorded expedited treatment in the manner set forth in section 204.4 of these Rules. . . .

(b) The public arbitration panel shall not make any award on issues, the arbitrability of which is the subject of an improper practice charge, until final determination thereof by the Board or withdrawal of the charge. . . .

The availability of arbitration to unions has deprived public employers of the posture, "I will negotiate, but I will not yield on this demand." This has increased the pressure for PERB decisions specifying mandatory subjects of negotiations. Nevertheless, in the first year since these amendments became effective, few cases came before the board. A partial explanation is found in the fact that constitutionality of the arbitration amendments has only recently been sustained.[30] Since this decision the number of cases has increased substantially. The growing list of board decisions implementing the principles recited above are summarized in Appendix 4A.

Changing Bargaining Strategies

Bargaining strategies adopted by the parties obviously change from time to time and are influenced by economic and revenue conditions. Problems concerning the scope of bargaining and related legal issues vary, to a certain extent, with the ebb and flow of these events.

In the early days of the Taylor law, some public employers adopted a strategy analogous to one developed by many private-sector unions. The resolution of real or apparent conflicts between the public policy of collective negotiations and the large body of law enacted prior to the Taylor law became a major source of litigation. An analysis prepared by R.L. Epstein and P.R. Braunsdorf in 1969 suggested upwards of 200 separate "points of contact" between the Taylor law and other preexisting New York statutes affecting terms and conditions of employment.[31]

A not atypical stance by a public employer was to agree to a benefit and then to refuse to implement the contract provision on the grounds that it was illegal. When the employee organizations sought to grieve and finally to arbitrate the matter, the public employer would seek to stay arbitration. Occasionally public employers relied upon opinions of the state comptroller who, pursuant to his function of rendering opinions as to the propriety of local-government expenditures, sometimes advised that local governments were precluded from actions for which a specific statutory authorization could not be found, that the Taylor law did not enlarge the authority of public employers to grant benefits to their employees, and that article VIII, section 1 of the New York State Constitution, which prohibits the "gift" of public monies, was applicable.

The impact of this approach was much broader than the actual number of cases brought. While such cases were pending, public employers could plead lack of authority to negotiate on this or that matter. Since it was not until 1972 that a decision of the court of appeals upset this bargaining tactic, it had a life of about three years. This may explain why relatively few cases involving issues of bargainability were brought to PERB under the 1969 improper-practice amendments during these years.

The court of appeals, in *Board of Education, Town of Huntington* vs. *Associated Teachers of Huntington*,[32] substantially resolved the question of conflicts between the Taylor law and other "contact points." The court stated:

Under the Taylor Law, the obligation to bargain as to all terms and conditions of employment is a broad and unqualified one, and there is no reason why the mandatory provision of that act should be limited, in any way, except in cases where some other applicable statutory provision explicitly and definitively prohibits the particular employer from making an agreement as to a particular term or condition of employment. . . .

Public employers must, therefore, be presumed to possess the broad powers needed to negotiate with employees as to all terms and conditions of employment. The presumption may, of course, be rebutted by showing statutory provisions which expressly prohibit collective bargaining as to a particular term or condition [of employment] but, "[i]n the absence of an express legislative restriction against bargaining for that term of an employment contract between a public employer and its employees, the authority to provide for such [term] resides in the [school board] under the broad powers and duties delegated by statutes." [Citation omitted.] It is hardly necessary to say that, if the Board asserts a lack of power to agree to any particular term or condition of employment, it has the burden of demonstrating the existence of a specific statutory provision which circumscribes the exercise of such power. It has failed to meet this burden in the present case.[33]

Lower courts, even before *Huntington*, had rejected the notion that retroactive-pay increases are constitutionally prohibited and are not gifts, approved provisions providing for termination pay, and payments to a union-administered welfare fund. Opinions of the comptroller subsequent to *Huntington* reversed earlier opinions on the same or similar subjects. Thus it became clear that if public employers wanted to avoid certain contract terms, the consequences of rejection at the bargaining table had to be faced. Reliance could rarely be placed on contentions of illegality.

Actually, the parties were, for the most part, able to work out bargainability issues at the table. Such issues, for example, did not come before fact finders with any great frequency.[34] In 1970 PERB commissioned a study that, among other things, examined contracts and the attitudes of the parties. The categories surveyed included teacher contracts, contracts with school nonteaching personnel, municipal employee contracts, and public authorities. Because of the large number of teacher contracts and those of school nonteaching personnel, a sample based on size and geography was employed. Other types of employment were analyzed on the basis of all available contracts.

Analysis of contracts by type of employer and employee indicates some variation and practice toward management-rights clauses and related matters; no real problem emerged because of the broad scope of bargaining under the Taylor law. There was, of course, some variance between attitudes expressed at the table and those expressed away from the table:[35]

In summary, school public employers for the most part held views similar to other public employers. Except for school boards in most of the larger cities, they decried the fact that formal collective bargaining for teachers had developed, and viewed PERB, along with the mediators and fact-finders, as an extension of the labor organizations. They felt that certain issues were beyond the reach of collective bargaining both for legal reasons and because they intruded on managerial rights. Yet, many of these issues were dealt with in negotiations, and despite some apprehension over future developments, the schools felt they could continue to deal with them on a bilateral basis. As was the case with other public employers, there was very little support for legislative changes in the Taylor Act that would exclude certain items from negotiation and thus establish more precise limits on the scope of bargaining.

The basic conclusion of the report was as follows.[36]

The experience in New York State indicates that the broad scope of bargaining under the Taylor Act has not created numerous problems. The contract study showed that very few impasses have arisen over the bargainability of issues; the parties have frequently adopted clauses which in a general way recognized management rights and the supremacy of certain existing laws and regulations. Numerous joint study committees have been established, especially in teacher contracts, in areas which might have been interpreted as being outside the scope of bargaining if certain legislative exclusions were included in the Taylor Act.

Finally, the interviews did not reveal any really strong sentiment for legislative exclusions, even though various public employers expressed reservations concerning formal collective bargaining for public employees and some apprehension concerning future developments.

The bargaining commencing in 1968, 1969, and 1970 can basically be described as negotiations in which employees made substantial gains, economic and other. Although the 1969 round was slower than the other rounds, employees still made gains. In late 1970, both state and most local jurisdictions began to face a substantial financial crunch as the result of recession and inflation. Thus, the 1971 negotiating round took place against a different background—threats of layoffs and finally wage and price controls (imposed in August 1971). In this round government in general and public education in particular had ceased to be a growth industry.

It was against this background that the initial group of improper-practice charges were filed raising substantial negotiability questions. This same fiscal crisis produced the previously discussed legislative attempt to limit the scope of bargaining. This negotiating round—1971—produced the board decisions promulgating the general ground rules defining the scope of bargaining. It may be that emergence of these ground rules tended to blunt the legislative drive for a statutory limitation on the scope of bargaining.

The period of wage and price controls—August 1971 to April 1974—produced a greater employee interest in nonmonetary subjects that might otherwise have been the case. Also, employee organizations became more accustomed to using improper-practice charges for defensive and aggressive purposes.

The bargaining strategies of certain public employees, particularly professionals, often have a different thrust:[37]

The basic problem of collective bargaining in public employment, and particularly of collective bargaining in public education, is the inapplicability of the concept of terms and conditions of employment as we know it in the private sector. It is relatively rare that professional employees have organized in the private sector, but professional employees—teachers in particular—are probably the group that is most organized in the public sector. For professional employees, job satisfaction is a term and condition of employment of great priority. . . .

It is true, as has been suggested by management representatives, that teachers are not likely to offer to trade off economic benefits in return for concessions regarding their professional objectives. This does not diminish the sincerity with which they pursue those objectives. A more likely explanation is that while teachers recognize that their economic objectives are for themselves, they often see their professional objectives as being in the interest of their students and the school system for which they work. Accordingly, they expect and are willing to make compromises while bargaining over their economic package, but they expect their professional objectives to be accepted *in toto* on their merits. Even so, there are situations—admittedly rare—when professional employees have been willing to compromise economic objectives in order to achieve professional ones, provided that they are shown that the price tag of the professional objectives cannot be met if their economic objectives are satisfied.

Because professional employees do consider job satisfaction to be a term and condition of employment, we may anticipate increased pressure from them to negotiate over matters that, in the blue-collar employment, would not be thought of. Hence, demands regarding class size are not only workload demands but also job quality demands, and teachers will attempt to bargain over course offerings, choice of textual materials, and the availability of supplemental services to students. . .

As professional employees in the private sector continue to pressure for expansion of the concept of the scope of negotiations, there will undoubtedly be more stress on such issues than there has been in the immediate past. Professional employees, driven by their desire for enhanced job satisfaction and their views on how best to accomplish their particular mission, will continue to attempt to bargain on such subjects, perhaps incrementally rather than by wholesale assault. Public-employment management will, of course, continue to resist these developments as an intrusion upon management prerogatives. In many instances, such public-employee pressure will be resisted by the community as an assault upon its political prerogatives.

During the financial emergencies facing many municipalities, there were several decisions that a public employer may disavow an agreement that imposes undue financial burden upon it. One example is *Schwab* vs. *Bowen*, 51 AD 2d 574 (2d Dept. 1976) which involved the city of Long Beach. The court said:

Even were we to accept the concept that a public employer may voluntarily choose to bargain collectively as to a nonmandatory subject of negotiation, the public interest or welfare in this case demands that the public employer's job abolition power remain unfettered [cf. *Susquehanna Valley Cent. School Dist.* vs. *Susquehanna Valley Teachers Ass'n*, 37 N.Y. 2d 614 (dec. Oct. 28, 1975)]. Regardless of fault, the fact remains that the fiscal crisis facing the City of Long Beach threatens its very ability to govern and to provide essential services for its citizens.

This analysis, if it were to prevail, would doom collective bargaining in the public sector. No public-employee organization could enter into an agreement if the public employer were free to disavow that agreement because it became burdensome. There would be no incentive for public employees to accept small, or, perhaps, even zero increases in return for guarantees of job security if those guarantees were meaningless. The possibilities of union-management cooperation in finding ways to meet the financial emergency that is afforded by collective bargaining would be frustrated. Fortunately, in *Board of Education, Yonkers Central School District* vs. *Yonkers Federation of Teachers* (40 NY 2d 268 [1976]), the New York State Court of Appeals rejected the analysis of the appellate division. It reaffirmed its holding in *Susquehanna* that the "matters in controversy [which], although not subject to mandatory bargaining, may voluntarily be included within a collective agreement by a public employer" [citation omitted].

As to the substantive issues in dispute, the court reasoned:

A job security provision insures that, at least for the duration of the agreement, the employee need not fear being put out of a job. Such absence of fear may be critical to the maintenance and efficiency of public employment, just as the fear of inability to meet its debts may destroy the credit of the municipality. A job security clause is useless if the public employer is free to disregard it when it is first needed.

Finally, it held that the collectively negotiated labor agreements enjoy the same status as other contractual obligations of a municipality, saying:

In bankruptcy all obligations may suffer impairment or dissolution, job security clauses included. But the collective agreement in question, negotiated before a legislatively declared emergency, short-term in length, and indistinguishable from the city's other contractual obligations which remain enforceable, is not yet vulnerable to attack as in violation of public policy.

Summary and Conclusions

Litigation represents only the tip of the iceberg, whether the subject is scope of negotiations or other matters. Since the Taylor law became effective, about 23,000 contracts have been negotiated. Each year up to 70 percent are negotiated without third-party assistance. Of the 400 to 500 improper-practice charges filed annually, relatively few involve significant scope-of-negotiations questions. The parties have, for the most part, been able to resolve most of these issues at the table.

Since PERB did not have improper-practice jurisdiction in the early negotiating rounds, the parties were left to their own devices and some employers resorted to the tactic of agree now and litigate later. A PERB-sponsored study of this period indicated that scope-of-negotiations questions were not among the issues frequently faced by fact finders.

The anticipated problem of conflict between the Taylor law and other statutes, for the most part, did not materialize. Judicial determinations resolved part of the problem in establishing the principle that public employers could negotiate on subjects unless expressly prohibited from doing so.

Even the expected clash between civil-service laws and procedures and bargaining did not take place, at least not in the manner and on the scale that some anticipated.[38] Although it is not possible to conclude precisely why this has been so, several factors have contributed to this situation. One is that the major union representing public employees outside of New York City was instrumental in the evolution of the present civil-service system and has a vested interest in its preservation. Another is that to the extent that broad-based units have been created, either by agreement or by PERB decision, there has been some tendency to negotiate across-the-board increases rather than specific occupational rates. When the need to negotiate specific rates has emerged, there has been a tendency to submerge the existing job classification by creating more classifications by contract than exists under civil-service law.[39]

An example of the extent to which the accommodation between the negotiated- and statutory-benefit structures pertains is teacher-salary increments. The teacher minimum-salary law was repealed in 1971[40] but the impact so far has been minimal. This law had long ceased to have any impact on actual salary levels, but it did mandate the traditional teacher-salary grid. By the time of repeal, the grid had become so institutionalized that neither party has been able to negotiate a substitute that holds up over the long term.

PERB decisions on scope-of-negotiations questions, although fully recognizing the fundamental differences between the public and private sectors, have generally adapted many private-sector concepts into public-sector terminology. Codification yields a list not unlike that found in the laws of other states where attempts have been made to do the same thing through legislation.

In brief, New York State's Taylor law represents an approach to define conditions of employment in only the broadest of terms. There is no management-rights clause and no specific list of mandated or prohibited subjects of bargaining.

The anticipated emotional and controversial struggle over what is and what is not bargainable has just not materialized. Generally, parties have been able to agree on their own management-rights clauses or settle such issues by negotiation. The state legislature has, by its creation of the improper-practices machinery, left dispute settlement of these issues to PERB and to the courts. PERB has generally held that the overall mission and level of services a government wishes to provide its constituency is a management prerogative and thus not a mandatory subject of bargaining. Where such decisions affect the employees conditions of employment, that effect is bargainable. The dividing line is imprecise at best. The board draws the line on a case-by-case basis subject to a review by the state courts, and thus this line becomes sharper with the passage of time.

The state legislature and the parties seem to be reasonably satisfied with this approach since almost no serious legislative attempts to change the system have emerged in the last three or four years. Although the advent of interest arbitration will place increasing importance on these decisions, an independent, bipartisan and competent administrative board may well provide its best expertise in making these critical judgments.

Changing economic and political conditions influence the bargaining strategies of the parties. The scope-of-bargaining issues remain dynamic rather than static. New issues will arise and old questions will have to be reexamined in new and different contexts. The continuing and perhaps increasing militancy of the professional employee can be expected to introduce new and larger pressures for both expanding and reducing the scope of bargaining. From this conflict, one can foresee the potential for major alteration of the way in which the public enterprise is managed, but these issues, if they indeed do emerge, are not likely to be resolved in this context but more likely in the political arena.

Notes

1. CSL sec. 203.

2. Final Report, Governor's Committee on Public Employee Relations, p. 17.

3. Ibid., p. 18.

4. Ibid., pp. 45-46.

5. CSL sec. 205.5(g).

6. Final Report, pp. 25-26.

7. Governor's Committee on Public Employee Relations, Interim Report, June 1, 1968; Governor's Committee on Public Employee Relations, Report of January 23, 1969.

8. Ch. 24, Laws of 1969.

9. 1969 Report, Select Joint Legislative Committee on Public Employee Relations, Legislative Document (1969), Number 14, p. 19.

10. CSL sec. 209-a.3.

11. Legislative Document (1969), Number 14, p. 19.

12. Assembly 7796, introduced by Assemblymen J.E. Kingston and C.A. Jerabek on May 3, 1971.

13. 1971-72 Report, Joint Legislative Committee on the Taylor Law, Legislative Document (1972), Number 25, pp. 33-34.

14. Ch. 382, Laws of 1973.

15. Ch. 383, Laws of 1973.

16. Ch. 158, Laws of 1970. It should be noted that reallocations have taken place shortly after the completion of negotiations, including the dispute out of which this legislation came.

17. *In the Matter of the City School District of New Rochelle*, 4 PERB 3705, 3706.

18. Presentation by Jerome Lefkowitz, Conference on Public Education Bargaining, sponsored by Rutgers University, March 4, 1975.

19. See concurring opinion in *Fibreboard Paper Products Corp.* vs. *NLRB*, 379 U.S. 203, 220 (1964); 57 LRRM 2616:

It is important to note that the words of the statute are words of limitation. The National Labor Relations Act does not say that the employer and employees are bound to confer upon any subject which interests either of them; the specification of wages, hours, and other terms and conditions of employment defines a limited category of issues subject to compulsory bargaining.

20. *In the Matter of Monroe-Woodbury Teachers Association*, 3 PERB 3632, *affirmed* 68 Misc. 2d 952, 4 PERB 7097.

21. *In the Matter of Mrs. Lloyd Herdle et al., constituting the West Irondequoit Board of Education*, 4 PERB 3728, *affirmed* 35 N.Y. 2d 46, 7 PERB 7028.

22. Ibid.

23. *In the Matter of Board of Higher Education of the City of New York*, 7 PERB 3044.

24. *Schwab* vs. *Bowen*, 80 Misc. 2d 763; see also *Matter of Lippman* 48 App. Div. 913 (2nd Dept.), NYLJ 7/8/75, p. 17, col. 5; and *DeLury* vs. *City of New York*, 48 App. Div. 595 (1st Dept.), NYLJ 7/14/75, p. 6, col. 1.

25. *Matter of Susquehanna Valley School District at Conklin [Susquehanna Valley Teachers' Association] 37 NY 2d 614, 8 PERB ¶ 7515, 7562.*

26. *In the Matter of City School District of the City of New Rochelle*, 4 PERB 3706.

27. Ibid., p. 3707.

28. *In the Matter of Yorktown Faculty Association* 7 PERB 3054.

29. Rules of Procedure, 7 PERB 2128.

30. *City of Amsterdam* vs. *Helsby et al., City of Buffalo* vs. *PERB et al.* 37 N.Y. 2d 19 (June 5, 1975).

31. Barr, Martin L., "The Power to Agree After Huntington," *PERB News*, Vol. 6, No. 3 (March 1973), p. 2.

32. 30 N.Y. 2d 122 (1972), 5 PERB 7507.

33. Ibid., p. 7510.

34. Sabghir, Irving H., *The Scope of Bargaining in Public Sector Collective Bargaining*, New York State Public Employment Relations Board, 1970, Chapter 4.

35. Ibid., pp. 107-108.

36. Ibid., pp. 113-114.

37. Presentation by Jerome Lefkowitz, Conference on Public Education Bargaining.

38. Helsby, R.D., and Joyner, T.E., "The Impact of the Taylor Law on Local Governments," *Unionization of Municipal Employees*, Proceedings of the Academy of Political Science, December 1970, pp. 35-36.

39. Ibid., p. 36.

40. Ch. 123, Laws of 1971.

Appendix 4A:
PERB Decisions: Mandatory
and Nonmandatory

Index

Court Decisions

Mandatory

General

1. Death Benefits (*Albany PPFA*, 7 PERB ¶3079; *Albany Police*, 7 PERB ¶3078; affirmed 38 NY 2d 778, 9 PERB ¶7005).

Benefits such as those authorized by Retirement and Social Security law §360-b, which is only applicable to employees who joined a public-retirement system before July 1, 1973, are negotiable. (See *Kingston PFA*, 9 PERB ¶ 3069.)

2. Parking Fees at Work Locations Controlled by the Employer (*New York State* 6 PERB ¶ 3005).

It was found that free parking is a term and condition of employment. This decision was based on the application of such criteria as the nature of the benefit, the proportion of the work force at a given location and as a whole receiving the benefit, the relative value of the benefit, the availability of alternatives to employees receiving the benefit, and the extent to which the decision of whether or not to provide or continue to provide the benefit is an essential part of the employer's mission as an enterprise.

3. Retirement (*Albany PPFA* 7 PERB ¶ 3079; *Albany Police*, 7 PERB ¶ 3078; affirmed 38 NY 2d 778, 9 PERB ¶ 7005).

The Laws of 1974, Chapter 510, Section 31, permits employee organizations to negotiate for improvements in retirement between July 1, 1974 and June 30, 1975 (extended to June 30, 1976 by Laws of 1975; also extended to June 30, 1977 by Laws of 1976) provided the improved benefits are among those already available under state law. (See *Kingston PFA*, 9 PERB ¶ 3069.)

4. Wages and Hours (The Taylor Law).

College

26. Access to College Property and Equipment (*Orange County Community College Association*, 9 PERB ¶ 3068).

Mandatory subject insofar as it covers proper and legitimate official business relating to the association's role as the representative of employees in the bargaining unit. (See *Albany City School District*, 6 PERB ¶ 3012. See also Nonmandatory-College #26.)

27. Assignments for Extra Compensation (*Orange County Community College Faculty Association*, 9 PERB ¶ 3068).

Mandatory as it relates to the opportunity of employees within the negotiating unit to earn extra compensation in other teaching and related assignments.

28. Committees to evaluate faculty (*Orange County Community College Faculty Association*, 9 PERB ¶ 3068).

Requiring written statements of criteria for promotion, retention, and tenure, and a written rationale for all decisions denying promotion, reappointment, and tenure is a mandatory subject except to the extent that, in the absence of necessary reasons for such specification, the requirement would impose a management duty upon particular member of management.

29. Pay for Absence Due to On-the-Job Injury (*Orange County Community College Faculty Association*, 9 PERB ¶ 3068).

This is a demand for compensation and therefore a mandatory subject of negotiation.

30. Professional Development Plan that Would Constitute Basis for an Annual Evaluation and for Reappointment (*Schenectady County Community College*, 6 PERB ¶ 3027).

It cannot be said that the implementation of the college's professional-development plan would not have an impact on terms and conditions of employment. Therefore, the college had a duty, upon request, to negotiate with the union on the impact on terms and conditions of employment. Failure to do so constitutes a violation of its duty to negotiate in good faith.

Fire Fighter

51. Death Benefits (*Albany PPFA* 7 PERB ¶ 3079).

See Mandatory-General #1. (See also *Kingston PFA*, 9 PERB ¶ 3069.)

52. Establishment of Labor-Management and Joint Safety Committees (*Albany PPFA*, 7 PERB ¶ 3079).

The establishment of labor-management committees to discuss matters of mutual concern is a mandatory subject of negotiations to the extent that the matters to be discussed are themselves mandatory subjects of negotiations, as is employee safety.

53. Exclusivity of Representation (*Albany PPFA*, 7 PERB ¶ 3079).

According to PERB's Rules of Procedure Sec.201.12(h), whether an employee organization is granted exclusive rights of representation is subject to agreement between the organization and the public employer.

54. Parity (*Albany PPFA*, 7 PERB ¶ 3079).

The board said that to the extent it is a demand for a wage reopener and for subsequent negotiations, it is a mandatory subject of negotiations. However, if the demand is not to reopen the agreement for negotiations but to reopen it for the mechanical change of instituting the dollar value of benefits obtained later by the police in their negotiations, it is not negotiable.

55. Retirement (*Albany PPFA*, 7 PERB ¶ 3079).

See Mandatory-General #3. (See also *Kingston PFA*, 9 PERB ¶ 3069.)

56. Safety (*White Plains*, 9 PERB ¶ 3007).

Safety as a general subject is a mandatory subject of negotiations. Demand to establish a joint safety-policy committee would be a mandatory subject of negotiations.

57. Seniority Rights

(*Albany PPFA*, 7 PERB ¶ 3079). This is manifestly a term and condition of employment; does not involve the decision of a government with respect to the carrying out of its mission or the manner and means by which its services ought to be rendered to its constituency.

(*White Plains*, 9 PERB ¶ 3007). Assignment of jobs by seniority is a term and condition of employment.

58. Time to Process Grievance without Loss of Pay (*Albany PPFA*, 7 PERB ¶ 3079).

Reasoning same as "Paid Leave." (See Mandatory-Police #111.)

59. Tours of Duty

(*White Plains*, 5 PERB ¶ 3008; *Niagara Falls*, 8 PERB ¶ 3030; *Malone*, 8 PERB ¶ 3045). The board said it is the city alone that must determine the number of firemen it must have on duty at any given time. It cannot be compelled to negotiate with regard to this matter. However, there are many ways in which the schedules of individuals and groups of firemen may be manipulated to satisfy the city's requirement for fire protection. Within the framework that the city may impose unilaterally that a specified number of fire fighters must be on duty at specified times, the city is obligated to negotiate over the tours of duty of the fire fighters within its employ.

(*Buffalo PBA*, 9 PERB ¶ 3024). The availability of long weekends on a rotating basis involves hours of work and therefore is a mandatory subject of negotiations.

See also Nonmandatory-Fire Fighter #57.

60. Tuition Reimbursement (*Kingston PFA*, 9 PERB ¶ 3069).

Same as Mandatory-Schools #169.

61. Work Schedules (*Albany PPFA*, 7 PERB ¶ 3079).

Found to be mandatory for same reasons as Tours of Duty (#59) except to the extent that it would require the employer to call in off-duty personnel and would preclude the reassignment of on-duty personnel.

62. Unpaid Leave of Absence for Union Activity (*Albany PPFA*, 7 PERB ¶ 3079).

Reasoning same as for "Paid Leave." (See Mandatory-Police #111.)

Police

101. Air-Conditioning in Cars (*Scarsdale*, 8 PERB ¶ 3075).

Air-conditioning affects employees' comfort and is thus a term and condition of employment.

102. Death Benefits (*Albany Police*, 7 PERB ¶ 3078; affirmed 37 NY 2d 778; 9 PERB ¶ 7005).

See Mandatory-General #1. (See also *Kingston PFA*, 9 PERB ¶ 3069.)

103. Department Rules and Regulations (*Albany Police*, 7 PERB ¶ 3078; affirmed 38 NY 2d 778, 9 PERB ¶ 7005).

Rules and regulations of a police department may involve the mission of the department within the meaning of the board's *New Rochelle* decision. If restricted to work rules, however, it is a mandatory subject of negotiations.

104. Discipline and Discharge

(*Albany Police*, 7 PERB ¶ 3078). A mandatory subject of negotiations so long as it does not deny employees an opportunity to use the statutory procedures in Civil Service law sections 75 and 76.

(*Scarsdale*, 8 PERB ¶ 3075). Discretionary-discipline procedures, such as investigation, must be negotiated.

(*Buffalo PBA*, PERB ¶ 3024). Period of time of service after which police detectives become subject to Civil Service law section 75 removal proceedings must be negotiated.

105. Dismissal of Probationary Employee, Decision and Procedures for Accomplishment (*Albany Police*, 7 PERB ¶ 3078).

The duration of probationary service is within the jurisdiction of the municipal civil service commission and not of the city itself, and therefore a nonmandatory subject of negotiations. A decision to dismiss a probationary employee, however, and the procedures by which such a decision might be accomplished are subject to the discretion of the municipality and are, therefore, subject to mandatory negotiations.

106. Establishment of Labor-Management and Joint Safety Committees (*Albany Police*, 7 PERB ¶ 3078).

Same as Mandatory-Fire Fighter #52.

107. Exclusivity of Representation (*Albany Police*, 7 PERB ¶ 3078).

Same as Mandatory-Fire Fighter #53.

108. Extra Work Outside Regular Hours of Duty (*Albany Police*, 7 PERB ¶ 3078).

To the extent the demand is for authorization under General Municipal law section 208-d for authorization to engage in extra work for all employees outside of regular hours of duty, it is a term and condition of employment and mandatory.

109. Impact of Management Decisions (*Buffalo PBA*, 9 PERB ¶ 3024).

Requirement that police officers carry service revolvers while off duty. (See also Nonmandatory-Police #106.)

110. Job Duties (*Scarsdale*, 8 PERB ¶ 3075).

Job content, such as repairing own equipment, is a mandatory subject of negotiations. (See Mandatory-Schools #157. See Nonmandatory-Police #108; Nonmandatory-Schools #161.)

111. Paid Leave (*Albany Police*, 7 PERB ¶ 3078; affirmed 38 NY 2d 778, 9 PERB ¶ 7005).

Paid leave may be occasioned by bereavement, personal concerns, jury duty, military service, and other reasons. Time off is a term and condition of employment and therefore mandatory.

The ability of an employee organization to provide effective representation to its constituency is predicated upon having employee leaders of that organization available to devote time to the work of the organization. The question of whether or not such employee leaders are to be compensated, and if so, how much, are mandatory subjects of negotiations.

112. Procedures Relating to Layoff (*Albany Police*, 7 PERB ¶ 3078).

A provision for notice of layoff is not unreasonably related to the requirement that a public employer negotiate over the impact of its decision to eliminate or curtail a service. However, to the extent that the duration of the notice proposed by a union would impinge on an employer's obligation to provide services to the public, it is not a matter to be dealt with in negotiations.

113. Promotional Procedures for Unit Employees (*Albany Police,* 7 PERB ¶ 3078).

In a decision involving promotion and filling of vacancies in noncompetitive classification, the board said that but for the enactment of the Taylor law, this would be subject to the discretionary authority of the employer. Such matters, to the extent that they are terms and conditions of employment, are mandatory subjects of negotiations. To the extent promotion is sought to higher paying positions within the negotiating unit, this also is a mandatory subject of negotiations.

114. Retirement (*Albany Police*, 7 PERB ¶ 3078; affirmed 38 NY 2d 778, 9 PERB ¶ 7005).

See Mandatory-General #3.

115. Time to Process Grievance without Loss of Pay (*Albany Police* 7 PERB ¶ 3078).

Reasoning same as for "Paid Leave." (See above Mandatory-Police #111.)

116. Tours of Duty (*Buffalo PBA*, 9 PERB ¶ 3024).

See Mandatory-Fire Fighter #59.

117. Unpaid Leave of Absence for Union Activity (*Albany Police*, 7 PERB ¶ 3078).

Reasoning same as for "Paid Leave." (See above Mandatory-Police #111.)

118. Use of Unsafe Equipment (*Scarsdale*, 8 PERB ¶ 3075).

Union may demand that unit employees not ride in unsafe vehicles.

119. Zipper Clause (*Albany Police*, 7 PERB ¶ 3078).

This refers to the fact that the total agreement supercedes any and all personnel rules, regulations, local laws, or regulations, and will be amended by mutual agreement. The board said zipper clauses per se are mandatory subjects of negotiation.

Schools

151. Arbitration as Last Step of Disciplinary Proceedings against Tenured Teachers (*Huntington*, 30 NY 2d 122, 5 PERB ¶7507).

Called a term and condition of employment by court of appeals. Court said it is a provision commonly found in collective-bargaining agreements in the private and public sectors and carries out federal and state policy favoring arbitration as a means of resolving labor disputes. It assures teachers with tenure that no disciplinary action will be taken against them without just cause and that any dispute as to the existence of such cause may be submitted to arbitration.

152. Cash Payment for Accumulated Unused Sick Leave (*Board of Education Central High School District No. 3, Nassau County*, 34 AD 2d 351, 3 PERB ¶8012).

See Mandatory-Court Decisions #200.

153. Change in Conference Hours (*Jamestown*, 6 PERB ¶3075).

This case arose on a charge that the school board during negotiations had unilaterally changed certain aspects of the school calendar including the number of parent-teacher conference hours for the elementary schools. PERB endorsed the hearing officer's ruling that the school board did not violate the law because the calendar, which was unilaterally decreed, was tentative and subject to change based on bilateral agreement. Adoption is something that must be done during a particular period, and the unilateral action was based on necessity of the moment. With regard to the change in the parent-teacher conference hours, PERB said there was no compelling reason for a unilateral change in May when the conferences would be held the following November.

154. Compulsory Retirement (*Harrison*, 6 PERB ¶3017).

The employer conceded that compulsory retirement is a term and condition of employment, but relied on language of section 510.1b of the Education law for the conclusion that school districts have nondelegable authority to decide whether or not to request a member of the Teachers' Retirement System to retire at age 70. PERB disagreed saying this section of the law neither obligated the Board of Education to retire a member of the Teachers' Retirement System at 70 nor does it vest a board of education with an absolute right to require such a teacher to retire at a predetermined age. The applicable language of Ed. Law Section 510 is, "Any member who has attained age seventy *may* be retired at his own request or at the request of the employer...." PERB said this language was designed to be permissive. The court of appeals in *Board of Ed Huntington* vs. *Teachers*, 30 NY 2d 122 (1972), ruled that when explicit language of a statute circumscribes the exercise of power by a board of education, as is the case with respect to the involuntary retirement of teachers younger than 70, there is no Taylor law duty to negotiate, but when there is no such explicit statutory circumscription of the exercise of power by a board of education, there is a duty to negotiate.

155. Impact of Management Decisions

    A.   Abolishing Positions Claimed to Exist by Employee Organization (*North Babylon*, 7 PERB ¶3027).

The gravamen of the charge is that the employer abolished a number of teaching positions and refused to negotiate with the teachers on the impact of such action on the terms and conditions of employment. The employer claimed there was no impact and that there was no obligation to negotiate. PERB said, "An employer cannot avoid a duty to negotiate by simply making a unilateral determination that there is no impact any more than an employer could avoid an obligation to discuss a grievance on the ground that in its judgment the grievance is without merit. The employer has an obligation to meet with the teachers and discuss the issue of impact. The act of meeting and discussing would not constitute a concession on the employer's part that there is an impact on terms and conditions."

Severance pay, continued medical and other fringe benefits, employment in other positions and retraining of laid-off employees must be negotiated (*Somers*, 9 PERB ¶ 3014).

B.   Modification of Class Size (*West Irondequoit*, 4 PERB ¶ 3070; affirmed 35 NY 2d 46, 7 PERB ¶ 7014).

The line of demarcation between a basic policy decision and the impact on terms and conditions of employment may not always be clear. For example, a policy decision may have an impact on teaching load. At first look, class size and teaching load may seem the same, but they are not. The first represents a determination by the public employer as to an educational policy made in the light of its resources and other needs of its constituency. This decision may have an impact on hours of work and the number of teaching periods that are clearly mandatory subjects of negotiations.

In affirming the board decision, the court of appeals adopted and approved the reasoning of the board that the impact of a policy decision, such as class size, is negotiable.

C.   Reduction in Work Force for Unit Members (*New Rochelle*, 4 PERB ¶ 3060).

The decision of the school superintendent involving budgetary cuts with concomitant job eliminations is not a mandatory subject of negotiation. The board concluded, however, that the employer is obligated to negotiate with the union on the impact of such decisions on the terms and conditions of employment of the employees affected.

Examples of such negotiable matters are order of layoff, severance pay, and work load for the remaining employees.

156. Incentive-Pay Plan (*North Hempstead School District and Carle Place Teachers*, 6 PERB ¶ 7510).

See Mandatory-Court decisions #202.

157. Job Duties of Unit Employees (*West Irondequoit*, 4 PERB ¶ 3070).

The board affirmed the hearing officer who referred to job duties when dealing with the issue of promotional policy for unit positions. She said "Insofar as a promotional policy for unit positions is concerned the duties of a position and the procedures for promotion, as distinguished from the qualifications for promotion, are matters having a direct and significant relationship to working conditions. . . ." (See Mandatory-Police #110. See Nonmandatory-Schools #158, #161; Nonmandatory-Police #108.)

158. Length of Work Year (*Oswego*, 4 PERB ¶ 4520).

The length of an employee's work year no less than the hours he may work each day is a term and condition of employment. With regard to the latter subject, the law expressly requires good-faith negotiations. With regard to the former, good-faith negotiations are also required unless the length of the work year is a subject that involves a decision concerning the basic goals and direction of the employer.

159. Procedures for Evaluating Probationary or Untenured Teachers (*Monroe-Woodbury*, 3 PERB ¶3104).

The employer contended that such proposals are in derogation of the authority of school superintendents and boards of education as granted in the Education law, section 3012 and section 3013, relating to the granting or denial of tenure. PERB said that although the procedures proposed in this case go beyond that required by the Education law, it does not appear that the procedures contravene the provisions of the Education law. PERB ruled that this is not barred by existing law and as it deals with a term and condition of employment is mandatory.

160. Promotional Procedures for Unit Employees (*West Irondequoit*, 4 PERB ¶3070).

The board upheld the hearing officer who said "insofar as a promotional policy for unit positions is concerned, the duties of a position and the procedures for promotion, as distinguished from the qualifications for promotion, are matters having a direct and significant relationship to working conditions. At the same time, these matters do not as heavily bear upon the fundamental goals and direction of the employer. . . ."

161. Reallocation of Job Grades (*New Rochelle*, 7 PERB ¶3021).

The employer's argument that it complied with various sections of the contract was not persuasive since there was no provision in the agreement granting to the employer the right to change wages and other terms and conditions of employment unilaterally and without prior negotiations as required by Section 204 of the law. Moreover, in further reference to that part which alleged that a local ordinance by implication excluded job reallocations for local employees from their terms and conditions of employment, it is noted that local laws are not in *pari materia* with the Taylor law.

162. Reimbursement for Job-Related Personal Property Damage (*Huntington*, 5 PERB ¶7507).

The court of appeals said this provision constitutes a term or condition of employment. It went on to say, "It is certainly not uncommon for collective agreements in the public sector, as well as in the private sector, to contain 'damage reimbursement' provisions similar to the one before us. If, during the course of performing his duties, an employee has his clothing, eyeglasses, or other personal effects damaged or destroyed, it is certainly reasonable to reimburse him for the cost of repairing or replacing them."

163. Reimbursement of Tuition for Graduate Courses (*Huntington*, 5 PERB ¶7507).

The court of appeals said tuition reimbursement clearly relates to a term and condition of employment. School boards throughout the state pay teachers a salary differential for completing a specified number of credit hours above the baccalaureate degree. Since graduate work tends to increase teacher skills and is beneficial to the school district, there is no reason why the board should not encourage such work by absorbing one-half of the tuition expense.

164. Sabbatical Leave (*East Meadow*, 4 PERB ¶ 3018).

The board ruled that sabbatical leave is a term and condition of employment and thus a proper subject of collective negotiations. The provisions of section 1709, subdivision 16 of the Education Law do not negate this conclusion.

165. Safety (*Somers*, 9 PERB ¶ 3014).

Teachers may negotiate over means of protection from gross misconduct and acts of violence by students.

166. Sick-Leave Bank (*Syracuse*, 7 PERB ¶ 7513).

Decision by court of appeals upholding validity of a contract provision for a "sick-leave bank." The court said that "One should construe the language in *Board of Education, Huntington* vs. *Teachers* (30 NY 2d 122, 130) to mean that collective bargaining under the Taylor Law (Civil Service Law, Section 204, subd. 1) has broad scope with respect to the terms and conditions of employment limited by plain and clear, rather than express, prohibitions in the statute or decisional law. . . ."

167. Special Salary Increment in Last Year of Service before Retirement (*Huntington*, 30 NY 2d 122, 5 PERB ¶ 7507).

Called a term and condition of employment by the court of appeals. "Employers, both in the public and private sectors, have traditionally paid higher salaries based upon length of service and training. In addition to the fact that the payment was to be for service actually rendered during their last year of employment, the benefit provided for served the legitimate purpose of inducing experienced teachers to remain in the employ of the school district. It is not, therefore, a constitutionally prohibited 'gift' of public moneys since the retiring teachers who benefit from this provision have furnished a 'corresponding benefit or consideration to the State.'"

168. Subcontracting

(*Somers*, 9 PERB ¶ 3014; *Buffalo*, 9 PERB ¶ 3015). The decision to subcontract does not contemplate a change in the employer's operating method or the nature or extent of its services and is bound to other mandatory negotiating subjects; it must be negotiated.

(*Northport*, 9 PERB ¶ 3003). The reassignment of unit work to nonunit employees must also be negotiated.

169. Tuition Reimbursement (*Huntington School District*, 38 NY 2d 122).

Tuition reimbursement clearly relates to a term and condition of employment. (See *Kingston PFA*, 9 PERB ¶ 3069.)

170. Work Load (*Yorktown*, 7 PERB ¶ 3030).

In this matter the board referred to its decision in the *Matter of West Irondequoit Board of Education*, 4 PERB ¶ 3070, in which it distinguished between matters of education policy that are not terms and conditions of employment such as class size and the impact of such decisions on terms and conditions of employment, such as teacher work load. Class size is but one factor in the calculation of WSCM (weighted student contact minutes); a demand for limitations on the WSCM is a work-load demand and a mandatory subject of negotiations. The formula for the determination of WSCM includes not only class size but also hours of work and the number of teaching periods.

Court Decisions

The following are items termed mandatory subjects of negotiation by the courts.

200. Cash Payment for Accumulated Unused Sick Leave (*Teacher Association Central High School District #3* vs. *Board*, 34 A.D. 2d 351 [3 PERB ¶8012]).

The appellate court said that "... sick leave as a condition of employment offers an inducement to competent and efficient workers to enter public service and the right to accumulate unused sick leave encourages them to stay in public service and at the same time deters absenteeism for trifling ailments. There is no constitutional barrier to the payment of a sum equivalent to a percentage of accumulated unexercised sick leave when the employee dies in service or severs his relationship." The court also said the Board of Education did not lack the authority to make the contract for the payment of the amount attributable to the unused sick leave.

201. Medical, Dental, and Life-Insurance Benefit Payments by Employer to a Union-Administered Welfare Fund (*Local 456 IBT* vs. *Town of Cortlandt*, 68 Misc. 2d 645 [PERB ¶8012]).

The court said that a town has power to make payments, as called for by a collective-bargaining agreement with the union to a trusteed welfare fund (Insurance Law, Art. 3-A) of moneys to provide medical, dental, hospital, eyeglasses, and life-insurance benefits to its members. Such payments accord with the public policy of the state as embodied in the Insurance law (Art. 3-A) and the Taylor law.

202. Incentive-Pay Plan (*North Hempstead School District and Carle Place Teachers*, 6 PERB ¶7510).

The court decided that the incentive-compensation plan was a valid negotiable term and condition of employment. In doing so, the court said, "It would appear that before the Taylor Law was enacted the school authorities were empowered to reward superior performance of its teachers in the manner plaintiff here devised. Was this power eliminated by the Taylor Law?" In approaching a solution to this query, the court referred to the court of appeals decision in the *Huntington* case (5 PERB ¶7507) saying in part "... there is no reason why the mandatory provisions of that act should be limited, in any way except in cases where some other applicable statutory provision *explicitly and definitively* prohibits the public employer from making an agreement as to a particular term or condition of employment."

Index

Nonmandatory

General

1. Agency Shop

(*Monroe Woodbury*, 3 PERB ¶ 3104 [affd. 68 Misc. 2d 957, 4 PERB ¶ 7014]). The board found agency shop unlawful. Agency shop that subjects nonmember employees to discharge is inconsistent with the statutory grant of the Taylor law of right that employees may refrain from "participation in" an employee organization. Also barred by other statutes—Education law § 3012.2, which would preclude the dismissal of a tenured teacher on grounds other than that set forth in that subsection and General Municipal law § 93-b, which, in substance, provides that dues may be deducted from an employee's salary only upon written authorization from the employee and that such authorization may be withdrawn at any time.

(*Albany Police*, 7 PERB ¶ 3078). PERB ruled nonmandatory a demand to negotiate inclusion in a contract of agency shop when authorized by state enabling legislation. Given the current status of the law to mandate negotiations on such a matter would unnecessarily impede negotiations.

(*Erie County*, 5 PERB ¶ 3021). The language of the Taylor Law is clear. Public employees have the unfettered right to refrain from forming, joining, or participating in any employee organization. Such language is absolute. This right may not be infringed upon by a collective agreement. The "maintenance-of-membership" provision in the contract in this case, the board said, clearly "interferes with" the rights of those blue-collar employees who are members of the intervenor but who, during the term of the contract, no longer desire to participate in the affairs of the intervenor union by continuing their membership. Thus the mere execution of a contract containing such a clause constitutes unlawful interference.

2. Civil Service or Other Statutory Requirements

(*Albany Police*, 7 PERB ¶ 3078). Matters within the discretion of a local civil service commission or mandated by Civil Service law are not negotiable.

(*Scarsdale*, 8 PERB ¶ 3075). Inclusion of statutory provision or provision contrary to statutory mandate in contract is not mandatorily negotiable.

3. Death Benefits (*Albany Police*, 7 PERB ¶ 3078).

Death benefit authorized by the appropriate sections of the Retirement and Social Security law available only to employees hired before July 1, 1973 and prohibited for those hired after July 1, 1973.

4. Employment Qualifications (*Nassau County*, 8 PERB ¶ 3058).

New employees to furnish own tools.

5. Overall Policies and Mission of Government (*Albany Police*, 7 PERB ¶ 3078).

A public employer exists to provide certain services to its constituents, be it police protection, sanitation, or education. Of necessity, the public employer, acting through its executive or legislative body, must determine the manner and means by which such services are to be rendered and the extent thereof, subject to the approval or disapproval of the public so served, as manifested in the electoral process. Decisions of a public employer with respect to the carrying out of its mission, such as a decision to eliminate or curtail a service, are matters that a public employer should not be compelled to negotiate with its employees.

6. Reduction in Work Force

See Nonmandatory-Schools #164.

7. Residency Requirements

(*Rochester*, 4 PERB ¶ 3058). A residency requirement is not a condition of, but a qualification for, employment. Like other employment qualifications, it defines a level of achievement or a special status deemed necessary for optimum on-the-job performance. Traditionally, qualifications for employment have been matters of managerial prerogative, and no cogent reason appears to justify a departure from this rule.

(*Buffalo*, 9 PERB ¶ 3015). Residency requirement for prospective, but not existing, employees is a management prerogative.

8. Vacancies

(*Albany Police*, 7 PERB ¶ 3078). This subject matter covered in part by mandatory language in Civil Service law and in part lies within the discretionary authority of the local civil service commission. As to matters set forth in proposal, employer has no power or discretion.

(*Albany PPFA*, 7 PERB ¶ 3079; *New Rochelle*, 4 PERB ¶ 3060; *Scarsdale*, 8 PERB ¶ 3075). Filling of vacancies within 30 days goes to the mission of the employer and is a management prerogative.

(*Orange County Community College Faculty Association*, 9 PERB ¶ 3068). Screening and interviewing candidates for teaching vacancies deals with responsibility for administrative operation of the institution.

See Nonmandatory-College #31.

College

26. Access to College Facilities and Equipment (*Orange County Community College Faculty Association*, 9 PERB ¶ 3068).

Demand for right to use employer facilities and equipment such as typewriters, duplicating equipment, mail, telephone, and computer services seeks assistance from employer in the operation and conduct of the business of the association. If granted, it could raise questions of improper public employer support of an employee organization.
Giving faculty keys to buildings is a management prerogative as it may affect security of the premises.
See also Mandatory-College #26.

27. Assignments for Extra Compensation (*Orange County Community College Faculty Association*, 9 PERB ¶ 3068).

Giving full-time faculty first priority in teaching assignments and counselors and librarians first priority to work one summer-school session nonmandatory to extent it would limit the assignment of faculty where necessary to accomplish the mission and educational program of the employer.

28. Attendance at Board Meeting; Also Access to Minutes of All Board Meetings (*Orange County Community College Faculty Association*, 9 PERB ¶ 3068).

Attendance of association representative at board meetings does not pertain directly to association's appropriate role as employee representative in matters relating to working conditions. Moreover, neither party is entitled to access to the internal affairs of the other.

29. Class Size (*Orange County Community College Faculty Association*, 9 PERB ¶ 3068; *West Irondequoit*, 4 PERB ¶ 3070).

   See Nonmandatory-Schools #153. Same principle applies to postsecondary education.

30. College Calendar (*Orange County Community College Faculty Association*, 9 PERB ¶ 3068).

   Encompasses broad nonmandatory area dealing essentially with the administrative organization of the overall academic program.

31. Faculty Evaluation

   (*City University*, 7 PERB ¶ 3028). Composition of the Personnel and Budget Committees of the City University of New York were determined to be a management prerogative. In a split decision two members ruled that designation of membership on committees, which have as a part of their function faculty retention and promotion policies, is not mandatory. In a dissenting opinion, the third member found the makeup of these committees to be a term and condition of employment and, therefore, mandatory.

   (*Orange County Community College Faculty Association*, 9 PERB ¶ 3068). Structure of Committee on Reappointment, Promotion and Tenure is matter of administrative organization and operation of institution.

   (*Orange County Community College Faculty Association*, 9 PERB ¶ 3068). A faculty association may insist upon negotiation of a demand for due process in the application of an evaluation system. Permitting faculty members to establish their own evaluation system each year goes beyond due process and intrudes upon a management prerogative.

   See Nonmandatory-General #8.

32. Course Offerings, Outlines, and Evaluations (*Orange County Community College Faculty Association*, 9 PERB ¶ 3068).

   Deals with educational policy.

33. Faculty Advisors

   (*Orange County Community College Faculty Association*, 9 PERB ¶ 3068). Whether students should have access to members of the teaching faculty for advice on academic pursuits and course-related matters is an aspect of educational policy.

   (*West Irondequoit*, 4 PERB ¶ 3070). The ratio of professional counselors to students covered in this decision.

34. Hiring of Part-Time Faculty (*Orange County Community College Faculty Association*, 9 PERB ¶ 3068).

   Demand goes beyond hours of work and preservation of unit work and extends to manpower policies and hiring policies. (See *New Rochelle*, 4 PERB ¶ 3060.)

35. Hours and Days of Work and Work Location (*Orange County Community College Faculty Association*, 9 PERB ¶ 3068).

Demand for no evening or weekend teaching deals with the kind of work to which faculty may be assigned and when they may be required to perform it. It is a management prerogative to decide how many employees it needs on duty at any given time and where teachers may be required to teach, whether on or off-campus. (See Nonmandatory-Fire Fighter #53.)

36. Reappointment of Faculty (*Orange County Community College Faculty Association*, 9 PERB ¶ 3068).

Administrators return to bargaining unit upon recommendation of search committee. To extent it would require delegation to a search committee of the authority to appoint or reappoint employees, it deals with the administrative organization and operation of an institution of higher education. (See also *City University*, 7 PERB ¶ 3028.)

37. Teaching Materials (*Orange County Community College Faculty Association*, 9 PERB ¶ 3068).

Involves educational policy.

38. Vacancies (*Orange County Community College Faculty Association*, 9 PERB ¶ 3068).

See Nonmandatory-General #8; Nonmandatory-College #31; Nonmandatory-Fire Fighter #58; Nonmandatory-Police #116; Nonmandatory-Schools #167.

Fire Fighter

51. Call in of Off-Duty Personnel

(*Albany PPFA*, 7 PERB ¶ 3079). In previous decisions, the board ruled that work load is a mandatory subject of negotiations. In this case the board determined to the extent that the employer would have to call in off-duty personnel and that this would preclude the reassignment of on-duty personnel, this is a nonmandatory subject of negotiations.

(*Scarsdale*, 8 PERB ¶ 3075). Work-schedule posting requirement insofar as it would prevent employer from calling in staff to work in an emergency is not mandatorily negotiable.

52. Equipment Safety Committee (*Kingston PFA*, 9 PERB ¶ 3069).

Vesting committee with duties to investigate complaint that equipment is inadequate or unsafe and to certify condition of equipment to union and the fire chief could give committee veto power over equipment selected by the city. Its ambiguity requires resolution against the party demanding it.

53. Manning Levels

(*White Plains*, 9 PERB ¶ 3007; *Niagara Falls*, 9 PERB ¶ 3025; *Johnson City*, 9 PERB ¶ 3042; *Kingston PFA*, 9 PERB ¶ 3069). The board held that manning requirements, such as the number of men assigned to a police car or fire truck, or to be on duty, even though related to safety, is not a mandatory subject of negotiations. Safety as a general subject is mandatorily negotiable, however.

(*Johnson City*, 9 PERB ¶ 3042). Similarly, the board held that a demand for a minimum manpower standard for a certain number of paid firemen to be on duty at all times is not a mandatory subject of negotiation.

(*White Plains*, 5 PERB ¶ 3008). The board said it is the city alone that must determine the number of firemen it must have on duty at any given time. It cannot be compelled to negotiate with respect to this matter. (See Mandatory-Fire Fighter #59.)

(*Kingston PFA*, 9 PERB ¶ 3069). Demand that only a specific number may be on vacation at the same time would restrict the authority of the city to decide how many fire fighters it requires on duty at any given time. See also Mandatory-Fire Fighter

See also Mandatory-Fire Fighter #59.

54. Negotiating Team (*New Rochelle*, 8 PERB ¶ 3071).

Employer may not seek to negotiate contract limiting the composition of the union's negotiating team and specifically to exclude from it a certain class of unit employees.

55. Parity (*Albany PPFA*, 7 PERB ¶ 3079).

If the demand is not to reopen the agreement for negotiations but to reopen it for the mechanical change of instituting the dollar value of benefits obtained later by the police in their negotiations, it is not negotiable. The fire fighters can no more insist that during the life of their agreement the wage provisions thereof will be adjusted upwards automatically to equal those obtained thereafter in police negotiations than the police can insist that the wage provisions of their agreement be reopened to guarantee that they receive some amount more than the fire fighters have obtained thereafter by negotiations. Such a demand concerns terms and conditions of employment outside their own negotiating unit. In effect, the fire fighters seek to be silent partners in negotiations between the employer and employees in another negotiating unit. Moreover, an agreement of this type between the city and one employee organization would improperly inhibit negotiations between the city and another employee organization representing employees in a different unit. (See *Doyle* vs. *City of Troy*, 51 AD 2d 845, 9 PERB ¶ 7510; *Voight* vs. *Bowen*, 53 AD 2d 277, 9 PERB ¶ 7525.)

56. Supervision (*White Plains*, 5 PERB ¶ 3008).

The board said that the fire fighters in this case have a legitimate interest in adequate supervision because it is directly related to their safety while fighting fires, but it is not for them to determine the rank of the persons assigned to supervise them. Rank of supervisors assigned is a management prerogative.

57. Vacancies (*Albany PPFA*, 7 PERB ¶ 3079).

See Nonmandatory-General #8; Nonmandatory-College #31; Nonmandatory-Police #116; Nonmandatory-Schools #167.

Police

101. Agency Shop (*Albany Police*, 7 PERB ¶ 3078).

See Nonmandatory-General #1.

102. Civil Service or Other Statutory Requirements (*Albany Police,* 7 PERB ¶3078).

See Nonmandatory-General #2.

103. Criminal Investigation of Police-Unit Employee (*Scarsdale,* 8 PERB ¶3075).

Policeman who is investigated for criminal conduct is in the same position as a civilian, nor is employee entitled to accusatory statements before a preliminary investigation.

104. Death Benefits (*Albany Police,* 7 PERB ¶3078).

See Nonmandatory-General #3.

105. Dismissal of Probationary Employee, Decision and Procedures for Accomplishment (*Albany Police,* 7 PERB ¶3078).

The duration of probationary service is within the jurisdiction of the municipal civil service commission and not of the city itself, and therefore a nonmandatory subject of negotiations.

106. Equipment.

(*Albany Police,* 7 PERB ¶3078). Even if a demand for shotguns in police cars has safety implications, those implications are overcome by the consideration specified in *New Rochelle* (4 PERB ¶3060) decision that the manner and means by which a city should render services to its constituencies is a management prerogative. The selection of weapons and their tactical deployment is a management prerogative. The preservation of public order is involved.

(*White Plains,* 9 PERB ¶3007). Increase in number of operational police cars would make job safer but is a basic managerial decision involving level of services and thus is not a mandatory subject of negotiations.

(*City of Buffalo,* 9 PERB ¶3024). Carrying of service revolver off duty not mandatorily negotiable, but impact of such requirement is.

(*Scarsdale,* 8 PERB ¶3075). Union cannot demand removal of an unsafe vehicle from service rather than its assignment to a nonunit employee.

107. Extra Compensation (*Albany Police,* 7 PERB ¶3078).

Employer intercession to obtain work from other employers is not a mandatory subject of negotiations to the extent that an employer would be required to make available to employees work for other employers at extra compensation.

108. Job Duties (*Buffalo PBA,* 9 PERB ¶3024).

See Nonmandatory-Schools #161. See also Mandatory-Police #110; Mandatory-Schools #157.

109. Manning Levels (*White Plains,* 9 PERB ¶3007).

Same as Nonmandatory-Fire Fighter #53.

110. Organizational Structure (*Scarsdale*, 8 PERB ¶ 3075).

   Demand that employer maintain a particular organizational structure is not a mandatory subject of negotiations.

111. Overall Policies and Mission of Government (*Albany Police*, 7 PERB ¶ 3078).

   See Nonmandatory-General #5.

112. Assignment of Union Officers (*Buffalo*, 9 PERB ¶ 3024).

   Assignment of union officers to specific jobs is not a mandatory subject of negotiations.

113. Pistol Permits (*Albany Police*, 7 PERB ¶ 3078).

   As in the *New Rochelle* case, this is a decision of the public employer with respect to the carrying out of its mission. To the extent that the demand is that employees be permitted pistol permits for reasons not connected with their official duties (such as after they retire), it is not a term or condition of employment.

114. Political Activities (*Albany Police*, 7 PERB ¶ 3078).

   This demand deals with matters that are covered by Election law section 426.3 and Second Class Cities law section 144. We do not regard this forum as the appropriate one to deal with the social and constitutional issues involved. Therefore, not mandatory subject of negotiation.

115. Test Requirements (Breathalizer, Blood, Polygraph) (*Buffalo*, 9 PERB ¶ 3024).

   Requirement that police officers, who have a higher standard of compliance with law, submit to such tests or to stand in a line-up as part of investigation for violations of law is a management prerogative.

116. Vacancies (*Albany Police*, 7 PERB ¶ 3078; *Scarsdale*, 8 PERB ¶ 3075).

   See Nonmandatory-General #8; Nonmandatory-College #31; Nonmandatory-Fire Fighter #58; Nonmandatory-Schools #167.

Schools

151. Agency Shop (*Monroe-Woodbury*, 3 PERB ¶ 3014).

   See Nonmandatory-General #1.

152. Civil Service or Other Statutory Requirements (*Scarsdale*, 8 PERB ¶ 3075).

   See Nonmandatory-General #2.

153. Class Size (*West Irondequoit*, 4 PERB ¶ 3070; affirmed 35 NY 2d 46, 7 PERB ¶ 7014).

In the *New Rochelle*, decision (4 PERB ¶ 3060), the board held that budgetary cuts with concomitant job eliminations were not mandatory subjects of negotiations. Underlying this determination was the concept that basic decisions as to public policy should not be made in the isolation of a negotiations table, but rather should be made by those having the direct and sole responsibility therefor, and whose actions in this regard are subject to review in the electoral process. It would appear that class size is also a basic element of education policy.

In affirming the board decision, the court of appeals adopted and approved the reasoning of the board that the impact of a policy decision, such as class size, is negotiable. The court, using an example, indicated that although the number of pupils in a class is a policy decision, the compensation and other benefits to be received by a teacher, depending on the class size, is a mandatory subject of negotiations.

154. **Demand that Each Student Have Specific Number of Contact Periods with Teaching Specialists (*Yorktown*, 7 PERB ¶ 3030).**

This is a management prerogative going to the mission of employer. (See *New Rochelle*, 4 PERB ¶ 3060.)

Hours of instruction for students, however, *may* be negotiated. (*NYC Bd. of Ed.*, 39 NY 2d 111, 9 PERB ¶ 7512.)

155. **Demand for Greater Role in the Formulation of Policy Relating to Student Guidance in High Schools (*Yorktown*, 7 PERB ¶ 3030).**

This is a management prerogative going to mission of employer. (See *New Rochelle*, 4 PERB ¶ 3060.)

156. **Demand for Union to Have Greater Role in Making of Decisions Relating to Development of Curriculum, the Evaluation of Principals, the Assignment of Paraprofessionals and Other Educational Matters (*Yorktown*, 7 PERB ¶ 3030).**

This is a management prerogative going to the missions of employer. (See *New Rochelle*, 4 PERB ¶ 3060.)

157. **Prohibition against Employer Consultation with Unit Employees (*New Rochelle*, 8 PERB ¶ 3071).**

Since such consultation is a violation of section 209-a.1(d) of the act, it would be a redundant provision, insistence upon which is not permitted.

158. **Employment Qualifications**

(*Rochester*, 4 PERB ¶ 3058). Same reasoning as "Residency Requirements." (See Nonmandatory-General #7.)

(*Queensbury*, 9 PERB ¶ 3057). Assignment of duties in new programs to unit employees only.

159. **Inspection of Employee-Personnel Files by Employer (*Great Neck*, 52 AD 2d 573, 9 PERB ¶ 7515).**

Employer Board of Education may agree to limit its right to inspect personnel files of its teachers.

160. New Programs (*Queensbury*, 9 PERB ¶ 3057).

See Nonmandatory-Schools #158.

161. Nonunit Duties (*Somers*, 9 PERB ¶ 3014; *Queensbury*, 9 PERB ¶ 3057).

Union has no standing to negotiate job duties of employees not in the unit or assignment of job duties of new positions.

162. Policies and Mission of Government (*New Rochelle*, 4 PERB ¶ 3060).

See Nonmandatory-General #5.

163. Promotional Policy for Job Titles not within the Negotiating Unit (*Monroe-Woodbury*, 3 PERB ¶ 3104).

Promotional policy for job titles outside the negotiating units, as well as the determination of qualifications for promotion into positions within the negotiating units, are not terms and conditions of employment.

164. Reduction in Force

(*New Rochelle*, 4 PERB ¶ 3060). Budget cuts and resultant economically motivated decision to reduce work force. A management decision that is a party of carrying out the employer's mission.
   Employer's budgetary cuts resulting in termination of services of substantial number of employees is a managerial decision relating to the carrying out of its mission and is not a mandatory subject of negotiations.

(*White Plains*, 5 PERB ¶ 3008). Demand that work force not be reduced except by attrition or disciplinary charge for cause. Having determined that a public employer may choose to eliminate or curtail a service, it necessarily follows that a public employer may abolish positions that had been necessary for the provision of that service and that it may not be required to negotiate with respect to that decision. Of course, the employer is required to negotiate with respect to the impact of its decision to curtail services and abolish positions.
   Job security, however, is a permissive subject of negotiations (*Yonkers City SD* vs. *Teachers*, 40 NY 2d 268, 9 PERB ¶ 7519; *Burke* vs. *Bowen*, 40 NY 2d 264, 9 PERB ¶ 7520).

165. Seminar or Conference Designed to Enrich the Professional Staff at which Attendance Is Not Compulsory (*Gates-Chili*, 6 PERB ¶ 3065).

The board upheld the hearing officer's determination that the ostensibly optional workshop days were, indeed, optional and that the unilateral establishment of them by the employer did not violate the law. The board agreed that an employer may unilaterally establish seminars or conferences designed to enrich the professional experience of its staff at which attendance is not compulsory. (If such conferences or seminars require attendance and thus expand the work year, their establishment is a mandatory subject of negotiation).

166. Substitutes (*Somers*, 9 PERB ¶ 3014).

Demand that recommended substitutes be hired need not be negotiated since the offer of employment is a management prerogative.

167. Unit Definition (*Southern Cayuga CSD*, 9 PERB ¶4523, aff'd 9 PERB ¶3056).

Inclusion of job title or position in a negotiating unit is a permissive subject of negotiations.

168. Vacancies (*New Rochelle*, 4 PERB ¶3060).

See Nonmandatory-General #8; Nonmandatory-College #31; Nonmandatory-Fire Fighter #58; Nonmandatory-Police #116.

The Scope of Bargaining in the Public Sector in Pennsylvania

J. Joseph Loewenberg
and
James W. Klingler

Scope of bargaining was not supposed to be a problem in Pennsylvania. Persons responsible for formulating and implementing the statutes that authorized collective bargaining for public-sector employees believed that the limits of scope of bargaining were made explicit. Yet scope of bargaining has remained a problem for the parties, administrators, and interpreters of law in the public sector.

The discussion of scope of bargaining in Pennsylvania must follow along dual lines because of the existence of two separate laws governing public-sector bargaining: Act 111 of 1968 governs labor relations for police and fire fighters in the state, and Act 195 of 1970 applies to all other state and local employees. These two laws present radically different approaches to the issue of scope of bargaining. Neither approach, however, has proven immune to challenge.

Legislation

Act 111 of 1968 was the result of intense pressure and lobbying by organized public-safety employees. The inadequacy of prior bargaining procedures, which terminated in fact finding, led police and fire fighters to seek legislation with binding arbitration as the final impasse step. It was first necessary to amend the state constitution, however, to ensure that the constitutionality of compulsory arbitration would be upheld in the courts. The police and fire fighters persisted in their efforts, which culminated in a constitutional amendment and the subsequent passage of Act 111.

The focus of Act 111 is arbitration. Most of the brief act is devoted to the arbitration procedure. No attention is given to such matters as bargaining-unit composition, administrative agencies, or unfair-labor practices. Act 111 provides for bargaining on employees' "terms and conditions of employment, including compensation, hours, working conditions, retirement, pensions and other benefits . . . " There is no further elaboration or restriction of "terms and conditions of employment." To uphold the inviolability of arbitration awards, the law stipulates: "No appeal therefrom shall be allowed to any court." Presumably this provision could give wide latitude to arbitration panels to determine the appropriate scope of bargaining. It was also the intent of the advocates of Act 111 to insulate the bargaining process and results from further review and litigation. The extent to which these expectations have been met are explored in the next section of this chapter.

97

The legislative history and formulation of Act 195 is quite different from those of Act 111. Although many public employees throughout Pennsylvania were eager for legislated bargaining rights, the initiative for such a statute in the late 1960s came from the governor. In 1968 Governor Shafer appointed a commission, which was composed of representatives of labor, public employees, the state legislature, and the general public. The commission, popularly known by the name of its chairman Leon E. Hickman, held hearings in various parts of the state and submitted unanimous findings. With respect to scope of bargaining, the commission recommended:

Bargaining should be permitted with respect to wages, hours, and conditions of employment, appropriately qualified by a recognition of existing laws dealing with aspects of the same subject matter and by a carefully defined reservation of managerial rights.

This recommendation was the kernel of the scope-of-bargaining section of the statute authorizing collective bargaining for all employees of public jurisdictions and nonprofit institutions in the state.

Act 195 of 1970 is perhaps best known for permitting public employees to strike under certain conditions. Even in this section, however, the rights of the public and the public employer are protected because a strike is prohibited if it "creates a clear and present danger or threat to the health, safety or welfare of the public." Similarly, in the section on representation, the law attempts to balance the interests of public employees and public employers by requiring consideration of two criteria in the determination of bargaining units: "(i) public employes must have an identifiable community of interest, and (ii) the effects of overfragmentization." It is in the area of scope of bargaining, however, that management considerations are most pronounced. The text of Article VII, Scope of Bargaining, of Act 195 is presented as Appendix 5A. The first section of this article defines the scope of bargaining in terms reminiscent of the private-sector National Labor-Management Relations Act: ". . . wages, hours and other terms and conditions of employment . . . " The only additional subjects specifically authorized for bargaining appear in section 705, which permits bargaining on two matters of importance to employee organizations: membership dues deductions and maintenance-of-membership provisions. The breadth accorded to bargaining by these two sections are immediately restricted by Sections 702 and 703. The former section posits what to all intents and purposes is a management-rights clause: "Public employers shall not be required to bargain over . . . functions and programs of the public employer, standards of service, its overall budget, utilization of technology, the organizational structure and selection and direction of personnel. . . ." The restriction is somewhat meliorated by the requirement for the parties to meet and discuss matters excluded from bargaining that affect "wages, hours and terms and conditions of employment as well as the impact thereon . . . " An additional restriction in the scope of bargaining is presented in section 703 of the article, namely, that no bargained provision may conflict with legislation enacted by the state or a municipality with a home-rule charter.

The detail of the scope-of-bargaining provision is evidence of thought, deliberation, and compromise. Although the 1970 state legislature considered a number of bills, including separate bills based on the Hickman Commission recommendations and proposals of the Senate State Government Committee and of the administration, all of the proposed bills contained provisions similar to section 702 of Act 195, the management-rights provision. The first part of the provision was patterned after Executive Order 10988, which provided bargaining for federal employees in 1962. The members of the Hickman Commission and the governor's representative for labor relations were also affected by experience in other states, especially Michigan, where court decisions extended bargaining into areas they considered within government's authority. Granting employees the right to strike enhanced the importance of limiting the scope of bargaining to forestall the determination of policy decisions by coercion, they felt. The proponents of the legislation to authorize collective bargaining were not pleased with any restrictions on the scope of bargaining. Their principal argument was that restrictions on bargaining would exacerbate employee tempers and would encourage employees to strike over matters excluded from negotiations. Representatives of the American Federation of State, County and Municipal Employees (AFSCME), the Pennsylvania State Education Association, and administration spokesmen discussed the scope-of-bargaining issue. They finally agreed to provide employees an opportunity to talk about issues that concerned them, recognizing that the final determination of such issues would remain with the employer. Thus was born the compromise that appears in the last sentence of section 702, "to meet and discuss on policy matters affecting wages, hours and terms and conditions of employment as well as the impact thereon. . . ." Although the unions disliked any restrictions on bargaining, they feared that the legislature would not approve a basic bargaining law without the compromise.

By now it is evident that the two principal laws authorizing collective bargaining for public employees in Pennsylvania followed different courses with respect to scope of bargaining. Act 111 of 1968 was essentially legislation promoted by organized employees. The bill, although devoting little language to scope of bargaining, was intended to provide wide latitude to subjects that could be of interest to employees' terms and conditions of employment. Act 195 of 1970, on the other hand, was the product of considerable study, lobbying, and negotiations by those who would be affected by public-employee bargaining. The state, as the major public employer in Pennsylvania, and other public-employer representatives were determined to limit the scope of bargaining and preserve what they felt were management and public rights. Employee organizations were adamant about including all matters relating to employee welfare in talks with public employers. The result was a full-blown provision on scope of bargaining in the legislation, which to some extent accommodated the interests of all parties.

Administrative and Legal Determinations

How have the different legislative approaches to scope of bargaining worked out? Does a broad mandate and limitations on appeal rights encourage a wide-ranging variety of negotiated subjects, free of legal interference? Does a detailed provision on scope of bargaining prevent misunderstandings or give clear directions for interpretation? This section investigates the decisions of courts, arbitrators, and administrative agencies with respect to these questions. First the challenges under Act 195 are investigated, and then those under Act 111.

The decisions interpreting scope of bargaining under Act 195 derive from several sources: the state attorney general, the Pennsylvania Labor Relations Board, and the courts.

On occasion the attorney general issues opinions about areas of bargaining under Act 195. On July 7, 1972, for instance, he declared that school districts and employee organizations could bargain about the amount of salary to be paid employees if schools were closed before the scheduled end of the school-year because of lack of funds. The topic related to wages, hours, and other terms and conditions of employment, the attorney general found. Similarly, in an opinion issued April 9, 1973, the attorney general decided that sabbatical-leave benefits are within the permitted area for bargaining because such benefits are part of terms and conditions of employment. In this case, however, certain statutory provisions exempt areas of sabbatical-leave benefits from bargaining, such as requirements for eligibility in the granting of leave and the benefits to be provided while on leave. Consequently the only parts of such benefits that are bargainable are areas of school-district discretion. The attorney general opinions are important guidelines, but they have covered only a limited number of problem areas. Moreover, as the above opinions suggest, the attorney general has been more concerned with permissible areas for bargaining than with mandatory areas for bargaining.

The arena for resolving the determination of mandatory areas of bargaining is first and foremost the Pennsylvania Labor Relations Board, the administrative agency assigned responsibility for determining bargaining units, conducting representation elections and deciding unfair-labor practices. The board has received many charges of refusal to bargain, cases that in effect involved questions of scope of bargaining.

Most of the allegations concerning scope of bargaining have involved school districts and teacher associations. In each case the moving party charged a violation of section 702 of Act 195. The board has issued cease-and-desist orders to school districts and mandated that they bargain with teacher associations on a number of items:

1. Wages to be paid to employees supervising extracurricular activities[1]
2. Sick-leave bank in which sick leave of all teachers would be pooled into one fund
3. Compensation for teachers inflicted with an occupational disease
4. Compensation for teachers unable to serve due to court appearances
5. Allowed absences and compensation for leave due to family death or illness
6. Compensation for appearances before the School Board or secretary of education
7. Procedure for assaults on teachers
8. Teachers being parties to civil or criminal actions
9. Reimbursement for losses, damages, and/or medical expenses[2]

In the latter case the board's basis for determining negotiability was the initiation and impact of policy. Items that originate with employees and have a direct, immediate impact on employees are subjects for mandatory bargaining, the board argued.

The Pennsylvania Labor Relations Board (PLRB) used the precedent of Fibreboard Paper Products to hold that a school district must negotiate with the employees' representative about the dismissal of paid teacher aides and the transfer of their duties to volunteer aides. When this case was appealed, however, the court determined that the dismissals were within the managerial rights of the school district.[3]

Another case involving transfer of work occurred in a noneducational setting. The Borough of Wilkinsburg was considering subcontracting sanitation services while it was negotiating with its organized employees. The borough discussed the potential cost savings of subcontracting and requested that the employees suggest a plan with comparable cost reductions. When the employees were unable to evolve a satisfactory plan, the borough proceeded with the subcontracting. The employees filed an unfair-labor practice charge, but the PLRB held that the borough had not violated the law. A district court reversed the PLRB decision and ruled the borough had a duty to bargain collectively on subcontracting work previously performed by members of the bargaining unit. The commonwealth court, however, once again reversed, finding that the decision to subcontract, when arrived at in good faith and for sound reasons, is a matter of inherent managerial policy and therefore need not be bargained. Because the decision affects wages, hours, and terms and conditions of employment, the borough was obliged to meet and discuss the issue with employee representatives, which it had done.[4]

A similar interpretation of section 702 can be inferred from a series of board rulings that upheld the refusal of school districts to engage in bargaining on specific issues:

1. Teacher-preparation time[5]
2. Sick-leave bank
3. Binding arbitration
4. Sabbatical leave
5. School year
6. Teaching load
7. Class size
8. Notification of teaching schedule
9. Flexible scheduling[6]
10. School calendar and budget[7]

It should be noted that the board reversed itself on the issue of sick-leave bank and followed the attorney general's opinion in the matter of sabbatical leaves. The reason for excluding arbitration from the mandatory list of subjects was that section 804 of Act 195 *permits* the negotiation of arbitration provisions. The rationale for most of the remaining items excluded from mandatory subjects can be found in the best-known and most far-reaching case on scope of bargaining to date—that involving the State College Area School District.

The State College Area Education Association filed a charge of refusal to bargain against the State College Board of School Directors when the latter refused to bargain on 23 separate issues proposed by the association. Two issues were subsequently withdrawn. The Pennsylvania Labor Relations Board upheld the school board's refusal to bargain on the remaining 21 issues because they fell within the scope of inherent managerial policy. The issues excluded from mandatory bargaining were:

1. Availability of classroom instructional printed material
2. School time for planning required "innovative" program
3. Timely notice of teaching assignment for coming year
4. Separate desk and lockable drawer for each teacher
5. Cafeteria for teachers in the Senior High School
6. Elimination of nonteaching duties: bus duty, lunch duty, study hall, parking-lot duty
7. Elimination of requirement to teach two consecutive classes in different buildings
8. Elimination of substituting for other teachers during planning periods and teaching in noncertified subject areas
9. Elimination of requirement to chaperone athletic events, dances, etc.
10. Elimination of requirement for teachers to handle, store, and check supplies
11. One night per week free for association meetings
12. Free access to personnel file
13. Freedom to leave the school building during any nonteaching period
14. Prep time for special teachers equal to that for other staff members

15. Maximum class-size provisions
16. Consultation with association when determining school calendar
17. Noon closing before Thanksgiving, Christmas, spring and summer vacations
18. At least half of the time requested for staff meetings be held during the school day
19. Elimination of Tuesday afternoon conference with parents in favor of scheduled conferences
20. Secondary teachers to have a maximum of 25 periods per week, with a minimum of 1 planning period per day
21. Elementary teachers to have 1 period or 15 minutes per day for planning.[8]

The association filed an amended charge of unfair-labor practices on the same issues, and the Pennsylvania Labor Relations Board reversed its stand on five issues. The board ordered bargaining on:

1. Notifying teachers of upcoming assignments
2. Providing a cafeteria for teachers in the Senior High School
3. Eliminating requirement to chaperone athletic events
4. Providing free access to personnel file
5. Providing noon closing before holidays and vacations

The board also reaffirmed the prior findings that the other 16 items were within management's inherent authority and therefore need not be bargainable.[9] Part of the reason for the board's reversal may have been the appointment of two new members to the three-member board.

Both the State College Area School District and the State College Area Education Association appealed the board's decision to the courts. The Court of Common Pleas of Centre County and later the Commonwealth Court of Pennsylvania ruled fully in favor of the school district, finding nonmandatory not only the 16 issues held by the Pennsylvania Labor Relations Board but also the 5 other issues on which the board had reversed itself.[10] In effect, the courts felt that all of the proposals presented by the association were matters of inherent managerial policy and/or public policy issues. Again, the decision was appealed.

The latest chapter in this landmark case on scope of bargaining has been the decision of the Supreme Court of Pennsylvania, filed on April 17, 1975.[11] The court neither included nor excluded any of the outstanding issues from mandatory bargaining. Rather, the court remanded the case back to the Pennsylvania Labor Relations Board for further consideration. The court issued some principles and interpretations of the law that might guide the board (and perhaps lower courts) in its determinations. With respect to the conflict between the public policy to promote bargaining on wages, hours, and terms and conditions of employment and the policy to preserve inherent managerial policy, the court suggested weighing the relative effects:

Thus we hold that where an item of dispute is a matter of fundamental concern to the employees' interest in wages, hours and other terms and conditions of employment, it is not removed as a matter subject to good faith bargaining under Section 701 simply because it may touch upon basic policy. It is the duty of the Board in the first instance and the courts thereafter to determine whether the impact of the issue on the interest of the employees in wages, hours and terms and conditions of employment outweighs its probable effect on the basic policy of the system as a whole.

As for the conflict between negotiable subjects and legislated matters, the court announced that:

. . . items bargainable under Section 701 are only excluded under Section 703 where other applicable statutory provisions explicitly and definitively prohibit the public employer from making an agreement as to that specific term or condition of employment.

The refusal of the supreme court to endorse the lower court's rulings implies a broader interpretation of section 701 than the judiciary had favored heretofore. The decision was hailed by the Pennsylvania State Education Association. The full meaning of the supreme court decision remains unknown until the long process of PLRB decisions and appeals to the courts has been exhausted.

Although the State College Area School District case has captured much of the attention to date, another case will be heard by the supreme court of the state in fall 1975, the outcome of which may also affect scope of bargaining for public employees. This case involves social workers rather than teachers, and it is the first case on scope of bargaining where the state is the employer. The Commonwealth of Pennsylvania refused to bargain on case and patient loads of professional employees in the Department of Public Welfare on the grounds that such decisions are within discretionary management functions and affect organization structure and standards of service. The commonwealth did agree to meet with the union and discuss case and patient loads, but the union believed the subject was part of employees' terms and conditions of employment. The Pennsylvania Labor Relations Board and the commonwealth court have concurred in the commonwealth's interpretation of its obligation in this matter, relying on the line of reasoning used in the state college cases by the PLRB and the commonwealth court.[12] Since that line of reasoning has been undermined by the supreme court's State College Area School District opinion in the interim, it remains to be seen if this case will receive identical treatment at the hands of the supreme court in the upcoming term.

All the above cases have been instances of employer refusal to bargain or employee organizations insisting that employers bargain on particular issues. Rarely have the courts considered whether the parties *may* bargain over an issue. The principle guiding scope of bargaining in the private sector has generally been held to be applicable in the public sector; that is, although the parties are obliged to bargain on certain issues, they may voluntarily bargain over any other issue that is not prohibited by law. That principle was challenged in a civil suit.[13] The association and the school district had included in their collective-bargaining agreement a provision on procedures for transferring a student from one school to another for disciplinary reasons. The plaintiff, a parent of a disciplined student, challenged the merit of the provision and the right of the parties to negotiate such a provision. He later signed a consent decree permitting the provision to stand uncontested when he was convinced that the negotiated procedure was sound. The issue of negotiability was therefore not fully tested in this case.

Scope of bargaining has been interpreted differently under Act 111 than under Act 195, both because of the different substantive language in the statutes and the different procedures available to interpret the statutes. Act 111, it will be recalled, provided for no unfair-labor practices, no administrative agency, and no appeals of arbitration awards. These restrictions, however, have not rendered scope of bargaining a moot question. If a subject arises that the employer believes is beyond the mandatory or permissive scope of bargaining and that the employee organization wishes to pursue, the initial recourse is to submit the issue to the impasse procedure and let the arbitration panel decide.

Aside from innumerable econommic items, arbitrators have been asked to decide on such matters as granting police false-arrest insurance, residence requirements, promotion and suspension policies, shift assignments, manning of equipment, job duties, and composition of the bargaining unit. Arbitrators have generally been loathe to render awards that infringe on traditional management rights or public-policy areas. References may then be made to the kind of language employed in section 702 of Act 195. It is also possible to find awards that include most of the subjects just mentioned. In such cases, the employer may force the employee organization to sue for enforcement of the award in the courts, or the employer may sue directly to overturn the award.

Once courts have assumed jurisdiction over arbitration awards, they have determined the arbitrability of subjects contained in the award. Because arbitrators can only decide bargainable proposals, the courts in effect have been deciding the scope of bargaining under Act 111.

In the only Act 111 scope case thus far decided by the Supreme Court of Pennsylvania, the court established the principle: "An arbitration award may only require a public employer to do that which it could do voluntarily."[14] Application of the principle was the basis for vacating part of an arbitration award that granted hospitalization-insurance coverage to policemen's dependents in a third-class city. The court found that such cities did not have specific authorization to pay premiums for anyone other than city employees and officials and that the award therefore contravened the employer's authority. The same principle was used by a district court to invalidate the award of false-arrest insurance for policemen in another arbitration award.[15] Since the legislature gave various classifications of subordinate jurisdictions different authority, the scope of bargaining in each classification could differ. Moreover, the scope of bargaining could change legally over time. Shortly after the state supreme court had invalidated part of the arbitration award for the police of the city of Washington, the state legislature amended the Third Class City code to allow such cities to extend medical-insurance coverage to employee dependents. The import of the court's ruling was to tailor the scope of bargaining and arbitrability to the specific legal situation.

Another principle announced by the courts in testing the limits of scope under Act 111 was that awards could not contravene state legislation or administrative provisions. This principle is reminiscent of section 703 of Act 195. The court overturned part of an arbitration award that required union membership in good-dues-standing in the union as a condition of continued employment because such a provision would have violated civil-service laws.[16] The court also deleted an arbitration provision reducing retirement age, not because such a reduction was incorrect per se, but because the precondition of an actuarial study had not been completed before the award went into effect.[17]

The courts have considered the question of management rights with respect to scope of arbitrability under Act 111. A district court has held that a city could require police to pass a physical examination as a condition of continued employment and that the subject is therefore in the scope of bargaining or arbitration.[18] Pension rights, however, are not within the discretionary rights of the public employer, as Act 111 specifically authorizes bargaining on such rights.[19]

A final test employed by the courts is to measure the issue in question against the definition of "terms and conditions of employment." Such a test resulted in the inclusion of residency requirements and the exclusion of department vehicles to transport employees to and from work. In the former case, the commonwealth court argued that residency requirements are clearly a condition of employment and thus, if within the authority of the municipality, a bargainable and arbitrable item.[20] Using police cars to transport policemen from their homes to work and return, on the other hand, was judged to be beneficial to employees but not a benefit within the meaning of Act 111.[21] A decision with broader significance was rendered by the commonwealth court with respect to the award of binding grievance arbitration. In two separate decisions, the court declared that such arbitration was not within the meaning of terms and conditions of employment because the procedure was being made available for "currently unidentifiable disputes."[22] The court noted that grievance arbitration was a bargainable item under Act 195 but concluded that its specific absence from Act 111 excluded it from conditions of employment.

There has been no shortage of appeals to the courts concerning arbitration decision under Act 111. One analyst has explained the reason for the number:

Arbitrators view their function as that of determining equity. Where legal doubts are raised during the course of arbitration about the validity of awards, unless there is ample documentation, arbitration boards have been inclined to include the questionable item and leave it up to later appeals to the courts to establish or refute the legal propriety of the award.[23]

In comparing the decisions on scope of bargaining under Acts 195 and 111, it is evident that many of the same guiding principles have been employed. Differences in the language and provisions of the statutes, however, have resulted in different interpretations of the bargainability of an issue under these two statutes. The major concern under Act 195 has been the contents of inherent managerial rights as outlined under section 702 and the limitations of that section on mandatory subjects of bargaining. No real test of management rights under Act 111 has yet emerged. Instead, the problems of bargaining under Act 111 have for the most part been (1) a definition of "terms and conditions of employment" that determine the content of bargaining and (2) establishment of the employer's authority that limits the permissive areas of bargaining and arbitration.

Effect on Collective Bargaining

Recounting the cases and decisions involving scope of bargaining, one might think that the problem is so large and complex as to stifle meaningful bargaining. The impression would be faulty for two major reasons: (1) the list does not include areas that are clearly bargainable, and (2) the list does not include cases where questionable items have been bargained but not challenged.

Both acts 111 and 195 delineate areas of mandatory bargaining. These include items affecting the economic welfare of employee, hours, and other terms and conditions of employment. For the most part, issues of prime concern to most public employees have not been challenged as to bargaining status, or have not been successfully challenged. On occasion, some aspect of economic conditions has been viewed as part of managerial prerogatives or in conflict with other statutory provisions. Overall, however, the impact of such limitations on collective bargaining has generally not been insufferable for most parties.

Even the decisions of the PLRB or the courts need not restrict scope of bargaining, unless the topic is contrary to law. As has been pointed out repeatedly, removing an item from mandatory bargaining, even if it is considered part of inherent managerial authority, does not prohibit the parties from voluntarily including it in negotiations. Many parties have chosen to do so without seeking the interpretations of the courts or disregarding decisions exempting the item from mandatory bargaining. The changes in court decisions and uncertainties of the meaning of the law encourage the introduction of "gray-area" proposals. The relationship of mandatory and permissible subjects in the bargaining process has been raised with the Pennsylvania Labor Relations Board. The board has announced that an employer may set withdrawal of permissible items as a condition for bargaining on mandatory items.[24] The board also has ruled that a union may continue to ask for bargaining on permissible subjects, even after the employer has declared such subjects non-negotiable; however, the union cannot insist on bargaining on such subjects to the exclusion of other mandatory topics.[25] The fact that such cases are still brought to the board indicates continuing union insistence to bargain all subjects and continuing employer efforts to avoid bargaining on nonmandatory subjects. The pronouncements do not appear to offer any abatement in the testing of scope of bargaining.

The interest in subjects legally determined to be permissible at any point in time is far from academic. Parties can be quite insistent in their position at the bargaining table. A survey of strikes among public employees in 1971 revealed that negotiability of subjects was a factor in 50 percent of the 71 strikes.[26]

Despite the arguments and furor over negotiability, evidence exists that items until now considered nonmandatory have been incorporated into bargaining agreements. The Pennsylvania State Education Association claims that many of the items struck from mandatory bargaining by the lower courts in the State College Area School District case have been included in collective-bargaining agreements throughout the state. The only item that the association advises its constituents to propose that has not yet appeared in an agreement is one on student evaluation of teachers. The Philadelphia School District agreement with the American Federation of Teachers, which followed a lengthy strike in the 1972-73 school year, includes a provision on maximum class size and a provision granting elementary school teachers preparation time in school each day. The Pennsylvania School Boards Association, on the other hand, continues to advise local school districts not to bargain on nonnegotiable subjects. The Pennsylvania State Education Association has studied the frequency of 209 clauses in agreements between its members and Pennsylvania School Districts.[27] The following topics illustrate the frequency of subjects considered permissible by the Pennsylvania School Boards Association that have been included in the 518 agreements: school calendar appears in 115 agreements; preparation time in 172 agreements; and class size in 69 agreements. The gross figures do not permit measurement of the impact of the bargained provision, but the fact remains that the subject was negotiated. Moreover, only a case-by-case study would allow evaluation if the inclusion of such subjects indicates powerful employee organizations, weak or indifferent employers, tradition, or some other factor.

Adaptation of union proposals has permitted parties to include items in bargaining without violating management needs and existing procedures. The Commonwealth of Pennsylvania in its first agreement with AFSCME negotiated seniority to be applied in the event of layoffs and in shift assignments. Employee performance ratings determine the group from which layoffs are to take place, however, thereby affording management an input into the procedure. Likewise, in granting shift assignment preferences the Commonwealth retains the right to assign if it is necessary for the efficiency of the operation. Another example of adaptation is the tenure provision in the agreement between Temple University and the American Association of University Professors. The university refused to bargain over its tenure standards and procedure. In particular the university wanted to avoid placing tenure cases in the regular grievance procedure that ended in outside arbitration. The parties agreed to incorporate into the agreement the tenure statements of the Faculty Senate Handbook but to amend the final step in the procedure. Previously appeals of individual cases terminated by decision of the Board of Trustees. Now the final step is an arbitration panel composed of nine persons: three selected by the American Association of University Professors (AAUP), three selected by the university, and three selected by the other six members from within the university. The decision of the arbitration panel is final and binding.

Although adaptations may serve management interest, they can raise other problems. The seniority provision in the commonwealth agreement was at odds with the civil-service law at the time it was negotiated. The conflict occurred in the definition of seniority and its application to furloughs and promotions.[28] Civil-service regulations defined seniority as the first date of civil-service employment in class and periods of subsequent civil-service employment in the same or higher grade. The collective-bargaining agreement used length of continuous service in the employee's classification series as the basis for determining layoffs or furloughs. In a case of furlough, the Civil Service would select employees from the lowest quartile, based on employees' last regular performance ratings. The agreement stipulated an average of the employee's last three annual performance ratings to determine the lowest quartile. For promotions, the Civil Service advocated appointments from open competitive lists, lists established from competitive promotional examinations, and/or recognition of meritorious service and seniority if an employee completed probation and was qualified for next higher position. The bargaining agreement required promotion by seniority among all equally qualified employees or by seniority among employees whose examination ratings were within five points of the highest employee in the seniority group. This particular set of conflicts was removed by the passage of Act 266 of 1974, which authorized collective-bargaining agreements to take precedence over civil-service legislation in the areas of seniority, promotions, and furloughs. Not all conflicts are so readily resolved.

In some agreements the parties recognize the conflict between a bargained provision and existing legislation. The agreement may specify that the parties will work together to change the legislation and/or to hold the negotiated provision in abeyance until implementing legislation is passed. Other agreements do not give specific recognition to areas of conflict, however. In such cases it is difficult to know whether the negotiated provisions have been executed despite the conflict with extant legislation and the violation of section 703 of Act 195.

Aside from the continuing legal tests on scope of bargaining, new strategies might be available to unions bargaining under Act 195 that hope to encroach on areas previously protected by inherent management rights. One of these has been suggested by a justice of the commonwealth court. Judge Kramer in dissenting from the majority opinion in the State College Area School District case commented that the problem with the issues was the language and thrust of the demands; if the problems addressed by the demands were raised in other ways, the matters might be deemed negotiable under section 701. The judge's suggestion has been studied and discussed. Some leaders of employee groups believe that putting all demands in money terms would force employers to negotiate union proposals because the courts have consistently upheld the negotiability of such items under section 701. Other leaders, recognizing the likelihood of a continuing distinction between mandatory and permissible items, prefer to place a high price-tag on mandatory economic issues when they also present permissible topics for negotiations; the employer's agreement to negotiate the permissible items would then become the price for reducing the economic settlement. Undoubtedly these strategies have already been employed somewhere in the state. Official sponsorship of and education in such strategies would encourage more widespread adoption.

Prospects for Change

Given the fluctuation in court interpretations of scope of bargaining under Act 195 and the current uncertainty of the meaning of the supreme court's decision in the State College Area School District case, the prospects for changing standards are real and imminent. The outcome of the review process may well determine if legislative changes are likely to be forthcoming.

Management spokesmen have talked privately of the possibility of amending Article VII of Act 195 if the Pennsylvania Labor Relations Board and the courts liberalize extensively the previous interpretations of section 702 of the act. Such amendments would attempt to legislate a tighter and more detailed definition of the nonmandatory areas of bargaining. Of course the public-employee unions, now a political force in the state, would oppose any further legislative restrictions on scope of bargaining.

The likelihood of legislative changes regarding scope of bargaining appear dim. In 1973 the state legislature appointed a Special Joint Committee to Study Act 195 "to review its effect upon our society and economy and to invite and explore sound and reasonable suggestions for its amendment. . . ." The committee held hearings and issued its report in the following year. Overall the act received favorable comments from most of the witnesses heard by the committee. On the issue of scope of bargaining, the committee heard a range of views. A representative of the Pennsylvania Local Government Conference, a coordinating group of municipal associations, suggested a prohibition of strikes over non-negotiable subjects. The head of the Pennsylvania School Board Association requested more explicit guidelines with respect to managerial prerogatives. The delegate of the Pennsylvania State Education Association, on the other hand, wanted a broader scope of bargaining and elimination of terms applicable only to private-sector bargaining. To round out the picture, other witnesses cautioned against too much specificity in the law. The committee concluded:

[Sections 701 and 702] of the Act should be permitted to age without premature amendment. It is believed that the case law which will develop will be far more helpful in delineating the extent of managerial prerogatives than hasty legislative enactments.[29]

The committee also reviewed the conflict-of-bargaining agreements with other statutes, as governed by section 703 of Act 195. It noted that many agreements contain provisions that conflict with statutory provisions. The committee was particularly critical of agreements that dismissed any possible conflict between negotiated provisions and law with a general disclaimer at the end of the agreement. To overcome such conflicts, three alternatives were explored: (1) enforcement of section 703 by declaring items covered by existing legislation as nonnegotiable, (2) repeal of section 703, or (3) clear indication of conflicting provisions in agreements. The conclusion and recommendation was:

The Committee endorses the third alternative which allows the General Assembly to approach each separate question on its own merits without usurping legislative authority. This approach would also enable mature bargaining between the parties involved.

Although Act 111 was not within the formal authority of the committee's charge, the committee heard testimony on the effectiveness of that act as well. Much of the discussion centered about the lack of formal procedures, administrative supervision, and intermediary impasse steps. Scope of bargaining did not seem to trouble the witnesses. The committee decided to refrain from recommending any changes, perhaps because of the political repercussions from the police and fire fighters in making such recommendations as much as lack of jurisdiction.

There is no reason to believe that the state legislature has changed its view toward Act 195 and Act 111 in the last year. In short, no legislative changes in these acts can be anticipated at this time.

Summary

Scope of bargaining in Pennsylvania is still a murky, uncharted area. The legislative announcements of the scope of bargaining—restricted in Act 195, liberal in Act 111—have proven far from clear. Neither approach succeeded in stemming the need for interpretation and rulings. As collective bargaining has developed in the state, the challenges to scope of bargaining (and arbitration, under Act 111) have continued. Many of the union challenges under Act 195 have come from professional groups because their interests in bargaining frequently impinge closer to areas that management considers part of its authority in determining standards of service or directing the organization. Blue-collar groups have not been immune from problems involving scope of bargaining, however.

The administrative and judicial agencies in the state have not fully clarified the situation, and at times their efforts have left it in confusion. Few consistent principles to guide the parties have yet emerged. The uncertainty about subjects of bargaining under Act 195 has been heightened by the recent decision of the Pennsylvania Supreme Court in the State College Area School District case. Until the courts and the Pennsylvania Labor Relations Board have a common understanding of the law, the legal controversy about scope of bargaining is likely to continue.

Despite the ambiguity about scope of bargaining—or perhaps because of it—unions have continued to press for the negotiation of additional subjects. Many public employers have been circumspect and adamant in refusing to negotiate anything that could be considered inherent managerial rights, although they have recognized their legal obligation to meet and discuss some of these issues. Other public employers have adopted a more flexible attitude and been willing to negotiate permissible items as long as the results of those negotiations were not adverse to their interests. The statutory prohibition against negotiating items included in law has not prevented parties from including such items in their collective-bargaining agreements.

The uncertainty about scope of bargaining, although troublesome to particular parties in particular instances, has not proven so disturbing or unsettling to damage the image of collective bargaining for the parties or for the public. Nor have the problems associated with scope of bargaining been of such import as to encourage legislators to amend the existing legislation in major fashion. For the foreseeable future, then, scope of bargaining in the public sector in Pennsylvania promises to be more of the same: probing, litigation, interpretation, frustration, and accommodation.

Notes

1. *Cannon-McMillan School Board*, PLRB Case No. PERA-C-934-W. Affirmed by Commonwealth Court, January 28, 1975.

2. *Richland School District*, PLRB Case No. PERA-C-2169-C, November 20, 1972.

3. *PLRB* vs. *Mars Area School District*, PLRB Case No. PERA-C-2932-W, September 27, 1973. Court of Common Pleas, Butler County, August 21, 1974.

4. *PLRB* vs. *Employees' Committee of the Wilkinsburg Sanitation Department*, PLRB Case No. PERA-C-2007-W, Pa. Cmwlth. Ct., January 8, 1975, reversed by Allegheny Court of Common Pleas.

5. *Nazareth Education Association*, PERA-C-1884-C, August 10, 1972.

6. *Richland School District*, PLRB Case No. PERA-D-3610-C, January 4, 1974.

7. *Richland School District*, PLRB Case No. PERA-C-3611-C, January 4, 1974.

8. *State College Board of School Directors*, PLRB Case No. PERA-C-929-C, October 14, 1971.

9. *State College Area School District*, Case No. PERA-C-929-C, June 26, 1972.

10. *PLRB* vs. *State College Area School District*, 306 A.2d 404, 9 Pa. Cmwlth. 229 (1973).

11. *Government Employe Relations Report* No. 603, April 28, 1975, Section E.

12. *Pennsylvania Social Services Union* vs. *PLRB* PLRB Case No. PERA-C-3157-C, 15 Pa. Cmwlth. 441 (1974).

13. *Erie Education Association and School District of Erie* vs. *Jordan*, U.S. District Court for the Western District of Pa., Civil Action #34-75, February 5, 1974.

14. *City of Washington* vs. *Police Department of the City of Washington*, 436 Pa. 168. 259 A.2d 437 (1969).

15. *Garbin* vs. *Brentzel*, 54 DC 2d 364, 54 West.29 (1972).

16. *Allegheny County Firefighters, Local 1038, International Association of Firefighters* vs. *County of Allegheny, Pa.*, 299 A.2d 60, 7 Pa. Cmwlth. 81 (1973).

17. *Cheltenham Township* vs. *Cheltenham Police Department*, 301 A.2d 430, 8 Pa. Cmwlth. 360 (1973).

18. *City of Sharon* vs. *F.O.P. Lodge No. 3*, 814 Commonwealth Docket, November 8, 1973.

19. *Mase* vs. *City of Carbondale*, 74 Lack. Jur. 107, 65 Mun. 25 (1973).

20. *Cheltenham Township* vs. *Cheltenham Police Department*, supra.

21. *Cheltenham Township* vs. *Cheltenham Police Department*, 312 A.2d 835 (1973).

22. *Allegheny County Firefighters, Local 1038, International Association of Firefighters* vs. *County of Allegheny*, supra.; and *Cheltenham Township* vs. *Cheltenham Police Department* 301 A.2d 430, 8 Pa. Cmwlth. 360 (1973).

23. Patricia Crawford, "Act 111 and the Courts," *Pennsylvanian*, September 1974, p. 17.

24. *Littletown Education Association*, PLRB Case No. PERA-C-3534-C.

25. *Williamsport Education Association and Williamsport Area School District*, PLRB Cases No. PERA-C-5078-C and PERA-C-5392-C.

26. Memorandum of Vincent Carocci to State Senators Lamb and Arlene, May 16, 1973, citing a survey from the Pennsylvania Labor Relations Board.

27. P.S.E.A. Research Bulletin, *Negotiated Contract Clauses in 518 Pennsylvania School Districts, 1973-74*, mimeograph, August 15, 1974.

28. Testimony of Mrs. Grace Hatch, chairman of the Civil Service Commission, before the Special Joint Legislative Committee to Study the Public Employee Relations Act, August 9, 1973.

29. Report of the Special Joint Legislative Committee on the Effect of Pennsylvania Public Sector Bargaining Law, mimeograph, 1974.

Appendix 5A:
Article VII—Scope of
Bargaining

Section 701. Collective bargaining is the performance of the mutual obligation of the public employer and the representative of the public employee to meet at reasonable times and confer in good faith with respect to wages, hours and other terms and conditions of employment, or the negotiation of an agreement or any question arising thereunder and the execution of a written contract incorporating any agreement reached but such obligation does not compel either party to agree to a proposal or require the making of a concession.

Section 702. Public employers shall not be required to bargain over matters of inherent managerial policy, which shall include but shall not be limited to such areas of discretion or policy as the functions and programs of the public employer, standards of services, its overall budget, utilization of technology, the organizational structure and selection and direction of personnel. Public employers, however, shall be required to meet and discuss on policy matters affecting wages, hours and terms and conditions of employment as well as the impact thereon upon request by public employe representatives.

Section 703. The parties to the collective bargaining process shall not effect or implement a provision in a collective bargaining agreement if the implementation of that provision would be in violation of, or inconsistent with, or in conflict with any statute or statutes enacted by the General Assembly of the Commonwealth of Pennsylvania or the provisions of municipal home rule charters.

Section 704. Public employers shall not be required to bargain with units of first level supervisors or their representatives but shall be required to meet and discuss with first level supervisors or their representatives, on matters deemed to be bargainable for other public employes covered by this act.

Section 705. Membership dues deductions and maintenance of membership are proper subjects of bargaining with the proviso that as to the latter, the payment of dues and assessments while members, may be the only requisite employment conditions.

Section 706. Nothing contained in this act shall impair the employer's right to hire employes or to discharge employes for just cause consistent with existing legislation.

(Article VII of Public Employee Relations Act, Act 195 of 1970, as enacted by S.B. 1333)

6

Public-Employee Bargaining in Texas

Charles J. Morris

I. Introduction

Public sector collective bargaining in Texas is but embryonic in comparison with the practices and statutes existing in most other jurisdictions in the United States.[1] A survey of this subject in Texas reveals not only a sparsity of legislative authorization and relatively few examples of public employee unionism, but also an aura of mystery surrounding the subject. My purpose in this article is to attempt to dispel that mystery. The reason for the mystery is not hard to understand; indeed, it is the nature of the subject which results in inhibition of query. The reason one may be afraid to ask about public sector bargaining in Texas is that it may be embarrassing to inquire about a practice which seems to be flourishing in many parts of the state but which might also be illegal. For example, how does one inquire discreetly about the periodic negotiations between the San Antonio Transit System and Local 694, Amalgamated Transit Union? Such negotiations are often punctuated by work stoppages, extensive litigation, and even jail sentences for contempt, but they generally result in a settlement and execution of a document called a "statement of working conditions."[2] Does one ask the mayor of San Antonio if the city has been engaging in collective bargaining in violation of the law? Does one ask the officials of a dozen other cities[3] where agreements have generally been reached with unions without great fanfare whether de facto union recognition has been granted and if the agreements with those unions, though couched in euphemisms, are in reality collective bargaining contracts? I am happy to report that it will not be necessary to ask such embarrassing questions, for these cities have not engaged in any illegal conduct. This is the primary subject of this study, although it will also examine the structure and operation of the 1973 Texas statute which permits collective bargaining for firefighters and policemen in cities which adopt the process by local option elections.[4]

It is indeed important that responsible public officials in the state, and also the unions seeking to represent Texas public employees, understand the legal status and configuration of the public employee bargaining process permitted,

This article is a modified version of a paper presented at the George W. Taylor Memorial Conference on Public Sector Labor Relations, Temple University, Philadelphia, September 4, 1975. The author gratefully acknowledges the research assistance of Gary Crapster, and Robert Carrol, Southern Methodist University law students, in the preparation of this article. It is reprinted here with the permission of the *Houston Law Review*, Vol. 13, No. 2, pp. 291-323, January 1976. © 1976 by the Houston Law Review, Inc.

and to some extent required, by Texas statutes and by the United States Constitution. It is also desirable that these parties affix accurate labels to their conduct and to their work product. When thus properly confined and described, general public employee bargaining in Texas (aside from the statutory exceptions applicable to firefighters and policemen)[5] is both lawful and practicable. But it would be a mistake to characterize such general bargaining as the type of collective bargaining which prevails in the public sector in most other states, nor is such bargaining collective bargaining as practiced in the private sector pursuant to affirmative requirements of the National Labor Relations Act (NLRA).[6] Consequently, as will be explained in detail later, such bargaining is not collective bargaining within the meaning of the 1947 statute which declares public employee collective bargaining contracts to be null and void and against public policy and which prohibits recognition of "a labor organization as the bargaining agent for any group of public employees."[7] Nevertheless, this unique Texas brand of bargaining does consist of legal and enforceable rights and duties, and the agreements resulting from its practice are also enforceable, though not with the ease of private sector agreements under § 301 of the Taft-Hartley Act.[8] This article will describe a general system of public sector labor-management relations which, in my view, is superior to any thus far debated in the Texas Legislature. Until the time comes when the Texas Legislature is ready to adopt a truly modern and comprehensive public sector labor code—one with orderly procedures, adequate administration, and a fair and flexible impasse resolution mechanism protective of the public interest—the present law, if properly understood and applied, can offer a reasonable and workable structure in which public employers and labor unions may arrive at negotiated and enforceable settlements to govern wages and working conditions.

This analysis of public sector bargaining begins with an examination of the pertinent statutes and a review of the extent of union organization and bargaining now prevailing in many parts of the state despite the negative nature of most of the statutory provisions. Following that examination, it will be possible to piece together from interlocking legal principles, some of which are old but still valid, a viable basis for a public employee bargaining system for Texas.

II. Statutory Provisions

A. The 1947 Act Prohibiting Public Employee Collective Bargaining

The story opens with enactment of article 5154c,[9] one of a set of nine restrictive labor statutes which the Texas Legislature passed in 1947. Ostensibly a response to a 1946 strike of Houston city employees, this statute unequivocally declared that it was "against the public policy of the State of Texas for public employees to engage in strikes or organized work stoppages [and any] employee who participates in such a strike shall forfeit all civil service rights, re-employment rights and any other rights, benefits, or privileges which he enjoys as a result of his employment...."[10] And to make doubly certain that such strikes would not occur, the legislature added express prohibitions in §§ 1 and 2 of the Act against union recognition and collective bargaining contracts. Two other provisions of this statute which may not have been uppermost in the legislative mind at the time of the passage, now, ironically, provide guarantees for important employee rights. Section 4, intended as merely a reiteration for public employees of the state's "right-to-work" law, was couched in language which protected both the right of nonmembership as well as membership in a labor organization—language which was later to be used to protect the right of public employees to organize.[11] The other affirmative provision, § 6, a concession to conscience or Constitution, provided that:

The provisions of this Act shall not impair the existing right of public employees to present grievances concerning their wages, hours of work, or conditions of work individually or through a representative that does not claim the right to strike.[12]

As we shall see, it was these two provisions which, in time, became the statutory cornerstones for a meaningful public sector bargaining relationship in Texas, notwithstanding the express declaration in § 2 that it is "against the public policy of the State of Texas for any ... official or group of officials to recognize a labor organization as the bargaining agent for any group of public employees."[13]

Until recent years there was little deviation from the pattern of legislative hostility toward public employee unionization. But in 1967 the legislature authorized municipalities with populations exceeding 10,000 to grant check-off of union dues for consenting employees.[14] Two years later, a similar provision was passed for counties of 20,000 or more population.[15] Both of these check-off programs are voluntary with respect to the governmental employers. The anomalous situation was that although it was unlawful to grant union recognition or to bargain collectively with a union, a union could obtain consent to a check-off. The 1967 legislature also passed a statute which enabled teacher organizations to "consult" with school boards.[16]

B. The 1973 Fire and Police Employee Relations Act (FPERA)

The most significant departure from this hostile legislative policy occurred in 1973 with the passage of the "Fire and Police Employee Relations Act."[17] This was a legislative breakthrough which legitimatized collective bargaining for some of the state's public employees. The legislature severely hedged the Act with obstacles, however, in order to avoid the governor's veto. Chief among these obstacles was a local option proviso which limited the Act to those cities or other political subdivisions which by local election vote to adopt its provisions.

Since FPERA is unique in several respects, experience under this statute will be worth monitoring. Aside from the floor-added amendments—the local option feature, a "sunshine" provision applicable to the collective bargaining process, and mandatory severe penalties for strikes and mild penalties for lock-outs—the features of the statute which are most noteworthy are the following: First, a general legislative requirement in § 4 that wages and working conditions of firefighters and policemen be comparable to the wages and conditions prevailing in "other jobs, or portions of other jobs" in the same labor market area in the private sector. The Act focuses such comparability on similarity of skills, ability, and training and similarity of conditions under which the jobs are performed; similarity of entire jobs is not required for comparison purposes.[18] Second, an encouragement of arbitration as an impasse-resolution device. Arbitration is not mandatory, however, and if the public employer refuses arbitration, the state district court will enforce the prevailing wages and working conditions required by § 4.[19] These unique procedures reflected the legislators' dislike for compulsory arbitration and also their recognition of a need to encourage both collective bargaining and interest arbitration, for the Act contains an absolute ban on strikes. The prevailing-wage-and-conditions concept was deemed necessary, for as a last resort the court will set wages and conditions in accordance with this definite legislative standard, for an open-ended determination of wages and conditions by a court would have been a judicial exercise of legislative authority. The formula adopted in the statute avoids any such constitutional objection. While this comparability formula is suitable for judicial determination, it may be unduly confining, however, as to the scope of arbitral authority when the parties resort to arbitration to settle a collective bargaining impasse.[20]

Other provisions of the Act maintain familiar themes, but there are some interesting variations. A summary of the entire statute follows. Section 2 declares as public policy of the state that firefighters and police shall be provided "with compensation and other conditions of employment that are substantially the same as compensation and conditions prevailing in comparable private sector employment," and that such protective service employees "shall have the right to organize for purposes of collective bargaining."[21] The bargaining unit is broadly defined to include both rank and file and supervisory employees. As to fire departments, the statutory unit consists of all permanent employees, excluding only the chief of the department. As to the police unit, collective bargaining is applicable only to the "certified full-time paid employees . . . who regularly [serve] in a professional law enforcement capacity . . . ," excluding only the chief of the department. By these definitions, office-clerical employees of a fire department would be included, whereas similar clerical employees in a police department would be excluded. The Act leaves no substantial doubt as to the scope of the bargaining units: they are roughly the same as the groups included in the unions which have organized in these fields and which lobbied for passage of the Act.

Section 5 establishes a unique[22] local-option election procedure for voting *in* the provisions of the Act.[23] This is triggered by the filing of a petition signed by either 5 percent or 20,000, whichever is the lesser, of the qualified voters in the city or other political unit voting in the last preceding general election. The section also contains similar procedures for voting *out* coverage of the Act. The statutory provisions become applicable only after a city or other political unit votes to adopt the Act.

Section 6 provides for recognition of a union (termed an *association* in the Act) that has been selected by a majority of the bargaining unit. Since there is no employee relations board, there is no automatic requirement for an election of a bargaining agent. When there is a "question as to whether or not an association is the majority representative," however, the question is to be resolved by a "fair election conducted according to procedures agreeable to the parties"; but if the parties are unable to agree on such procedures the election is to be conducted by the American Arbitration Association. Election expenses are borne by the public employer unless two or more unions are seeking recognition, in which case the unions are required to share the costs of the election equally.[24]

Section 7 obligates the public employer to bargain collectively with the representative.[25] The bargaining obligation defined in the language of § 8(d) of the NLRA[26] includes the duty "to meet at reasonable times and confer in good faith with respect to wages, hours, and other terms and conditions of employment. . . ."[27] The scope of bargaining under FPERA will thus have the benefit of NLRA precedent as well as that of other states which have incorporated the NLRA language into their public employee relations acts. This language is sufficiently broad to allow mandatory bargaining subjects to be judicially defined in response to the practices and the needs of the parties as developed by experience in the public bargaining process. So far, there is only limited experience on which to report, but what bargaining has occurred will be noted below.

Section 7 of the Act also requires that when "wages, rates of pay, or any other matter requiring appropriation of money" are to be included in collective bargaining, the association must serve its request "at least 120 days before the conclusion of the current fiscal operating budget."[28] This provision was designed to provide sufficient time for bargaining on economic matters before the applicable budget is determined by the public authority, but it is also having another unanticipated effect. With the combination of time periods in the local option election provision and this 120 day requirement, initial bargaining is often delayed more than a year following a local option election.

Section 7(e) is the "sunshine law" provision which was added by floor amendment before passage. At least part of the provision is of dubious constitutionality:

All deliberations pertaining to collective bargaining between an association and a public employer or any deliberation by a quorum of members of an association authorized to bargain collectively or by a member of a public employer authorized to bargain collectively shall be open to the public and in compliance with the Acts of the State of Texas.[29]

This would appear to require the employees' union meetings to be open to the public—undoubtedly a violation of "the vital relationship between freedom to associate and privacy in one's associations" which the Supreme Court described as essential to first amendment freedom of association in *NAACP* vs. *Alabama*.[30] Most other states, with the exception of Florida, have excluded public sector collective bargaining from so-called "sunshine" legislation;[31] regrettably, Texas has not. There is a widespread belief that public negotiating sessions with the attendant press coverage inhibit the free exchange of views and tend to freeze the parties' positions.[32] This appears to be happening under the new Texas statute, for two of the first negotiations to be concluded since passage of the Act failed to produce complete contracts through voluntary bargaining, and the parties in those cities (Beaumont and San Antonio) resorted to arbitration and court action.[33] Commenting on the effect of the "sunshine" provision on recent negotiations, an official of the city of Beaumont stated:

Those knowledgeable in collective bargaining realize that "good faith" bargaining cannot be conducted in a public setting. Section 7(e) of the Law requires that bargaining collectively be open to the public. Meaningful bargaining cannot be conducted while under the watchful eye of the public. The City of Beaumont and Local 399 of the International Association of Firefighters carried on meaningless negotiations in public for sixty days prior to calling in the Federal Mediation and Conciliation Service. During the sixty day period, two issues were resolved and many taxpayer dollars wasted.[34]

The next legislature would be well-advised to eliminate § 7(e).

Although § 4 establishes a comparability standard applicable to all public firefighters and police in the state, the general applicability of that provision is limited by the local option feature in § 5. For units which have adopted the Act, voluntary agreement through collective bargaining is encouraged by § 8, which provides that when a collective bargaining agreement has been reached "on compensation and/or other terms and conditions of employment . . . the public employer shall be deemed to be in compliance with the requirements of Section 4" and the agreement shall be binding and enforceable.[35]

Section 9 outlines bargaining and mediation procedures and defines an impasse. An impasse occurs "when the parties do not reach a settlement of the issue or issues in dispute by way of a written agreement within 60 days after institution of the collective bargaining proceedings," although bargaining time may be extended by agreement for periods that do not exceed 15 days each.[36] Since Texas has no state mediation service, the Act encourages but does not compel mediation. The provision declares that the bargaining efforts "shall include mediation, provided a mediator can be appointed by agreement of the parties or by an appropriate agency of the state."[37] Federal Mediation and Conciliation Service mediators have in fact already assisted in the early efforts at collective bargaining under the statute. Section 9(c) defines the mediator's function and prohibits him from making a public recommendation, statement, or report evaluating the relative merits of the position of the parties. He can, however, "recommend or suggest to the parties any proposal or procedure which in his judgment might lead to settlement."[38]

If the parties are unsuccessful in resolving their differences through collective bargaining, the Act provides two avenues for impasse resolution, both of which have now been tested in practice. Both procedures are designed to satisfy the prevailing wages and conditions mandate of § 4.

The first impasse resolution device is interest arbitration. Although it is not compulsory, there are cost factors relating to the second device (which is recourse to judicial determination) designed to encourage use of arbitration. Arbitration, provided for in §§ 10 to 15, is binding when both parties agree to submit to arbitration. The scope of arbitrable issues is broad and includes "all matters which the parties have been unable to resolve through collective bargaining."[39] The arbitration board is tripartite with the impartial chairman either selected by agreement of the board members named by each party or by the American Arbitration Association. The board is charged with rendering an award which will comply with the prevailing wages and conditions requirement of § 4, and it has express authority to consider "hazards of employment, physical qualifications, educational qualifications, mental qualifications, job training and skills"[40] in determining private sector prevailing comparability standards. In practice, however, these limited standards may prove to be too confining in some arbitration cases, an issue to be further explored in connection with a review of the limited experience under the Act. The arbitration award, unless it is overturned or modified pursuant to narrowly defined grounds for judicial review,[41] will be binding and, as in the case of a collective bargaining contract, deemed to be compliance by the public employer with the § 4 comparability standards.

In the event the public employer refuses arbitration, § 16 authorizes the employee association to bring an action in state district court for enforcement of the prevailing wages and conditions requirement of § 4.[42] The FPERA was written to avoid the fate suffered in 1951 by a state prevailing wage law for public construction projects.[43] In *Texas Highway Commission* vs. *El Paso Building Construction Trade Council*[44] the Texas supreme court held the state highway commissioner's determination of prevailing wages to be final and nonreviewable, notwithstanding their apparent inaccuracy.[45] In contrast the FPERA grants the court "full power, authority, and jurisdiction to enforce the requirements of Section 4." A court proceeding is likely to be considerably more expensive to a public employer than arbitration, for court costs, including costs for a master if one is appointed, must be taxed against the public employer. And if the public employer is found in violation of the prevailing wages and/or conditions standard, the court will: (1) order the public employer to make the affected employees whole as to past losses; (2) declare the compensation and/or other terms and conditions of employment required by § 4 for the period as to which the parties had been bargaining, but not to exceed a period of one year; and (3) award the employees' association reasonable attorney's fees.

Section 17 prohibits "strikes, lockouts, work stoppages and slow-downs,"[46] and provides for injunctions and fines for violations. Individual public employer violators *may*, in the court's discretion, be fined not more than $2,000; an employee association which "has called, ordered, aided, or abetted in a strike of firefighters or policemen," however, *shall* be fined not less than $2,500 nor more than $20,000 for each day of violation, a sum determined by a statutory fraction (1/26) of the total amount of the association's annual membership dues. Forfeiture of dues check-off is also required. The mandatory nature of the fine against an association is tempered, however, by a provision allowing the court to reduce the amount of the fine on a finding that the municipality or its representatives "engaged in such acts of extreme provocation as to detract substantially from the responsibility of the association for the strike."[47] If an individual firefighter or policeman engages in a strike or related conduct he shall not be allowed an increase in compensation for a year, and he shall be placed on probation for two years "with respect to civil service status, terms of employment, or contract or employment. . . ." This is a lesser penalty than provided in article 5154c, which required a total forfeiture of all reemployment rights and benefits, although such harsh penalties apparently have never been invoked in the numerous public sector strikes which have occurred since 1947.

The possibility of conflict with civil service provisions is avoided by § 20(b), which provides that:

Provisions of collective bargaining contracts made pursuant to this Act shall take precedence over state or local civil service provisions whenever the collective bargaining contract, by agreement of the parties, specifically so provides. Otherwise, the civil service provisions shall prevail. Civil service provisions, however, shall not be repealed or modified by arbitration or judicial action; although arbitrators and courts, where appropriate, may interpret and/or enforce civil service provisions.[48]

Firefighters and police in Texas have traditionally received substantial employment benefits through effective lobbying, particularly by the well-organized Texas State Association of Firefighters. The foregoing provision protects those existing statutory benefits, but allows collective bargaining to make changes in the benefits at the local level when mutually agreeable. Further protection of existing benefits is provided by § 20(c), which expressly retains all existing employment benefits, such as "pension and retirement plans" and "other emoluments," and declares the Act to be "cumulative and in addition to" the existing benefits provided by statutes or ordinances.

The final provision of the Act, § 20(d), could have an impact on the scope of bargaining. It provides that nothing contained in the Act "shall be deemed a limitation on the authority of a fire chief or police chief" as defined by the Firemen's and Policemen's Civil Service Act "except to the extent the parties through collective bargaining shall agree to modify such authority."[49] This language would appear to make such authority permissibly bargainable, but if the parties have reached no agreement modifying those duties, neither an arbitration board nor a court could independently effect a modification in a chief's statutory authority.

III. Public Sector Bargaining Experience

A. Background

There are at least 61 Texas municipalities, counties and school districts in which public employees belong to a union or employee association.[50] According to a 1970 survey, the firefighters and police are the most highly organized of the municipal employees—the firefighters had locals in 45.6 percent of the municipalities and the police had associations in 42.1 percent; other municipal employees were organized in 26.3 percent of the municipalities.[51] Not only are the police and firefighter association present in more Texas cities, they also have been more successful than other municipal employee unions in attracting members.[52]

This high degree of organization by the police and firefighters has led to substantial legislative gains for these groups—particularly in state civil service coverage,[53] with many statutory benefits being added regularly to the Civil Service Act,[54] and most recently in the collective bargaining rights made available under FPERA.[55] In the absence of established bargaining opportunities, both groups, but especially the Texas Association of Firefighters, have engaged in intensive lobbying at each legislative session. In effect, they have bargained with the legislature, the result of which is the much-amended Firemen's and Policemen's Civil Service Act[56] that resembles a collective bargaining contract. For example, it contains provisions for wages,[57] longevity pay,[58] severance pay, classifications,[59] educational incentive pay,[60] hours of work,[61] extra hours,[62] exchange of hours,[63] overtime,[64] vacations,[65] holidays,[66] paid sick leave,[67] leave of absence,[68] and procedures for promotion,[69] discipline and dismissal.[70] Organized municipal and school employees operate under the strictures of article 5154c[71] and are not covered by either of the preceding statutes. Teachers are the subject of three additional labor relations provisions contained in the Texas Education Code bearing on organizational and representational rights. Section 13.216 provides that any certified teacher who violates article 5154c shall be suspended by the commissioner of education.[72] Section 13.217 guarantees the right of certified teachers to join or refuse to join any "professional association or organization."[73] Section 13.901 allows school boards and administrative personnel to "consult with teachers with respect to matters of educational policy and conditions of employment . . . and make reasonable rules, regulations and *agreements* to provide for such consultation."[74]

Ever since the legislative authorization in 1967 for check-off of union dues,[75] that device has served as informal indication of union recognition, although many public employee organizations have been unable to obtain public employer adoption of the check-off. The American Federation of State, County and Municipal Employees (AFSCME) presently has check-off rights from 7 counties, 16 cities, and 4 hospital districts[76]—not a very large number in view of the size of Texas, but nevertheless AFSCME seems to be increasing its membership and influence in the state. Teacher organizations are not particularly strong in Texas, though the National Education Association has a large membership, a carry-over from its long-standing status as the leading professional association representing Texas teachers. The American Federation of Teachers also has several locals in the state. Neither organization, however, has been able to arouse much militancy among Texas teachers, and bargaining by teachers' unions is still at a relatively primitive level.[77]

There is evidence to suggest that there is now a more tolerant view toward public employee unionization in the state. One indication is the passage of the 1973 Fire and Police Employee Relations Act.[78] Another is the increasing willingness of public employers to grant dues check-off. And still another is a report released recently by the Texas Public Employees Study Commission of the Texas State Legislature.[79] The latter pointed out not only an increasing management interest in union recognition but also a growing desire for change in the mechanics of the public sector labor relations process and indicated that public employee collective bargaining is now a popular topic of discussion.[80] As a result of that study, the Texas Legislature was urged to increase state employee compensation, improve fringe benefits, change salary administration procedures, promulgate a uniform state personnel administration act, provide new Equal Employment Opportunity Complaint remedies, and enact a public employer-employee relations statute. Although no specific guidelines for a bill were spelled out by the Study Commission, labor and management groups each submitted legislative proposals, but no public employee legislation was enacted in the 1975 legislative session.[81]

B. De Facto Bargaining

A 1971 study of public employer-employee relations in Texas by I.B. Helburn asserted that despite the prohibition of collective bargaining under article 5154c, there were at the time at least four situations in Texas where the negotiation process over wages and working conditions "may only be described as one of collective bargaining."[82] Helburn has since identified nine additional municipalities where de facto collective bargaining is taking place.[83]

The process generally operates in the following manner. Although the union or association is not formally recognized, bilateral discussions occur and result in verbal agreements, which are not reduced to bilaterally signed contracts but are reproduced in documents variously entitled *working conditions for employees* (San Antonio Transit System), *employees work policy* (Texas City), *personnel policy* (Texas City), *personnel policies* (Deer Park Independent School District), or *memoranda of understanding* (Pasadena).[84]

What happens when the Texas de facto system breaks down? Absent formal statutory procedures, strikes occur. The sanitation workers seem to have been the most active, having participated in 80 percent of the public employee strikes in Texas during the years 1966-1970.[85] The transit service workers were the next most active striking group during this period. In the past six years in San Antonio alone the transit service workers have struck five times.[86] The primary issues in the strikes are familiar: wages, hours, working conditions and grievance procedures. The firefighters and police have not formally struck in the recent past; this may be related directly to their legislative gains referred to earlier; however some "sick-ins" have occurred,[87] and the Dallas Police Association has recently talked about a possible strike.[88] Resolution of the disputes involved in the various public employee strikes has been handled in intensive bargaining sessions in which the Federal Mediation and Conciliation Service has sometimes participated.[89]

C. Case Study

Recent negotiations between the San Antonio Transit Service and the Amalgamated Transit Union, Local 694,[90] illustrate how the de facto process functions. The parties had been meeting since early in October, 1974. During the week of November 11, the Transit System offered to raise the operator's wage rate by fifty cents per hour; the union rejected the offer and countered by asking for a raise of 68 cents per hour. Later in the same week the San Antonio City Council voted to cut the San Antonio Transit Service offer to a 25 cent increase in order to keep increases uniform for all city employees, and on the following day the union struck. The Transit Service promptly obtained an injunction from the state district court ordering the striking employees back to work. The union and the strikers ignored the order, and the Transit Service filed a motion for contempt with a hearing to follow in four days. In the interim, the Transit Service made two more offers which were rejected by the union. The court found the union in contempt and fined it $500 per day; however, individual union members were not found in contempt. Intensive bargaining continued throughout the week with the aid of an FMCS mediator; the union made two counter-offers, both of which were rejected by the Transit Service. With the strike continuing into its second week, the Transit Service went back to court with a request that fines and jail sentences be imposed on individual union members. The hearing was to be held in ten days.

Meanwhile, the union made a third counter-offer and proposed that the entire dispute be submitted to binding arbitration. Both suggestions were rejected by the Transit Service, the latter for the reason that it would have been "illegal collective bargaining." The strike continued. The district court then found 28 individuals guilty of contempt, and two days later 21 of them were jailed. The union then filed suit, contending that article 5154c was unconstitutional as it denied nonpublic safety employees equal protection of the laws, citing the fact that police and firefighters had been given the right to bargain collectively under the 1973 FPERA.[91]

Considerable public opinion had now been aroused, mostly in favor of strike settlement. Settlement was finally reached with the granting of a sixty cent per hour raise, and individual union members were released from jail. Bus service was resumed—fully 25 days after the strike began. The mayor of San Antonio and several council members spoke out against the current system calling it "almost unworkable," and indicated their support for repeal of the prohibition against collective bargaining in article 5154c.[92]

Clarence Long, an official of the Amalgamated Transit Union, Local 694, also stated that he believed article 5154c should be amended or repealed, for "the A.T.U. would like to see the prohibition on collective bargaining lifted and the right to strike instituted." Recognizing the realities of the recent events, Long stressed that "we're negotiating with the Transit Service all the time legally or illegally; the fact that strikes have occurred is a matter of record."[93]

Taking a different view, an official of the San Antonio Transit Service declared that "the right to bargain collectively and the right to strike should not be legitimized because public sector employment is very different from employment in the private sector." But conceding that the process outlined in article 5154c is "obviously not working," he stated, "nevertheless the legislative intent is there and the law should be enforced."[94]

Bargaining situations not unlike the San Antonio scenario are occurring with increasing frequency, most recently in Galveston (county hospital), San Antonio (water board), and Houston (sanitation workers).[95] Though the process is not characterized as "collective bargaining," bargaining does occur, and there are resulting agreements—though not bilaterally signed—which fairly track the substance of negotiations.

D. Early Experience under the 1973 Fire and
Police Employee Relations Act

The 1973 FPERA, now officially designated as article 5154c-1, has not been in effect long enough to provide meaningful experience. Because of the local election feature, application of the Act is cumbersome. To date, elections have been held in twenty-one cities; the voters in eleven adopted the Act and in ten rejected it.[96] The first successful negotiations under the FPERA were concluded at Texas City on July 18, 1975, with the signing of a contract with Local 1259 of the Texas State Association of Fire Fighters.[97] Negotiations have also been concluded with the Fire Fighters in San Antonio and Beaumont. In those two cities, however, the parties bargained to an impasse without reaching a complete agreement. In San Antonio, impasse resolution was sought in state district court; in Beaumont, both sides agreed to binding interest arbitration pursuant to § .0 of the Act.

The Texas City contract, which was concluded with the assistance of an FMCS mediator, was made retroactive to July 1, 1975. It is for a term of two years but contains pay and pension reopeners after the first year. Features of this first contract include a 15 percent across-the-board wage raise for all classifications of firefighters, call-back pay of a minimum of eight hours at time-and-a-half pay, liability insurance for all employees who drive, paid sick-leave calculated on the basis of one day per shift, nine annual holidays, and four weeks annual vacation after eighteen years of service. Another feature, seemingly indicative of a positive attitude toward the bargaining relationship by both parties, is a contractual provision for a regular monthly communications meeting between a union committee and the city to discuss any interim problems that might arise.[98]

In San Antonio the initial negotiations with the Fire Fighters Association produced a bilaterally signed contract, though not a complete agreement. Bilateral agreement was reached on twenty-four of twenty-six issues, with two issues, wages and parking, remaining unresolved. The twenty-four issues agreed to were included in the signed contract, which the city then incorporated into an ordinance.[99] The contract included provisions for deduction of union dues, definition and limitation of union activity, maintenance of standards, a management-rights clause, rules and regulations, a nondiscrimination clause, a no-strike pledge, a grievance procedure and arbitration (including expedited arbitration administered by the American Arbitration Association), a successors and assigns clause, a joint occupational safety and health program, call-back pay, working hours, city liability and legal protection for acts of firefighters in lawful performance of their duties, sick leave, a "death in family" clause, a working-out-of-classification clause, paid holidays, clothing allowance, and reclassification of certain positions. As to the unresolved issues, the union proposed arbitration under § 10 which the city rejected, citing its fear of the outcome by an arbitrator from some other part of the country.[100] Resort was therefore made to § 16 of the Act (judicial enforcement in state district court) which produced a finding that the city had been in violation of the prevailing wage requirements of § 4 of the Act. The court awarded the same 5 percent across-the-board wage increase that the city had been proposing, but because of the finding of a § 4 violation, the increase was made retroactive from August 1, 1975, the date of the collective agreement; the city's proposal would have been effective only from November 1975. It also granted employee parking and awarded the union $5,000 in attorney's fees.[101] Both sides have appealed.

The City of Beaumont and Fire Fighters Local No. 399, singularly unsuccessful in resolving issues through the bargaining process, submitted a long list of issues to arbitration. The board of arbitration denied most of the union's positions because of insufficiency of evidence, but did grant a dues check-off, a one percent increase in the city's pension fund contribution, a provision for time-and-a-half overtime pay computed on the basic rate of pay (which the board defined as annual salary divided by 2,080 hours), two hours minimum call-back pay computed at overtime rate, double-time pay for firefighters responding to industrial fires outside the city, and a general wage increase of 7 percent, which was the amount that the city had offered.[102]

The Beaumont arbitration case pointed up several problems in the administration of the statute's comparability standards. The board's majority, consisting of the neutral arbitrator and the city-appointed arbitrator, expressed an inability to make findings based on private sector comparability in the absence of precise evidence of private sector wages and practices; the union's proffered evidence had consisted only of unsupported written statements. The majority also declined to read the statutory standards in §§ 4 and 13 to permit comparison with "different kinds of jobs involving a comparable degree of difficulty, training and skill."[103] The board seemed to require that the nature of the proceeding be more adversarial and judicial rather than informal. The statute specifies "[t]hat the hearing shall be informal, and the rules of evidence prevailing in judicial proceedings shall not be binding";[104] thus, in the opinion of this writer, it contemplates an informal proceeding. Furthermore, the board may not refuse to make findings for lack of evidence, for § 13(a) expressly provides that "[i]t shall be the duty of the arbitration board to render an award in accordance with the requirements of Section 4";[105] thus, the board has an affirmative and official duty to determine the facts even if compliance necessitates using its ample powers to require attendance of witnesses and production of other evidence "relative or pertinent to any issue presented to them for determination."[106] In no sense should this statutory arbitration proceeding be equated with an ordinary grievance arbitration or with burden-of-proof concepts familiar to the latter type of arbitration. Arbitration under the Act is not open-ended; the board is not authorized to exercise an unrestrained judgment—even if "good" judgment—rather, it must guarantee that the covered public employees be treated the same as private sector employees, for that is the mandate which § 4 imposes on the public employer. Nor does the Act require that private sector comparisons be made only with identical jobs, although the majority of the board in the Beaumont case seemed to read such a narrow approach into its view of the board's statutory responsibility. They expressly declined to read the statutory standard as permitting comparison with "different kinds of jobs involving a comparable degree of difficulty, training and skill."[107] Sections 4 and 13(a), however, seem to contemplate just such a comparison. Section 4 explicitly refers to "other jobs, *or portions of other jobs*, which require the same or *similar* skills, ability, and training, and which may be performed under the same or *similar* conditions,"[108] and § 13(a) expressly requires consideration of "hazards of employment, physical qualifications, educational qualifications, mental qualifications, job training and skills"[109] in determining comparable wages and conditions. Accordingly, the Beaumont board should have isolated the component factors in private sector jobs in order to establish a basis for adjusting compensation and other employment benefits for the Beaumont firefighters. It would seem that in the Beaumont area particularly, it would have been relatively easy for the board to have found not only comparable private sector job components but also some reasonably exact job counterparts among industrial firefighters. This was the first time the arbitration provision of the new Act had ever been used, however, and there were no guiding precedents.

The Beaumont experience suggests that the legislature might wish to reconsider the arbitration plan contained in FPERA. Perhaps recent experience in other states[110] with compulsory arbitration for firefighters and police will serve to eliminate or at least diminish the stigma which has traditionally adhered to compulsory arbitration—certainly Texas should now fully consider compulsory arbitration for fire and police services where the public welfare cannot tolerate a strike. Adoption of true compulsory, or legislated, arbitration would eliminate the need for the relatively inflexible comparability standard now required under FPERA because of the judicial role imposed on the court when the public employer refuses to arbitrate.

The local option feature of FPERA seems to be another serious defect in the Act. Local option elections have been costly and often bitterly fought.[111] In Houston, the firefighters claim to have spent $200,000 on an election campaign which they lost. The Civil Service Act is another hurdle, for it too is available only by local option election. Once coverage is achieved, many local associations are either politically exhausted or disinterested in yet another election campaign. An official of the Texas Association of Firefighters has expressed the view that "any right subject to local option is no right at all, but simply a privilege which only those locals best funded, best organized and politically knowledgeable may exercise."[112] Furthermore, the local option elections represent a public expense of dubious value to municipal taxpayers.

IV. A Blueprint for Public Sector Bargaining
Under Existing Law

It is obvious that this article has been following two distinct paths, each of which leads by a different approach to public sector bargaining. One path is by way of a legislative code, exemplified by the 1973 Fire and Police Employee Relations Act. Most other jurisdictions have approached public employee bargaining by such a path and may have enacted comprehensive statutory codes establishing procedures and regulating bargaining relationships.[113] Texas has moved a few steps in that direction by passage of the FPERA.

The other path which Texas is following, the one which has yet to be recognized as a distinct route to public employee bargaining, is by way of an approach thus far identified only as de facto collective bargaining, a term which I find unsatisfactory, for the bargaining which occurs and the agreements which are produced have—or should have—a legality and enforceability fully sanctioned by law and practice. For want of a better term I would simply call the process "public employee bargaining," "union bargaining," "public employee union bargaining," or even "common law public employee bargaining"; and the agreements produced by the process might be called "union agreements," "public employee union agreements," or simply "labor relations agreements." Regardless of designation, the terms of these agreements can be fully enforceable as to all union members. *Union membership* is the key to the relationship. Perhaps in time the process might come to be called "common law public employee collective bargaining"; but to avoid confusion with the statutory prohibition against public officials entering into "a collective bargaining contract with a labor organization respecting the wages, hours, or conditions of employment of public employees,"[114] the term "collective bargaining" should probably be avoided. Certainly the bargaining to be described herein will not be collective bargaining of the type prohibited by article 5154c, nor will a resulting agreement be a collective bargaining contract of the type referred to in the statutory prohibition.

As suggested by the foregoing terminology, this second path to public employee bargaining is partly based on common law concepts. It is also based on statutory provisions, however; indeed article 5154c is essential for the definition of rights and duties which comprise this system of bargaining. The approach does rely on common law development and traditional common law doctrine, but underlying the system are specific legislative enactments. Certain fundamental rights and obligations, whether of common law, constitutional, or purely statutory origin, are grouped in a few short legislative paragraphs found therein. When coupled to basic contract and agency principles, those rights and obligations form a correlated and distinct legal system for public employee labor relations.

We start with article 5154c and notice in its language a significant ambivalence pervading the legislative intent. On reading the statute as a whole, it is apparent that its normative thrust was to outlaw public employee strikes, not public employee unions. The prohibition against collective bargaining contracts and union recognition concerned two concepts widely held at the time of passage; a concept of governmental sovereignty which left no room for shared decision-making[115] and a concept about union recognition and collective bargaining contracts which prevailed in the private sector. Collective bargaining had come to mean exclusive bargaining with a union representing all employees in a group or unit. The Texas Legislature could only have had the Wagner Act[116] model in mind, for under that model *majoritarianism* and *exclusivity* had become the hallmarks of American collective bargaining.[117] Although the legislature wanted to avoid "collective" representation, it took pains to legalize the right of public employees to exercise a free choice of belonging or not belonging to a union, and required the public employer to recognize an "existing" right of its employees to present their grievances, that is, to seek to set or adjust, "wages, hours of work, or conditions of work"[118] either individually or through a union representative. Thus, it was "collective" union representation only, not individual union representation, that was being proscribed. True, the legislature limited even individual representation to unions which did not claim the right to strike, but that limitation, which has constitutional overtones to be discussed later, does not affect the essential nature of the legislative scheme.

As noted earlier, § 4 guaranteed that public employment would not be denied "by reason of membership or nonmembership in a labor organization."[119] This was a restatement for public employees of the general "right to work" statute, article 5207a, § 2, which declared, "No person shall be denied employment on account of membership or nonmembership in a labor union."[120] Those two provisions, together with a provision of another general statute passed in 1955, established broad right-to-organize protection for Texas public employees. The 1955 provision, article 5154g, § 1 reads:

It is hereby declared to be the public policy of the State of Texas that the right of persons to work shall not be denied or abridged on account of membership or non-membership in any labor union or labor organization and that in the exercise of such rights all persons shall be free from threats, force, intimidation or coercion.[121]

These rights are comparable but not identical to rights guaranteed private sector employees under §§ 7, 8(a)(1), 8(a)(3), 8(b)(1)(A), and 8(b)(2) of the National Labor Relations Act.[122] Texas has no administrative board to enforce these provisions, but judicial enforcement by injunction or mandamus, with reinstatement and back-pay remedies, is available.

In *Lunsford* vs. *City of Bryan*[123] a unanimous Texas supreme court liberally construed both article 5154c, § 4, and article 5207a, § 2, holding that the statutory language protected not only consummated union membership but also acts leading to membership.[124] The court noted that "when the intent and purpose of the legislature is manifest from a consideration of the statute as a whole, words will be restricted or enlarged in order to give the statute the meaning which was intended by the lawmakers."[125] These "right to work" provisions, which since the *Lunsford* case have been augmented by article 5154g, § 1, now provide a wide range of legal protection for the organizational rights of public employees.

Recently, in *Balderas* vs. *La Casita Farms, Inc.*,[126] the Fifth Circuit applied article 5154g, § 2 in upholding the reinstatement of an employee who had been active in support of a union though not himself a full-fledged union member, and ordered damages to compensate the employee "fully for the entire differential between pre- and post-discharge income."[127] The holding in *Russell* vs. *Edgewood Independent School District*[128] is not to the contrary. In that case a Texas court of civil appeals held that the doctrine of sovereign immunity, applicable to a public school district, prevented the granting of "actual damages, exemplary damages and damages for mental anguish and humiliation" in a tort action brought by a school teacher allegedly discharged in violation of articles 5154c and 5207a.[129] The court, however, carefully distinguished the suit, "a damage suit sounding in tort," from "a suit for reinstatement of a teacher who has been discharged, or for back pay for the time during which she was discharged. . . ."[130]

The foregoing provisions furnish reasonable protection for public employees who desire to join a union. But the right to join a union would be meaningless unless the union could be of benefit to the employee. The legislature recognized that a union representing public employees has a legitimate function to perform. What the legislature wished to avoid, in addition to strikes, was compulsory union representation as well as compulsory union membership. The focal point of article 5154c, § 6, was therefore on the employee's right to choose: He could either represent himself or he could authorize a union to provide such representation for him. The language which the legislature used to achieve this result is significant. It did not confer a new right of representation, rather it confirmed an "existing" right:

The provisions of the Act shall not impair the existing right of public employees to present grievances concerning their wages, hours of work, or conditions of work individually or through a representative that does not claim the right to strike.[131]

It is pertinent to examine existing common law concepts of representation. Except for the express statutory proscriptions, common law rights regarding a union's representation of its members remained unimpaired. Section 6 described a principal and agent relationship. It is familiar common law in Texas that:

When a person acts through an agent, the agent is the representative of the principal for the conduct of the transaction. Consequently, acts done by the agent, whenever they are within the scope of his actual or apparent authority, are binding on the principal. In other words, the agent's acts in such cases are the acts of the principal himself.[132]

Unquestionably the legislature by the language in § 6 had authorized individual public employees to present grievances, in other words to bargain and reach settlements concerning their employment relationship *through a union agent* which the statute defined as "a representative that does not claim the right to strike."

"Grievances" in § 6 were defined broadly enough to cover the entire public employee relationship. The phrase "wages, hours of work, or conditions of work" had an established private sector meaning. A similar phase: "rates of pay, wages, hours of employment, or other conditions of employment," had been in § 9(a) of the National Labor Relations Act since 1935;[133] the corresponding phrase in § 2 of the Railway Labor Act referred to "rates of pay, rules, or working conditions."[134] Whereas the NLRA and the RLA mandated *collective bargaining* as to such subject matter with the *exclusive and majority* representative of the employees, the Texas statute limited the process to individual bargaining, which could be conducted through the individual employee's union representative. The statute described a meaningful right, not an empty gesture.

In *Beverly* vs. *City of Dallas* [135] the city challenged the statute on the ground that § § 1 and 2, which prohibited collective bargaining, were in conflict with § 6. A court of civil appeals rejected the challenge, holding that the statute was not contradictory because "presentation of a grievance is in effect a unilateral procedure, whereas a contract or agreement resulting from collective bargaining must of necessity be a bilateral procedure culminating in a meeting of the minds involved and *binding the parties to the agreement.*"[136] The court correctly characterized the union as a *party* to a collective bargaining contract, which contract would be binding on the parties and enforceable directly by them. By contrast, the *parties* involved in settlement of a grievance under § 6 would not be the public employer and the union but rather the public employer and the individual employee. This would be true even when the employee was acting through a union representative.

In *Dallas Independent School District* vs. *AFSCME, Local 1442,*[137] another court of civil appeals upheld a judgment which declared the right of several local unions to present grievances to the school district on behalf of school employees who were members of those unions. The court rejected the school district's challenge that § 6 only contemplated individual grievances and that a declaratory judgment "as to a class or collective group is tantamount to designating said labor organization as the bargaining agent for public employees contrary to the Statutes."[138]

It seems clear enough from the statutory language that § 6 also contemplates, indeed requires, that if the employee is represented by a union the public employer must affirmatively meet with the union representative when employee grievances are presented. The "right . . . to present grievances" implies that the public employer will hear and consider them. As Chief Justice Hickman noted in *Lunsford*[139] regarding the same statute, "when the intent and purpose of the legislature is manifest from a consideration of the statute as a whole, words will be restricted or enlarged in order to give the statute the meaning which was intended by the law-makers."[140] Thus, it comes as no surprise that the Texas attorney general has recently issued a formal opinion in which he construed § 6 as follows:

Under Article 5154c . . . public employees are given a right to present grievances, either individually or through a representative which does not claim the right to strike. This right, given as an alternative to collective bargaining, is of little value if public employers are entitled to refuse to *hear or discuss* grievances. Having the right to present grievances necessarily implies that someone in a position of authority is required to hear them even though he is under no compulsion to take any action to rectify them. Otherwise the right to present grievances would be rendered meaningless. Therefore it is our opinion that implicit in Article 5154c, Sec. 6 is the notion that public officials should meet with public employees or their representatives *at reasonable times and places* to hear their grievances concerning wages, hours of work, and conditions of work.[141]

Section 6 may appropriately be compared to the duty to bargain definition in § 8(d) of the National Labor Relations Act,[142] but with the important difference that the Texas public employer's duty is to deal with the employee individually or with his union representative. This may be union bargaining but it is not collective bargaining. But like § 8(d) of the federal statute, the duty does not require the employer to take any action, although it does require that the employer and the union meet at reasonable times and places.

The foregoing statutory provisions have set the stage for the establishment of a legal relationship between the public employer and the public employees' union representative. For a definition of that relationship, we turn again to the common law.

Absent union intervention through collective bargaining, terms of employment in the public sector are governed by the employee's individual contract of employment[143] just as would be true in the private sector. The public sector employment contract may be one at will, in rare situations it may be a written contract for a definite term, in many cases it may be subject to supervening civil service regulations, and in every case its monetary terms will be set directly or indirectly by legislative appropriation. Governmental bodies are bound by the contracts which they are authorized to make,[144] and employment contracts are no exception. The capacity of parties to enter into employment contracts is governed on the whole by the same rules as are applicable to other common law contracts. Accordingly, rules determining capacity of principal and agent are also applicable to the employer-employee relationship.[145] When a public employee in Texas exercises his right to present grievances concerning his wages, hours of work, or conditions of work through a union representative, that representative is the employee-principal's agent and, assuming the existence of broad agency authorization, has full legal capacity to bind the employee. Thus, adjustments agreed to between the union representative and the public employer in the settlement of a grievance become adjustments in the terms of the employee's contract of employment.

The legislature did not confine grievance representation to limited subject matter; instead, as noted above, virtually the entire employment relationship was embraced by the operative phrase: "wages, hours of work, or conditions of work," and the scope of bargaining on grievances became comparable to the mandatory subjects of bargaining under the National Labor Relations Act.[146]

Because public employees within the same classification, or employees whose duties and responsibilities are similar, will generally have similar wage scales, fringe benefits, and other working conditions, it may be expected that most public employee grievances will involve groups of employees whose jobs are related. It is inevitable, therefore, that a typical grievance settlement by a union representative will affect many individual contracts of employment. Consequently, if a union is authorized individually by the members of a group to settle their job-related grievances—authorization that would normally inhere in the agency relationship expressed in the ordinary contract of union membership—the public employer must meet and treat with the union regarding the common grievances, for it is still the grievance of each individual employee. This would seem to be clearly required by § 6 and is consistent with the facts and holding in the *Dallas Independent School District* case.[147] When a grievance meeting produces a satisfactory settlement and provides for future action, the result is an amendment to each of the individual contracts of employment. Such a settlement, which normally would take the form of an agreement between the public employer and the union, is therefore enforceable, not directly as a collective bargaining contract, but as a series of individual employment contracts.

The arrangement thus described is neither awkward nor strange. If it seems strange, it is only because we in the United States have grown accustomed to union representation and collective bargaining contracts which conform to the NLRA model. But prior to the passage of the Wagner Act, and even later as to union-employer relationships which operated without benefit of NLRA representation procedures, such *members only* contracts were relatively common.[148] This was an agency relationship between employee and union which was consensual rather than statutory. By virtue of his membership in the union, the employee authorized the union to represent him, and the union only had a duty—essentially a contractual one based primarily on the union's constitution—

to represent its members; unlike the duty of fair representation mandated by § 9(a) of the NLRA,[149] the union had no duty to represent nonmembers.

The validity of a *members only* contract was assumed and recognized by the United States Supreme Court as recently as 1961 in the case of *Bernhard-Altman Texas Corp.* vs. *NLRB* decision.[150] The Court there distinguished recognition of a minority union as "exclusive" representative of the employees, which it held to be unlawful under the NLRA, from "an employer's bargaining with a minority union for its members only."[151] The latter practice is lawful and was common during the early days of the Wagner Act. For example, the contract between the Chrysler Corporation and the United Auto Workers renewed in March 1938 provided for recognition of the union as bargaining representative of its "members only."[152]

Unions and employers who bargained and contracted over wages and working conditions in the United States prior to the Railway Labor Act amendments of 1934[153] and the Wagner Act of 1935—as is still the practice in the United Kingdom—did not concern themselves as to whether a majority of the employees had authorized the union to represent them. Representation was based on union membership only, not on majoritarian concepts. The requirement of majority and exclusive representation was a creature of federal statutory law. Secretary of Labor Perkins testified in congressional hearings[154] that the idea of majoritarian and exclusivity feature in the Wagner Act was thought of accidentally as a result of experience under the old § 7(a) of the National Industrial Recovery Act of 1933.[155] In other words, without the benefit of a statutory mandate that a union be the exclusive and majority representative of the employees, no such requirement exists in American labor law. And such a requirement was expressly rejected for Texas public employees in article 5154c. But that statute did not prohibit common law *members only* representation, a fact which may have been forgotten over the years but which should now be recalled in view of the burgeoning growth of public employee unions and the need to give legal definition to the relationship authorized by § 6 of article 5154c.

That relationship is simply a common law agency relationship; and a union bargaining agreement, agreed to in settlement of grievances under § 6, records terms which are incorporated by reference into the union member's individual contract of employment. Even when the incorporation is not express, or when the terms of the union agreement are applied to an entire group of employees without regard to union membership, the incorporation occurs as a matter of usage or custom. The bargaining agreement is not itself an enforceable contract. That describes the situation which still prevails in England in both the private and public sectors; a situation which was not substantially disturbed by passage of the 1971 Industrial Relations Act[156] and in any event has certainly been fully restored by repeal of that Act.[157] In the United Kingdom, collective bargaining contracts are generally not contracts at all. According to Otto

Kahn-Freund: "This can be explained by the lack of that intent to conclude a legally binding contract which is an indispensable element of contract making as much as offer and acceptance and consideration."[158] This is not to say, however, that the terms of the British collective agreement are unenforceable— they may be unenforceable as a collective agreement but not as terms incorporated within individual contracts of employment.[159] Professor Kahn-Freund has described the legal status of the British collective agreement at common law as follows:

The terms of a collective agreement are likely to be "crystallized custom" and as such automatically implied in the relevant contracts of employment. "Automatically"—this means that there is no need for anything being said by either side. Unless something to the contrary has been (in the legal sense) "agreed" upon between employer and worker, the wage rates, the prescribed and permitted hours, the holidays, etc., laid down in the collective agreement thus become terms of the contracts of employment. It is still good for clarification if the parties expressly refer to the collective agreement, but there is no need for this to be done. This is the effect which, on general principles of the common law, must be attached to the collective agreement as a source of custom. . . .[160]

As I have said, there may be an automatic link between collective agreement and contract of employment. But I am under the impression that it is becoming more and more usual to dispense with the automatic link and to make an express reference to the collective agreement, a practice which should be encouraged. . . . An increasing number of employers seem . . . to adopt the wise practice of formulating a set of "work rules" or a "handbook"—a "codification" of terms—and of handling a copy of this document to each worker on engagement, sometimes of having it signed by him. This may, and no doubt often does, refer to the relevant collective agreement or agreements. [An] express reference [will], on established legal principles, leave no doubt that the collective terms are incorporated in the contract. . . .[161]

In Britain, when the individual contract of employment contains an express term at variance with the collective agreement, the term in the employment contract "would probably have priority."[162] Just the opposite would be true of a collective contract entered into pursuant to the National Labor Relations Act. As the Supreme Court explained in *J.I. Case Co.* vs. *NLRB*:[163] "The very purpose of providing by statute for the collective agreement is to supersede the terms of separate agreements of employees with terms which reflect the strength and bargaining power and serve the welfare of the group."[164] Also, § 301 of the Taft-Hartley Act,[165] as interpreted by the Supreme Court in the landmark case of *Textile Workers Union* vs. *Lincoln Mills*,[166] provides direct judicial enforcement of the private sector collective bargaining contract without regard to the individual contract of employment.[167]

The legal status of agreements negotiated between Texas public employers and unions in the settlement of grievances under § 6 of article 5154c is thus comparable to the situation prevailing in England and which prevailed in the private sector in the United States prior to the passage of the Railway Labor Act and the Wagner Act. The case law which reflected the latter situation was described in 1931 as follows:

[A] collective agreement establishes a rule which, unless negatived, is a term of every employment relation established between any employer and any worker when each is a member of some organization which negotiated it . . . it is a usage or, since knowledge of it is probably not necessary, a custom. . . .[168]

The conclusion which may be drawn from the above is that § 6 provides a viable mechanism through which a Texas governmental unit can bargain and enter into a formal agreement with a labor organization concerning wages and working conditions of public employees. Whether or not the union represents a majority of the employees in any particular grouping has no special legal significance, though it may have significance regarding the bargaining strength of the unionized employees. Notwithstanding, the public employer is under a statutory duty—perhaps even a constitutional one[169]—to meet and treat with the employees' union representative, a duty which does not depend on majority status. As a practical matter, however, a union's bargaining strength will normally reflect the size of its membership, but a public employer will have no legal excuse to avoid dealing with a union representative just because the union does not have membership authorizations from a majority of the employees.

Under this system, bargaining and resulting agreements will undoubtedly be shaped by practical considerations, such as relative organizational strength, appropriate employee groupings within the scope of the intended agreement, and the negotiating abilities of the parties. The law does not countenance strikes by public employees, but as noted earlier in this paper, strikes have occurred even when there was no theory of legal bargaining being applied. With a legal basis to support bargaining as here presented, the parties will at least have a means to establish a legal form of recognition and a device to achieve labor-management communication—factors which could help avoid some strikes. It is expected, however, that appeal to public opinion and the political process will continue to supply the principal bargaining pressures, on both sides, leading to a meeting of the minds between the public employer and the union representing its employees.

As previously noted, agreements under this system will be *members only* agreements. Although they will not be directly enforceable, they will be legal agreements, and the corresponding changes reflected in individual contracts of employment will be legally enforceable—although legal enforcement should hardly ever be necessary. Such agreements may include the full range of subject matter typically found in collective bargaining contracts; however application of these terms and benefits would be for union members only. Right-to-work advocates would have no reason to complain about unwanted union membership or compulsory union representation, and unions would have no obligation to represent nonmember employees. In all probability, however, a city or other public employer might be expected to apply union-bargained economic benefits to all employees uniformly within the same category or classification. But some benefits, such as grievance and arbitration procedures for discipline and dismissal cases and other disputes relating to interpretation or application of the terms of the employment agreement, could lawfully be applied to union members only, for such procedures would represent a form of grievance presentation by a union representative as contemplated within the § 6 statutory right.

Pursuant to this system of union bargaining, organized public employees of all classifications (even including those in police and fire departments where the city has not adopted FPERA by local option election) could legally achieve bargaining and execution of formal agreements with their respective cities concerning wages and working conditions. This system would thus be immediately available and would cover their operations until the time, if ever, that formal collective bargaining was instituted either under the 1973 FPERA or under some future legislative plan that the state legislature might enact.

V. A Postscript on Union Recognition and Unions which Claim the Right to Strike

I am not unmindful that § 2 of article 5154c declares that it is against public policy "to recognize a labor organization as the bargaining agent for any *group* of public employees,"[170] or that § 6 of that statute provides for grievance presentation "through a representative that *does not claim the right to strike.*"[171] In the interest of tidying up after putting together the pieces of a bargaining system, attention must now be given to these two statutory phrases.

It should be obvious that the proscription against union recognition in § 2 concerns recognition for collective bargaining purposes, referring to *exclusive* union recognition and the signing of an enforceable collective bargaining contract of the type previously distinguished. The lawful recognition provided for in the system described herein is of the type expressly permitted in § 6—an interpretation which is fully supported by the limiting reference to "bargaining agent for any *group.*" The proscription is thus for "collective" bargaining, that is, "group" bargaining, whereas bargaining, or grievance settling, under § 6 is confined strictly to individuals and their individual contracts of employment. These individuals cannot comprise a "group" within the meaning of § 2 because settlement of grievances must be on an individual basis, and that would be true even though many separate individuals are involved with similar or even common grievances. Any other interpretation would render meaningless the union representation expressly allowed by § 6. It is the "members only" feature of the bargaining contract which distinguishes lawful union recognition from recognition of a union for a group; the latter would be recognition for all employees within an employing or bargaining unit, and it is that which is not allowed by § 2.

The other language to be noted, the reference in § 6 to "unions which do not claim the right to strike," does not change the described bargaining system in any way. Even if the phrase is constitutional, it would simply mean that a union could satisfy the requirement by announcing an intent not to strike.[172] But there are grave doubts about the constitutionality of the limitation. The Texas attorney general has already issued an opinion that a similar limitation in article 4528c, § 10 A which denied the right of licensed vocational nurses "to be a member of any group, organization, association, or union which advocates or recognizes the right to strike," is unconstitutional since it "infringes unnecessarily on the freedom of association protected by the First Amendment to the United States Constitution."[173]

VI. Conclusion

The two paths to public sector bargaining outlined in this paper are both experimental; it will be interesting and instructive to watch further developments as to both approaches. Although I have told the reader more than he or she probably wants to know about public sector collective bargaining in Texas, I do so in order to stress that it is important that a legal way be found for governmental bodies in Texas to discuss and settle employment disputes with the unions which represent public employees.

It is much too early to assess performance under the FPERA. By adding the local option provision, which had been insisted upon by the governor, the legislature succeeded in "passing the buck" to local communities. These elections guarantee that collective bargaining will be a burning political issue in any locality choosing it even before it can be tried by the parties. Such elections tend to polarize local feeling, and the collective bargaining process is bound to suffer. Despite such obstacles, the FPERA contains sufficient flexibility in its procedures that, if constructive attitudes are adopted on both sides, the bargaining process under this statute can be a means of substantially improving employment relations with the unionized protective services, while at the same time protecting the public from either strikes or outrageous wage settlements. One can hardly quarrel with the proposition that firefighters and police, who are denied the right to strike, should receive compensation and employment conditions which are substantially the same as their counterparts in the private sector. It is to be hoped, however, that the impasse-settlement procedures in FPERA will in time be amended to provide for additional mediation and more flexible arbitration, including compulsory arbitration under adequate guidelines to be used where appropriate.

Unless a controlling federal statute is enacted, or until the FPERA is improved and until the state passes a fair and workable comprehensive code covering all public employees—a public employee relations act with adequate administrative machinery—the "members only" bargaining system outlined herein can offer a challenging opportunity for the parties to develop, through their own bargaining, an effective public sector labor-management system. That process could contribute valuable experience under an old form of bargaining—experience which conceivably might have an appeal beyond the public sector and beyond the boundaries of the Lone Star State.

Notes

1. See generally *U.S. Dept. of Labor, Summary of State Policy Regulations for Public Sector Labor Relations* (1975).

2. I.B. Helburn, *Public Employer-Employee Relations in Texas* 54 (1971) [hereinafter cited as Helburn].

3. *E.g.,* Houston, El Paso, Beaumont, San Antonio, Port Arthur, Texas City, Galveston, Pasadena, Fort Worth, Dallas, The Groves, Nederland.

4. *Tex. Rev. Civ. Stat. Ann.* art. 5154c-1 (Supp. 1975).

5. *Id.*

6. 29 U.S.C. §§ 141-68 (1970).

7. *Tex. Rev. Civ. Stat. Ann.* art. 5154c (1971). The only other jurisdiction in the United States with a similar prohibition is North Carolina. Its statute prohibits public employees from joining any union or organization which is affiliated in any way with national or international organizations and absolutely forbids the negotiation of any collective agreement or contract, violations of which is a misdemeanor. See *N.C. Gen. Stat.* 95-97, 95-98, 95-99 (1959). In *Atkins* vs. *City of Charlotte*, however, the prohibitions on becoming a member of any union or organization and the penalties therefor were struck down as an unconstitutional abridgement of the freedom of association, 296 F. Supp. 1068, 1075 (W.D.N.C. 1969). Nevertheless, the same case held the illegal contracts section to be a valid and constitutional exercise of legislative authority under the 10th Amendment. *Id.* at 1072. That section was also recently upheld in *Winston-Salem/Forsyth County Unit of the North Carolina Ass'n of Educators* vs. *Phillips.* 381 F. Supp. 644, 648 (M.D.N.C. 1974).

8. Labor-Management Relations Act (Taft-Hartley Act) § 301, 29 U.S.C. § 185 (1970).

9. *Tex. Rev. Civ. Stat. Ann.* art. 5154c (1971).

10. *Id.* See 14 Pub. Aff. Comm. No. 3 at 2 (May, 1968).

11. *Tex. Rev. Civ. Stat. Ann.* art. 5154c § 4 (1970). This article states: "It is declared to be the public policy of the State of Texas that no person shall be denied public employment by reason of membership or non-membership in a labor organization." *Id.*

12. *Id.* § 6.

13. *Id.* § 2. *See* Morris, *Public Policy and the Law Relating to Collective Bargaining in the Public Service*, 22 Sw. L.J. 585, 590-91 (1968).

14. *Tex. Rev. Civ. Stat. Ann.* art. 6252-3a (1971).

15. *Id.* art. 2372h-4.

16. Tex. Laws 1967, ch. 270, at 596, *as amended, Tex. Educ. Code Ann.* § 13.901 (1972). For a comprehensive discussion of the experience under that statute refer to Frels, *Teacher Consultation in Texas—The Last Frontier or a New Horizon,* 27 *Baylor L. Rev.* 233 (1975).

17. *Tex. Rev. Civ. Stat. Ann.* art. 5154c-1 (Supp. 1975).

18. *Id.* § 4.

19. *Id.* § 16.

20. Refer to accompanying text and notes 27, 102-09 *infra.*

21. *Tex. Rev. Civ. Stat. Ann.* art. 5154c-1 (Supp. 1975).

22. No other state conditions public employee collective bargaining on the outcome of local option elections.

23. *Tex. Rev. Civ. Stat. Ann.* art. 5154c-1 (Supp. 1975).

24. *Id.* § 6.

25. *Id.* § 7.

26. 29 U.S.C. § 158(d) (1970).

27. *Id.*

28. *Tex. Rev. Civ. Stat. Ann.* art. 5154c-1, § 7 (Supp. 1975).

29. *Id.* § 7(e).

30. 357 U.S. 449, 462 (1958).

31. *Fla. Stat. Ann.* § 447.023 (Supp. 1975). See also *ABA Labor Relations Law Section, Report of the Committee on State Labor Law and Public Employee Bargaining,* 1975 Comm. Rep't, Pt. I, 257, 274.

32. *ABA Labor Relations Law Section, Report of the Committee on State Labor Law and Public Employee Bargaining,* 1975 Comm. Rep't, Pt. I, 257, 274 (1975).

33. Letter from Howard McDaniel, Assistant City Manager, Beaumont, Texas to Charles Morris, June 2, 1975; Letter from Claude C. McRaven, Employee Relations Coordinator, San Antonio, Texas to Charles Morris, July 15, 1975. See also San Antonio, Tex., Ordinance 45470, Aug. 1, 1975.

34. Letter from Howard McDaniel, Assistant City Manager, Beaumont, Texas to Charles Morris, June 2, 1975.

35. *Tex. Rev. Civ. Stat. Ann.* art. 5154c-1, § 8 (Supp. 1975).

36. *Id.* § 9(b).

37. *Id.* § 9(c).

38. *Id.*

39. *Id.* § 10(a).

40. *Id.* § 13(a).

41. *Id.* § 14.

42. *Id.* § 16.

43. *Id.* art. 5159a (1971).

44. 149 Tex. 457, 234 S.W.2d 857 (1950).

45. 234 S.W.2d at 860.

46. *Tex. Rev. Civ. Stat. Ann.* art. 5154c-1, § 17(a) (Supp. 1975).

47. *Id.* § 17(c).

48. *Id.* § 20(b).

49. *Id.* § 20(d).

50. Helburn, *supra* note 2, at 33.

51. *Id.* at 35.

52. *Id.* Eight-five percent of police and 75 percent of firefighter locals have 75 percent of the respective forces organized. Less than 10 percent of municipal union locals have 75 percent of employees organized. *Id.* at 36.

53. *Tex. Rev. Civ. Stat. Ann.* art. 1269m (1971).

54. *Id.* §§ 8, 9, 14D, 22, 26(b) (Supp. 1975).

55. *Id.* art. 5154c-1.

56. *Id.* art. 1269m-r.

57. *Id.* art. 1269f.

58. *Id.* § 1.

59. *Id.* § 3.

60. *Id.* art. 1269m, § 8.

61. *Id.* art. 1269o; *id.* art. 1269p, § 6.

62. *Id.* art. 1269p, § 7.

63. *Id.*

64. *Id.* art. 1269p, § 6A.

65. *Id.* § 3.

66. *Id.* § 3a.

67. *Id.* art. 1269m, § 26(b)(a).

68. *Id.* § 22.

69. *Id.* § 14.

70. *Id.* §§ 20, 21 (1963).

71. *Id.* art. 5154c (1971).

72. *Tex. Educ. Code Ann.* § 13.216 (1972).

73. *Id.* § 13.217.

74. *Id.* § 13.901 (emphasis added).

75. *Tex. Rev. Civ. Stat. Ann.* art. 6252-3a (1970) (cities over 10,000 population) and art. 2372h-4 (1971) (counties over 20,000 population).

76. The counties are: Dallas, El Paso, Galveston, Harris, Jefferson, Orange, Tarrant. The cities are: Beaumont, Dallas, El Paso, Fort Worth, Galveston, The Groves, Houston, La Marque, Nederland, Pasadena, Port Arthur, Port Neches, San Antonio, South Houston, Texas City, Waco. The Hospital Districts are: Bexar County, Galveston County, Harris County, Tarrant County. Letter from Don McCullar to Charles Morris, June 26, 1975.

77. *See generally* Helburn, *supra* note 2, at 16. *See also* Frels, *Teacher Consultation—The Last Frontier or a New Horizon*, 27 *Baylor L. Rev.* 233 (1975).

78. *Tex. Rev. Civ. Stat. Ann.* art. 5154c-1 (Supp. 1975).

79. 1:2 D. Barnum, *Texas Employee Relations* 7 (March, 1975) [hereinafter cited as Barnum].

80. *Id.*

81. *Id.* at 5; H.B. 761, 53d Legis. (1975) (Texas AFL-CIO); H.B. 739, 63d Legis. (1975) (Texas League of Municipalities). In February of 1975 two bills were introduced in the Texas Legislature on employer-employee relations in the public sector. H.B. 739 was drafted by the Texas Municipal League and designed to put all city employees on an equal basis. To this end it would repeal existing collective bargaining and civil service coverage for the firefighters and the police. It is of the *meet and confer* type and provides for no collective bargaining. H.B. 761 was drafted by the Texas AFL-CIO and mandates collective bargaining rights for public employees similar to those in the private sector. It contains no impasse resolution procedure, but would repeal all laws in conflict except Article 5154c-1, the 1973 act applicable to firefighters and police.

82. Helburn, *supra* note 2, at 53.

83. Barnum, *supra* note 79, at 8 (Port Neches, La Marque, Port Arthur, Nederland, The Groves, Vidor, Orange; Jefferson County, Nederland School District).

84. Helburn, *supra* note 2, at 54.

85. *Id.* at 55-59.

86. Telephone interview with Thomas Fuller, Assistant General Manager, San Antonio Transit Service, June 7, 1975.

87. Interview with Alton Bostick, Secretary, Texas State Association of Firefighters, in Fort Worth, Texas, May 14, 1975.

88. Dallas Morning News, Aug. 28, 1975, § A at 39.

89. Barnum, *supra* note 79, at 8.

90. *Id.* at 3.

91. *Tex. Rev. Civ. Stat. Ann.* art. 5154c-1 (Supp. 1975).

92. Barnum, *supra* note 79, at 3.

93. Telephone interview with Clarence Long, Amalgamated Transit Union, July 14, 1975.

94. Telephone interview with Thomas Fuller, Assistant General Manager, San Antonio Transit Service, July 14, 1975.

95. Barnum, *supra* note 79, at 8.

96. Interview with Alton Bostic, Secretary, Texas State Association of Firefighters, in Fort Worth, Texas, May 14, 1975. The FPERA has been adopted in: Texas City, Corsicana, Beaumont, Sherman, Corpus Christi, El Paso, Laredo, Brownsville, Bryan, Kingsville, San Antonio (firefighters preceded police by six months). The FPERA has been rejected by: (1) Firefighters and Police: Brownwood, Galveston, Grand Prairie; (2) Firefighters only: Victoria, Houston, N. Richland Hills, Wichita Falls, Baytown; (3) Police only: Dallas, Mesquite.

97. *Texas Fire Fighter*, July-Aug., 1975, at 8.

98. *Id.*

99. San Antonio, Tex., Ordinance 45470, Aug. 1, 1975.

100. Letter from Claude C. McRaven, Employee Relations Coordinator, San Antonio, Texas to Charles Morris, July 15, 1975.

101. Firefighters Local 624 v. City of San Antonio, Civ. No. 75CI-9447, Dist. Ct. of Bexar County, 150th Judicial Dist. of Texas, Sept. 16, 1975.

102. City of Beaumont v. Fire Fighters Local No. 399 (Sept. 24, 1975) (J. Bailey, Arbitrator).

103. *Id.*

104. *Tex. Rev. Civ. Stat. Ann.* art. 5154c-1, § 12(a) (Supp. 1975).

105. *Id.* § 13(a).

106. *Id.* § 12(a).

107. City of Beaumont v. Fire Fighters Local No. 399 (Sept. 24, 1975) (J. Bailey, Arbitrator).

108. *Tex. Rev. Civ. Stat. Ann.* art. 5154c-1 (Supp. 1975) (emphasis added).

109. *Id.* § 13(a).

110. E.g., *Iowa Code* Vol. 3A, § 20.1 [GERR RF-93, 51:2411] (1974); *Mich. Comp. Laws Ann.* § 423.231 (Supp. 1975); *Me. Rev. Stat. Ann.* tit. 26, 965 (3), § 979-D(3) (1974); *Neb. Rev. Stat.* § 48-810 (1974), *amended by* [GERR RF, 51:3613] (1974); *Ore. Rev. Stat.* § 243.742 (1973); *Pa. Stat. Ann.* tit. 43, § 217.4 (Supp. 1975); *Wis. Stat.* § 111.77(3) (1974); *Wyo. Stat. Ann.* § 27-269 (1967).

111. Interview with Alton Bostick, Secretary, Texas State Association of Firefighters, in Fort Worth, Texas, May 14, 1975.

112. *Id.*

113. E.g., Alaska, Arkansas, California, Connecticut, Delaware, Florida,

Georgia, Hawaii, Idaho, Illinois, Indiana, Iowa, Kansas, Kentucky, Maine, Maryland, Massachusetts, Michigan, Minnesota, Missouri, Montana, Nebraska, Nevada, New Hampshire, New Jersey, New York, North Dakota, Oklahoma, Oregon, Pennsylvania, Rhode Island, South Dakota, Utah, Vermont, Virginia, Washington, Wisconsin.

114. *Tex. Rev. Civ. Stat. Ann.* art. 5154c, § 1 (1971).

115. Beverly v. City of Dallas, 292 S.W.2d 172 (Tex. Civ. App.–El Paso 1956, writ ref'd n.r.e.). The court characterized the presentation of grievances under article 5154c, § 6 as "a unilateral proceeding resulting in no loss of sovereignty by the municipality," in contrast to strikes and collective bargaining prohibited by other sections of the statute. *Id.* at 176.

116. National Labor Relations Act, 29 U.S.C. §§ 141-68 (1970).

117. Neither concept characterizes collective bargaining in most other western industrial countries. See generally E. Kassalow, *Trade Unions and Industrial Relations: An International Comparison* (1969).

118. *Tex. Rev. Civ. Stat. Ann.* art. 5154c, § 6 (1971).

119. *Id.* § 4; refer to note 11 *supra.*

120. *Id.* art. 5207a, § 2 (1971).

121. *Id.* art. 5154g, § 1.

122. 29 U.S.C. §§ 157, 158(a)(1), (3), (b)(1)A, (2) (1970).

123. 156 Tex. 520, 297 S.W.2d 115 (1957).

124. 297 S.W.2d at 117.

125. *Id.*

126. 500 F.2d 195 (5th Cir. 1974).

127. *Id.* at 200. The case involved a farm worker, who like public employees was excluded from coverage of the National Labor Relations Act. Article 5207a, § 2 is also applicable to public employees. *See* Lunsford v. City of Bryan, 156 Tex. 520, 297 S.W.2d 115 (1957).

128. 406 S.W.2d 249 (Tex. Civ. App.–San Antonio 1966, writ ref'd n.r.e.).

129. *Id.* at 251.

130. *Id.* at 250.

131. *Tex. Rev. Civ. Stat. Ann.* art. 5154c, § 6 (1971).

132. 2 *Tex. Jur.* 2d *Agency* § 2 (1964).

133. 29 U.S.C. § 159(a) (1970); 1 *The Developing Labor Law* 379 (C. Morris ed. 1971).

134. 45 U.S.C. §§ 161-63 (1970).

135. 292 S.W.2d 172 (Tex. Civ. App.–El Paso 1956, writ ref'd n.r.e.).

136. *Id.* at 176 (emphasis added).

137. 330 S.W.2d 702 (Tex. Civ. App.–Dallas 1959, writ ref'd n.r.e.).

138. *Id.* at 707.

139. 297 S.W.2d 115 (1957).

140. *Id.* at 117.

141. *Tex. Att'y Gen. Op.* No. H-422 (1974) (emphasis added).

142. 29 U.S.C. § 58(d) (1970).

143. See Kourik v. English, 340 Mo. 367, 100 S.W.2d 901, 905 (1936). See generally J. Dunsford, R. Alleyne, & C. Morris, *Labor Relations and Social Problems: Individuals and Unions* 1-17 (1973).

144. E.g., Morris & Cummings v. State, 62 Tex. 728, 744-45 (1884).

145. 53 *Am. Jur.* 2d *Master and Servant* § 15 (1970).

146. See generally *The Developing Labor Law* 389-423 (C. Morris ed. 1971).

147. See generally Dallas Indep. School Dist. v. Local 1442, AFSCME, 330 S.W.2d 702 (Tex. Civ. App.–Dallas 1959, writ ref'd n.r.e.).

148. See, e.g., Douds v. Retail Wholesale Dep't Store Local 1250, 173, F.2d 764, 769 (2d Cir. 1949); Eastwood-Neally Corp. v. International Ass'n Machinists, 124 N.J. Eq. 274, 1 A.2d 477, 481-82 (1938) (holding that at common law employees had a right to bargain through a minority union). See also Rice, *Collective Labor Agreements in American Law*, 44 *Harv. L. Rev.* 572 (1931).

149. 29 U.S.C. § 159(a) (1970); see Vaca v. Sipes, 386 U.S. 171, 177 (1967); Ford Motor Co. v. Huffman, 345 U.S. 330, 338 (1953); Rubber Workers Local 12, 150 NLRB 312 (1964), *enforced*, 368 F.2d 12 (5th Cir. 1966), *cert. denied*, 389 U.S. 837 (1967). *But cf.* Steele v. Louisville & N.R.R., 323 U.S. 192, 204 (1944).

150. I.L.G.W.U. (Bernard-Altmann Texas Corp.) v. NLRB, 366 U.S. 731 (1961).

151. *Id.* at 736.

152. 2 L.R.R.M. 964-67 (1938).

153. Railway Labor Act, ch. 347, § 1, 44 Stat. 577 (1926), *as amended*, 45 U.S.C. §§ 161-63 (1970).

154. *Hearings on* S. 1958 *Before Senate Comm. on Education and Labor*, 74th Cong., 1st Sess., 1 Leg. His. N.L.R.A. 1434 (1934).

155. National Industrial Recovery Act, Act of June 16, 1933, ch. 90, § 7(a), 48 Stat. 195, 198.

156. Industrial Relations Act 1971, c. 72.

157. Trade Union and Labour Relations Act 1974, c. 52.

158. O. Kahn-Freund, *Labor and the Law* 131 (1972).

159. Ford Motor Co., Ltd. v. Amalgamated Union of Eng'r and Foundry Workers, [1969] 2 Q.B. 303, 330-31.

160. O. Kahn-Freund, *Labor and the Law* 141 (1972).

161. *Id*. at 143. See also R. Simpson & J. Wood, *Industrial Relations* 17 (1973). Simpson and Wood stated: "The substantive content of the [collective] contract is most frequently determined through some form of collective negotiation the content of an agreement so made being expressly or impliedly incorporated into the contract of employment." *Id*.

162. O. Kahn-Freund, *Labor and the Law* 144 (1972).

163. 321 U.S. 332 (1944).

164. *Id*. at 338.

165. Labor-Management Relations Act (Taft-Hartley Act) § 301, 29 U.S.C. § 185 (1971).

166. Textile Workers Union v. Lincoln Mills, 353 U.S. 448, 462 (1957) (Reed, J., concurring).

167. *Id*. *Contra*, Westinghouse Salaried Employees Ass'n v. Westinghouse Elec. Corp., 348 U.S. 437, 451, 456-57 (1955).

168. Rice, *Collective Labor Agreements in American Law*, 44 *Harv. L. Rev.* 572, 604 (1931). Copyright 1971 by the Harvard Law Review Association. See also Cox, *The Legal Nature of Collective Bargaining Agreements*, 57 *Mich. L. Rev.* 1, 19 (1958). Professor Cox stated:

[A]lthough a collective bargaining agreement gave no rights to individual workers, whenever a man went to work his individual contract incorporated the union agreement as a local custom or usage so that every failure to pay wages in accordance with the collective agreement was a breach of the individual contract of employment.

Id.; Hudson v. Cincinnati, N.O. & T.P. Ry., 152 Ky. 711, 154 S.W. 47, 49-50 (Ct. App. 1913).

169. *Cf*. Richmond Educ. Ass'n v. Crockford, 55 F.R.D. 362, 364 (E.D. Va. 1972).

170. *Tex. Rev. Civ. Stat. Ann.* art. 5154c, § 2 (1971) (emphasis added).

171. *Id*. § 6 (emphasis added).

172. Dallas Indep. School Dist. v. Local 1442, AFSCME, 330 S.W.2d 702, 707-08 (Tex. Civ. App.—Dallas 1959, writ ref'd n.r.e.).

173. *Tex. Att'y Gen. Op*. No. H-389 (1974). See United Fed'n of Postal Clerks v. Blount, 325 F. Supp. 879, 883 (D.D.C.), *aff'd*, 404 U.S. 802 (1971). *But see* Rogoff v. Anderson, 34 App. Div. 2d 154, 310 N.Y.S.2d 174 (1970), *aff'd*, 28 N.Y.2d 880, 271 N.E.2d 553, 322 N.Y.S.2d 718 (1971), *cert. denied*, 404 U.S. 805 (1972) (upholding a similar provision in New York's Taylor Act on grounds that it applied only to "certification" of unions). The author feels that *Rogoff* is either wrong or distinguishable.

7

The Scope of Bargaining in the Federal Sector

Henry B. Frazier, III

Title 5 of the United States Code is the basic statutory provision codifying the laws relating to the organization of the federal government and to its civilian officers and employees.[1] Although the conditions of employment established pursuant to these measures constitute a very competitive package of benefits, the result has been that a great deal of the normal substance of labor-management negotiations at the bargaining table, such as wages, hours of work, insurance, compensated time off the job, employment and retention, has been preempted in the federal service by law. Although unions have not negotiated these matters through collective bargaining, they have been active in political negotiations that resulted in the enactment of these benefits into law. The Lloyd-LaFollette Act of 1912 had assured to federal employees the rights to petition and to furnish information to Congress and had assured postal employees the right of membership in labor organizations that do not impose an obligation to engage or assist in a strike against the United States.[2]

The highly developed system of provisions governing personnel management in the federal service today began with the Pendleton Act of 1883, which established the U.S. Civil Service Commission (CSC) with the usual responsibilities assigned to statutory civil service commissions.[3] Over the years, the commission has acquired the responsibility for administration of most of the provisions found today in title 5.

To complete the statutory framework that bears on the subject of the scope of bargaining, I should mention that section 301 of title 5 provides that the head of an executive department or military department may prescribe regulations for the government of his department, the conduct of his employees, the distribution and performance of its business, and the custody, use, and preservation of its records, papers, and property. Section 302 provides, in addition to the authority to delegate conferred by other law, that the head of an agency may delegate to subordinate officials the authority vested in him by law to take final action on matters pertaining to the employment, direction, and general administration of personnel under his agency.[4]

The delineation of the boundary between this statutory right of an agency head to regulate and the scope of bargaining under Executive Order (E.O.) 11491, as amended, has been the concern of the Federal Labor Relations Council in a number of its decisions, as will be seen later.

151

History of the Scope of Bargaining under the Executive Orders

A formalized labor-management program applicable to all agencies of the executive branch was not introduced until January 17, 1962, with the issuance of Executive Order 10988. The President's Task Force, which developed Executive Order 10988, recognized that many of the most important matters affecting federal employees are determined by Congress and are not subject to "unfettered negotiation by officials of the Executive Branch."

In discussing "the scope of consultations and negotiations with employee organizations," the Task Force

recognized that a major and perhaps controlling distinction between the type of employee-management relations that have developed in private industry and those which are possible in the Federal service is that in the latter neither the employer nor his employees are free to bargain in the ordinary sense. . . . The employer in most parts of the Federal Government cannot negotiate on pay, hours of work or most fringe benefits. These are established by law.[5]

In issuing Executive Order 10988, President Kennedy carried out the recommendations of his task force. Thus, Executive Order 10988, in section 6(b), stated the basic scope of negotiation as follows:

(b) . . . The agency and such employee organization, through appropriate officials and representatives, shall meet at reasonable times and confer with respect to personnel policy and practices and matters affecting working conditions, so far as may be appropriate subject to law and policy requirements. This extends to the negotiation of an agreement, or any question arising thereunder, the determination of appropriate techniques, consistent with the terms and purposes of this order, to assist in such negotiation, and the execution of a written memorandum of agreement or understanding incorporating any agreement reached by the parties. In exercising authority to make rules and regulations relating to personnel policies and practices and working conditions, agencies shall have due regard for the obligation imposed by this section, but such obligation shall not be construed to extend to such areas of discretion and policy as the mission of an agency, its budget, its organization and the assignment of its personnel, or the technology of performing its work.

Section 7 expressed the rights reserved to management in every agreement:

Section 7. Any basic or initial agreement entered into with an employee organization as the exclusive representative of employees in a unit must be approved by the head of the agency or any official designated by him. All agreements with such employee organizations shall also be subject to the following requirements, which shall be expressly stated in the initial or basic agreement and shall be applicable to all supplemental, implementing, subsidiary or informal agreements between the agency and the organization:

(1) In the administration of all matters covered by the agreement officials and employees are governed by the provisions of any existing or future laws and regulations, including policies set forth by the Federal Personnel Manual and agency regulations, which may be applicable, and the agreement shall at all times be applied subject to such laws, regulations and policies;

(2) Management officials of the agency retain the right, in accordance with applicable laws and regulations, (a) to direct employees of the agency, (b) to hire, promote, transfer, assign, and retain employees in positions within the agency, and to suspend, demote, discharge, or take other disciplinary action against employees, (c) to relieve employees from duties because of lack of work or for other legitimate reasons, (d) to maintain the efficiency of the Government operations entrusted to them, (e) to determine the methods, means and personnel by which such operations are to be conducted; and (f) to take whatever actions may be necessary to carry out the mission of the agency in situations of emergency.

Section 8 specifically authorized the negotiation of grievance systems, including advisory arbitration, provided they conformed to standards issued by the Civil Service Commission, "and did not impair rights otherwise available."

The Presidential Study Committee, which examined the need for changes in the program in 1969, found one of six major areas in greatest need of change to be "[a]n enlarged scope of negotiation and better rules for insuring that it is not arbitrarily or erroneously limited by management representatives."[6]

The study committee went on to say:

Section 6(b) of the present order includes a proviso that the obligation to negotiate does not extend to "to such areas of discretion and policy as the mission of an agency, its budget, its organization, and the assignment of its personnel, or the technology of performing its work. . . ."

We believe there is need to clarify the present language in section 6(b) of the order. The words "assignment of its personnel" apparently have been interpreted by some as excluding from the scope of negotiations the policies or procedures management will apply in taking such actions as the assignment of employees to particular shifts or the assignment of overtime. This clearly is not the intent of the language. This language should be considered as applying to an agency's right to establish staffing patterns for its organization and the accomplishment of its work—the number of employees in the agency and the number, type, and grades of positions or employees assigned in the various segments of its organization and to work projects and tours of duty.

To remove any possible future misinterpretation of the intent of the phrase "assignment of its personnel," we recommend that there be substituted in a new order the phrase "the number of employees, and the numbers, types and grades of positions, or employees assigned to an organizational unit, work project or tour of duty." As further clarification, a sentence should be added to this section providing that agencies and labor organizations shall not be precluded from negotiating agreements providing for appropriate arrangements for employees adversely affected by the impact of realignment of work forces or technological change.[7]

The Study Committee also heard complaints from unions about the impact of agency regulations on the scope of bargaining. The study committee's answer was a reaffirmation of the firm belief that "agency regulatory authority must be retained." However, the report went on to urge that agencies increase, "where practicable," their delegations of authority on personnel policy matters to permit a wider scope for negotiation. Agencies were exhorted not to issue overly prescriptive regulations and to consider exceptions to agency regulations where both management and union representatives requested an exception and the agency found it feasible.

The committee recommended the establishment of a procedure whereby disputes as to the negotiability of a bargaining proposal could be resolved. Other recommendations by the study committee that affected the scope of bargaining included the following:[8]

1. Agencies and unions should be free to agree to engage in joint negotiations covering combinations of units at any level of the agency—thus making it possible to negotiate at higher levels of authority having broader authority to bargain.
2. Changes in agency policies and regulations (other than those required by law or outside authority) should not supersede conflicting provisions of existing negotiated agreements until they are renegotiated or extended (unless an exception is granted).
3. Any provision in an agreement relating to payment of money to a union must be based on voluntary, written authorization. This specifically prohibited certain forms of union security.
4. Official time should not be used for negotiation. Previously this had been optional with the agency.
5. Binding arbitration of grievances over the interpretation and application of the agreement should be negotiable, with challenges to awards sustained only on grounds similar to those applied by the courts in the private sector.

President Nixon issued Executive Order 11491 of October 29, 1969, as a result of the study committee's report and these recommendations were adopted. In addition, agency internal security practices were added to the list of matters not included in the obligation to bargain. Sections 11(a), (b), and (c) and 12(a), (b), and (c) became the basic provisions governing scope of bargains in the new order:

Section 11. *Negotiations of agreements.* (a) An agency and a labor organization that has been accorded exclusive recognition, through appropriate representatives, shall meet at reasonable times and confer in good faith with respect to personnel policies and practices and matters affecting working conditions, so far as may be appropriate under applicable laws and regulations, including policies set forth in the Federal Personnel Manual, published agency policies and regulations, a national or other controlling agreement at a higher level in the agency, and this Order. They may negotiate an agreement, or any question arising thereunder; determine appropriate techniques, consistent with section 17 of this Order, to assist in such negotiation; and execute a written agreement or memorandum of understanding.

(b) In prescribing regulations relating to personnel policies and practices and working conditions, an agency shall have due regard for the obligation imposed by paragraph (a) of this section. However, the obligation to meet and confer does not include matters with respect to the mission of an agency; its budget; its organization; the number of employees; and the numbers, types, and grades of positions or employees assigned to an organizational unit, work project or tour of duty; the technology of performing its work; or its internal security practices. This does not preclude the parties from negotiating agreements providing appropriate arrangements for employees adversely affected by the impact of realignment of work forces or technological change.

(c) If, in connection with negotiations, an issue develops as to whether a proposal is contrary to law, regulation, controlling agreement, or this Order and therefore not negotiable, it shall be resolved as follows:

(1) An issue which involves interpretation of a controlling agreement at a higher agency level is resolved under the procedures of the controlling agreement, or, if none, under agency regulations;

(2) An issue other than as described in subparagraph (1) of this paragraph which arises at a local level may be referred by either party to the head of the agency for determination;

(3) An agency head's determination as to the interpretation of the agency's regulations with respect to a proposal is final;

(4) A labor organization may appeal to the Council for a decision when—

(i) it disagrees with an agency head's determination that a proposal would violate applicable law, regulation or appropriate authority outside the agency, or this Order, or

(ii) it believes that an agency's regulations, as interpreted by the agency head, violate applicable law, regulation of appropriate authority outside the agency, or this Order.

Section 12. *Basic provisions of agreements.* Each agreement between an agency and a labor organization is subject to the following requirements—

(a) in the administration of all matters covered by the agreement, officials and employees are governed by existing or future laws and the regulations of appropriate authorities, including policies set forth in the Federal Personnel Manual; by published agency policies and regulations in existence at the time the agreement was approved; and by subsequently published agency policies and regulations required by law or by the regulations of appropriate authorities, or authorized by the terms of a controlling agreement at a higher agency level;

(b) management officials of the agency retain the right, in accordance with applicable laws and regulations—

(1) to direct employees of the agency;

(2) to hire, promote, transfer, assign, and retain employees in positions within the agency, and to suspend, demote, discharge, or take other disciplinary action against employees;

(3) to relieve employees from duties because of lack of work or for other legitimate reasons;

(4) to maintain the efficiency of the Government operations entrusted to them;

(5) to determine the methods, means, and personnel by which such operations are to be conducted; and

(6) to take whatever actions may be necessary to carry out the mission of the agency in situations of emergency; and

(c) nothing in the agreement shall require an employee to become or to remain a member of a labor organization, or to pay money to the organization except pursuant to a voluntary, written authorization by a member for the payment of dues through payroll deductions. The requirements of this section shall be expressly stated in the initial or basic agreement and apply to all supplemental, implementing, subsidiary, or informal agreements between the agency and the organization.

As a result of the 1971 general program review conducted by the council, several changes were made with respect to negotiating a grievance procedure:

1. A requirement was established that each negotiated agreement contain a grievance procedure, applicable only to grievances over the interpretation and application of the agreement and not to grievances over agency regulations. This was to provide an incentive to the union to negotiate broader agreements within the existing scope of negotiations.
2. The negotiated grievance procedure would no longer be subject to CSC standards.
3. The payment of the cost of arbitration, which E.O. 11491 had required to be shared, could be negotiated..

In addition to these changes in the area of grievance procedures, the council recommended that the use of official time for negotiation, prohibited by E.O. 11491, be made negotiable within specified limits and that the question of agency charges for making payroll deductions for unions dues be left to negotiation.

The recommended changes were issued in E.O. 11616, which amended E.O. 11491 on August 26, 1971. In the council's general program review of 1974-75, expansion of the scope of negotiation was again a major objective as it was in 1969. Among the major issues considered by the council was whether changes should be made with respect to the impact of agency regulations on the scope of bargaining, which had been considered in every program review beginning with the study by the 1961 task force.

Prior to the 1974-75 general review the council had issued several decisions providing additional guidance as to what constituted a "published agency policy or regulation," which may thus limit the scope of bargaining under section 11(a) of the order. The council held that the term "agency" includes not only the headquarters of the agency but also any subordinate level authorized to issue binding regulations or policies.[9] Also, the council had held that to constitute a "policy or regulation" an agency directive must have been issued to achieve uniformity and equality in the administration of matters common to more than one activity, and, by its fundamental nature and the circumstances surrounding its issuance, be designed to implement broader agency purposes.[10] However, experience under the order since 1970 and testimony received during the review led the council to conclude that some further modification of the impact of agency regulations on the scope of bargaining was needed to promote the purposes of the Executive Order.

The council found that the scope of bargaining had not expanded as much as anticipated. The council concluded that multiple levels of agency regulations had unduly restricted negotiations by their complexity and their diversity within agencies and across agency lines. Therefore, the council recommended that negotiations at the local level would be barred only by those agency regulations issued at the headquarters level or by a "a first-level organizational segment which has functions national in scope that are implemented in field activities."

Even as to such regulations, only those for which a "compelling need" exists would bar negotiations. Regulations that did not meet this test would continue to apply in a given exclusive bargaining unit except to the extent that the local agreement contained different provisions. Criteria for determining compelling need would be established in rules to be published by the council. Disputes as to whether a regulation, as interpreted by the agency head, met the standard of need would be resolved by the council in negotiability appeals filed under section 11(c) of the order and decisions in one case would not necessarily be dispositive as to a similar regulation in another agency.[11]

The council also recommended changes in two other areas where changes should affect bargaining: the consolidation of existing bargaining units and the negotiation of grievance and arbitration procedures. To expand the scope of bargaining and to reduce unit fragmentation, the council recommended that a policy facilitating the consolidation of existing bargaining units should be adopted. Specifically, the council recommended that the order be amended to permit an agency and a union to agree to consolidate, without an election, those bargaining units represented by the union within the agency so long as the unit conforms to the appropriate unit criteria contained in the order. When there is no bilateral agreement to consolidate, either party would be permitted to petition for an election on the question and election-bar, certification-bar, and agreement-bar rules would not apply. The union would not lose its status as the exclusive representative in the existing units should the employees reject the consolidation.[12]

The council also examined the question of the permissible scope of the grievance procedure in relation to agency regulations. It recommended that the coverage of the negotiated grievance procedure should be fully negotiable so long as it does not conflict with statute or the order or include matters subject to statutory-appeal procedures. This would enable the parties to agree to use the negotiated grievance procedure to resolve grievances over matters covered by agency regulations pertaining to personnel policies and practices and matters affecting working conditions and not included as part of the agreement, provided the grievances were not over matters otherwise excluded from bargaining by sections 11(b) and 12(b) of the order. To the extent that the parties made their negotiated grievance system the *exclusive* procedure for resolving grievances over agency policies and regulations not contained in the agreement, such grievances would no longer be subject to separate grievance procedures established unilaterally by the agency.[13]

Finally, the council considered the question of whether section 11(a) encompassed an obligation to negotiate with respect to midcontract changes in established personnel policies and practices and matters affecting working conditions, and concluded that it did.

The council's recommendations were approved and, where appropriate, were incorporated by President Ford in E.O. 11838, further amending E.O. 11491, as amended.[14]

The council has since issued illustrative criteria for determining when a compelling need exists for agency policies or regulations concerning personnel policies and practices and matters affecting working conditions.

A compelling need exists for an applicable agency policy or regulation concerning personnel policies and practices and matters affecting working conditions when the policy or regulation meets one or more of the following illustrative criteria:

(a) The policy or regulation is essential, as distinguished from helpful or desirable, to the accomplishment of the mission of the agency or the primary national subdivision;

(b) The policy or regulation is essential, as distinguished from helpful or desirable, to the management of the agency or the primary national subdivision;

(c) The policy or regulation is necessary to insure the maintenance of basic merit principles;

(d) The policy or regulation implements a mandate to the agency or primary national subdivision under law or other outside authority, which implementation is essentially nondiscretionary in nature; or

(e) The policy or regulation establishes uniformity for all or a substantial segment of the employees of the agency or primary national subdivision where this is essential to the effectuation of the public interest.[15]

Council Decisions Affecting the Scope of Bargaining

Limitations on the Council's Role

The council's role in the area of negotiability is considered and limited by specific references in the order. Section 11(a) permits the council to establish criteria about compelling need of published agency policies and regulations. Section 11(c) permits the council to receive appeals from labor organizations if such an organization:

1. Disagrees with an agency head's determination that a proposal would violate applicable law, regulation, or appropriate authority outside the agency, or this order, or
2. Believes that an agency's regulations, as interpreted by the agency head, violate applicable law, regulation of appropriate authority outside the agency, or this order, or are not otherwise applicable to bar negotiations under paragraph (a) of this section.

Section 4(c)(2) of the order empowers the council to consider, "subject to its regulations . . . appeals on negotiability issues as provided in section 11(c) of this Order." Consistent with this authority, the council has issued detailed rules of procedure governing the conduct of a negotiability dispute proceeding (5 CFR Part 2411, Subpart C, §§ 2411.21 to 2411.28), which rules incorporate and implement the precise language of section 11(c).[16] The amendments to the order made in 1971 and 1975 did not change the nature of the council's basic authority to decide negotiability appeals.

From the outset, under these provisions of the order, the council has rejected appeals on negotiability disputes that did not arise during the course of negotiations and did not identify a contract proposal and the request for, or rendering of, an agency determination on that proposal.[17] Further, the council has limited its decision to sustaining, setting aside, or remanding the agency head's determination on the proposal.[18] Where the council has found a proposal to be negotiable, the council has, since its inception, uniformly cautioned:

This decision shall not be construed as expressing or implying any opinion of the Council as to the merits of the union's proposal. We decide only that, as submitted by the union and based on the record before us, the proposals are properly subject to negotiation by the parties concerned under section 11(a) of the Executive Order 11491.

Of further significance, the council under section 2411.28 of its rules does not "enforce" its decision finding a proposal to be negotiable. Instead, if a party fails to negotiate on the proposal found to be negotiable by the council, such failure may be subject to an unfair labor-practice proceeding initiated by a party before the assistant secretary under section 6 of the order;[19] or, if an impasse develops and the proponent is unwilling to abandon the proposal, the mediation and impasse procedures available under sections 16 and 17 of the order may be invoked by a party.

Moreover, the council does not retain jurisdiction in a negotiability case to monitor the subsequent negotiations of the parties. If a negotiability dispute arises about any revised proposal, such dispute may be appealed to the council after an agency-head determination on such revised proposal. Or, if an agreement, is reached on a revised proposal, the council may be called upon to pass upon the validity of that agreement in a *separate* proceeding.

Basic Council Decisions Affecting the Scope of Bargaining

The subject matter of bargaining in the federal sector does not break down readily into simple categories primarily because of the effect of restrictions in statute and regulation and the rights optionally or absolutely reserved to management in sections 11(b) and 12(b) of the order. Certain broad principles elucidating the concepts of negotiability are, however, emerging from the council's decisions.

As has been indicated, section 11(a) of the order defines the scope of negotiations to include "personnel policies and practices and matters affecting working conditions, so far as may be appropriate under applicable laws and regulations, including policies set forth in the Federal Personnel Manual, published agency policies and regulations . . . and this Order."

One of the early principles established and consistently followed by the council dealt with the question of what effect, if any, would flow from the fact that earlier contracts may have contained provisions that are nonnegotiable under the order. The council stated:

Although other contracts may have included such provisions, as claimed by the union, this circumstance cannot alter the express language and intent of the Order and is without controlling significance in this case.[20]

Matters Outside Section 11(a)

The council has found that some proposals that ostensibly deal with "personnel policies and practices and matters affecting working conditions" fall totally outside the scope of bargaining under section 11(a). Thus, the council has held that a proposal that the food-service facilities for personnel be operated directly by an internal cafeteria board of directors rather than by an outside contractor is outside the scope of bargaining because it concerns the method of management of the food service and who would provide the service rather than such matters as the quality of the food and the services or the nature of the facilities.[21] In another case, a union proposed that a member of the National Guard, who is also a civilian technician, have the option to terminate his enlistment when he ceases to be employed as a technician. (Technicians must, as a prerequisite to their civilian employment, become members of the National Guard in a military capacity.) The council held that the proposal was outside the scope of 11(a) because it deals with the postemployment status of individuals who no longer possess the status of employees under the order and with a wholly separate military enlistment contract, which is established by statute as a precondition for the employment relationship (as a civilian technician).[22]

On the other hand, in a third case, the council has overruled an agency's determination that a proposal that would establish a procedure for the acceptance of voluntary applications for unit positions from nonunit agency employees outside the required minimum area of consideration was outside the scope of section 11(a) because it dealt with the rights of nonunit employees. The council found that the proposal did fall within the scope of bargaining under the order because it concerned the procedural context within which unit employees would have to compete with outside applicants for unit jobs and hence was within the scope of 11(a).[23]

Conflict of Proposals with "Applicable Laws"

In conformity with section 11(c)(4)(i), the council has on a number of occasions passed upon the question of whether a proposal conflicts with statute. Thus, for example, it has ruled that union proposals pertaining to the faculty-salary schedule at the Merchant Marine Academy were consistent with the Merchant Marine Act;[24] that union proposals concerning an activity's practice of assigning "swing" operators in such a way as to avoid overtime pay did not violate 5 U.S.C. 301, 302 or 305;[25] that a union proposal relating to the establishment of a basic workweek and limitations upon the starting time of that workweek would not violate statutory restrictions on the payment of overtime (5 U.S.C. 5542[a]); and that the agency's determination that the proposal violated the

Poultry Products Inspection Act and the Federal Meat Inspection Act were unsupported.[26] On the other hand, the council has upheld agency determinations that a proposal that National Guard technicians be granted either military leave or administrative leave when ordered to attend reserve drill meetings in an inactive duty status on their normal workdays was contrary to statute[27] and that a proposal that wage-grade National Guard technicians receive overtime pay for hours worked in excess of 8 hours a day or 40 hours a week violated 32 U.S.C. 709(g)(2).[28]

Conflict of Proposals with Outside "Regulations, Including Policies Set Forth in the Federal Personnel Manual"

The council has received a number of negotiability appeals that presented the issue of whether a proposal violates the regulations of some authority outside the agency, such as those of the Civil Service Commission. Since the Civil Service Commission has primary responsibility under statute for the issuance and interpretation of its own directives, the council has followed the practice of requesting from the commission interpretations of its directives as they pertain to the issues related in such cases.[29] Recently, the council extended this practice to the comptroller general of the United States. Where the determinations received from such outside agencies are found to be controlling, they are incorporated in the council's decisions.

In two cases, the council has found that the outside directive relied upon by the agency was not an "applicable . . . regulation" as that term is used in section 11(a). Thus, an Office of Management and Budget (OMB) letter was held to be policy guidance and not regulatory in form or content;[30] and an OMB circular was found to represent policy guidance of a general nature rather than a strict injunction and, therefore, did not constitute a regulation of appropriate authority under the order.[31]

Conflict of Proposals with "Published Agency Policy or Regulation"

The council's role in resolving negotiability disputes wherein the agency head has determined that the proposal is contrary to agency regulation has been limited by the specific provisions of the order. Thus, the council has repeatedly held, based on the express language of section 11(c)(3), that an agency head's determination about the interpretation of his own regulations is controlling on the council and that the council may not substitute its interpretation of an agency's regulations for the agency head's determination about the interpretation of those regulations with respect to a proposal.[32] However, the council has further held that the agency regulation, as interpreted by the agency head, is not dispositive if the agency head has misconstrued the bargaining proposal he has found to be contrary to the agency regulation.[33]

The council's role in resolving negotiability disputes concerning agency regulations is also limited by section 11(c)(4)(ii) in the order, which has restricted appeals in such cases to those in which the union contends that the "agency's regulations, as interpreted by the agency head, violate applicable law, regulation of appropriate authority outside the agency, or this Order." When it was contended that an agency regulation is contrary to law, the council analyzed the law claimed to be contravened by the agency regulation and held, for example, that certain agency regulations were not, in one case, violative of constitutional proscriptions[34] or, in another case, statutory requirements.[35] When it was contended that an agency regulation is contrary to the regulations of outside authorities, here again the council followed the practice of deciding such cases based upon the interpretation by the outside authority of its own regulations. The council has also refused, at least in negotiability cases, to pass upon the validity of such outside regulations where the union has alleged that the outside regulation itself is, for example, contrary to statute.[36] Finally, when the union contended that the agency regulation is contrary to the order, the council found the regulation to be inconsistent with the order and set aside the agency-head determinations of nonnegotiability[37] or found the regulation to be consistent with the order and sustained the agency-head determinations of nonnegotiability.[38]

The council has held that the term "agency" includes not only the headquarters but also any subordinate level authorized to issue binding regulations and policies.[39] However, to constitute a "policy or regulation," the directive must be issued to achieve uniformity and equality in the administration of matters common to more than one activity, and, by its fundamental nature and the circumstances surrounding its issuance, be designed to implement broader agency purposes. Thus, a higher level directive applicable only to the activity involved was held not to limit bargaining under section 11(a),[40] but a command directive applicable uniformly to the several subordinate activities within the command was held properly to limit such bargaining.[41] (Of course, the cases cited were decided prior to the recent amendments to the order concerning "compelling need" and "level of issuance" of agency regulations.)

Conflict of Proposals with "This Order"

Most of the cases in which it is alleged that a bargaining proposal conflicts with the order involve section 11(b) and/or section 12(b), although other provisions, such as section 13[42] and section 20,[43] have sometimes been relied upon.

A decision by the council that a bargaining proposal conflicts with section

12(b) is, in effect, a ruling that such a proposal is prohibited by the order and hence is illegal. Thus, the council has explained that section 12(b) dictates that in every labor agreement management officials retain their existing authority to take actions with respect to the matters enumerated in section 12(b). "The emphasis is on the reservation of management authority to decide and act on these matters, and the clear import is that no right accorded to unions under the Order may be permitted to interfere with that authority."[44] However, the council has also indicated that there is no indication in section 12(b) that "such reservation of decisionmaking and action authority is intended to bar negotiation of procedures, to the extent consonant with law and regulations, which management will observe in reaching the decision or taking the action involved, provided that such procedures do not have the effect of negating the authority reserved."[45] Moreover, proposals to establish appropriate procedures dealing with the impact on employees of actions or decisions taken pursuant to section 12(b) are likewise negotiable.[46] Of course, such proposals dealing with impact could not encompass matters that would have the effect of requiring the agency to bargain on the action being taken, such as the realignment of work forces itself.[47]

Although matters covered by section 12(b) may be categorized as "prohibited" or "illegal" subjects of bargaining, matters covered by section 11(b) could be categorized as "discretionary" or "optimal" subjects of bargaining. Thus, the council has indicated that when it finds a matter is covered by section 11(b), it is within the agency's discretion under section 11(b) whether it wishes to bargain on the matter;[48] that is, the agency may, but is not obligated to bargain over a proposal that conflicts with 11(b).[49] This distinction between matters covered by section 12(b) and those covered by section 11(b) is based on the literal language of the two provisions. It should be noted that a decision by management representatives at the bargaining table to negotiate over a proposal that falls within 11(b) is a final and binding exercise of management discretion with respect to that proposal and it is not subject to subsequent reversal under section 15 of the order by higher level management officials exercising the authority to review agreements for conformance with the order.[50]

Decisions under Section 11(b)

Most of the council's decisions regarding section 11(b) have dealt with the meaning and application of the "organization" of any agency: and "the number of employees; and the numbers, types and grades of positions of employees assigned to an organizational unit, work project or tour of duty"; which are collectively referred to as the "staffing patterns" of an agency.

One line of cases concerning the meaning and application of the "staffing-patterns" provisions of 11(b) has dealt with the negotiability of various proposals pertaining to workshifts and workweeks. In the first of these cases, *Plum Island,*[51] the agency operated a research facility and, to provide for round-the-clock operation and maintenance, it employed four crews who worked on three rotating, weekly shifts and who supplemented a regular, one-shift crew of maintenance employees. The agency had decided to eliminate the entire third shift in one of its laboratory buildings and to establish two new fixed shifts working on a five-day basis. Although the total number of workers employed by the agency would not be reduced thereby, the changes in the staffing on the first and second shift resulting from the termination of the rotating third shift were intended by the agency to result in improved staffing of those two shifts. However, the union proposed that any such changes in tours of duty (and hence the staffing of the new, fixed, first and second shifts and the restaffing of the rotating shifts) be proscribed unless negotiated with the union.

The council held that the union's proposal was excepted from the agency's obligation to bargain under section 11(b), and, more particularly under the exclusion in that section relating to "the numbers, types, and grades of positions or employees assigned to an organizational unit, work project or tour of duty." As observed by the council, this language of the order, according to section E.1. of the report accompanying E.O. 11491, clarified the right of an agency to determine the "staffing patterns" for its organization and for accomplishing its mission. The council found in substance that the number and duration of the workshifts, or tours of duty, as intended to be changed by the agency in *that* case, *were integrally related to and determinative of the numbers and types of employees assigned to those tours of duty of the agency;* and therefore that, under the facts of that case, the union's proposal to bargain on such changes was nonnegotiable under section 11(b).[52]

The next case in this line involved the *Charleston Naval Supply Center,*[53] which provided round-the-clock service to the fleet, seven days a week. The union proposed to establish a basic workweek of five eight-hour days, Monday through Friday, for employees (other than those having jobs required to be performed on a continuous basis or directly related to certain functions performed at an activity operating on a continuous basis). The council held that the proposal is negotiable, setting aside an agency determination that the proposal is nonnegotiable under section 11(b) of the order, because it did not appear that the proposed basic workweek for employees was integrally related in any manner to the numbers and types of employees involved. In the absence of this integral relationship to staffing patterns, the proposal was found not to conflict with section 11(b), and *Plum Island* was inapposite.

A subsequent case involving basic workweeks arose at the *Charleston Naval Shipyard,*[54] where the union offered the following proposal:

Basic work weeks other than Monday through Friday may be established for employees whose jobs are directly related to service-type functions which must be performed more than five days a week and cannot be performed during the normal working hours or days (Monday through Friday) of the Unit as set forth in Sections 2. and 6. of this Article. The Employer agrees that the number of such employees assigned to a work week of other than Monday through Friday will be the minimum necessary to perform the service-type functions and such assignments will not be utilized to meet temporary peak workloads. . . . The Employer agrees to schedule the nonwork days of employees so assigned such that whenever practicable they will be consecutive. . . .

The council held that the proposal, with the exception of the second sentence, was negotiable. The excepted sentence was found to be integrally related to the numbers of employees that the activity might assign to particular tours of duty; the remainder of the proposal was found not to be so integrally related to staffing patterns.

The most recent case in this line involved a proposal concerning the days of the workweek, and the starting times of the workweek, for meat and poultry inspectors in the Department of Agriculture.[55] The agency did not rely on the "staffing-pattern" provisions of section 11(b) in its determination of nonnegotiability, tacitly recognizing that the *Plum Island* decision, as explicated by the council in the *Charleston* case and subsequent related decisions, was without controlling significance. Likewise, the council, believing that no useful purpose would be served by raising, *sua sponte*, this "straw-man" issue, did not discuss it. However, in a subsequent decision by a federal district court, in which the case was remanded to the council for reconsideration, the court directed the council to explain why *Plum Island* was not cited and why the council had apparently departed from the policies exemplified in *Plum Island* in the later case. The council, applying the principles in the earlier cases to the union's proposal concerning the basic workweek and the starting times of that workweek for the food inspectors, concluded that the proposal is clearly not excluded from the agency's obligation to negotiate under the "staffing-pattern" provisions of section 11(b). The council noted that, unlike in *Plum Island*, the union's proposal had not been shown to be integrally related to and determinative of the types of employees assigned to the proposed tours of duty of the agency. Whereas in *Plum Island* the union proposal extended to changes in the types of the employees to be assigned to the new, fixed shifts and the rotating shifts, here all employees on each tour would continue to be food inspectors. The proposed changes also related only to the days of the basic workweek and the range of starting times of that workweek, which would affect overtime but not the numbers of employees assigned to tours.

To summarize this line of cases, a proposal relating to the basic workweek and hours of duty of employees is not excepted from an agency's bargaining obligation under section 11(b) unless the proposal is integrally related to and consequently determinative of the staffing patterns of the agency, that is, the numbers, types, and grades of positions or employees assigned to an organizational unit, work project, or tour of duty of the agency.

A second line of negotiability cases arising under the "staffing-pattern" provisions of 11(b) has dealt with proposals designed to place limits on the assignment of additional duties to employees. In the first of these cases, *Griffiss*,[56] the council ruled that proposals that would proscribe the assignment of civil-disturbance functions and other alleged "unrelated duties" to fire fighters in the bargaining unit were excluded from the obligation to bargain under 11(b).

The council found that job content in general is excluded from the obligation to bargain under "organization" and "numbers, types, and grades of positions or employees assigned to an organizational unit, work project, or tour of duty" in section 11(b) of the order. Further, it found that nothing in section 11(b) of the order renders the exception from the obligation to bargain on job content dependent in any manner on the *degree of relationship* of the assigned duties to the principal job function. Accordingly, the exception from the obligation to bargain on job content, under section 11(b) of the order, was held to extend to the assignment of allegedly unrelated duties. However, the council went on to emphasize that its decision did not mean that *conditions deriving from the assignment of unrelated duties* would be excepted from the obligation to bargain under section 11(b) of the order, for example, health and safety hazards.

In a subsequent case,[57] the union proposed that whenever the phrase "such other duties as may be assigned" or the like appears in a position description, it shall be defined to mean "tasks that are normally related to the position and are of an incidental nature." The council held that the proposal was negotiable. Here, unlike in *Griffiss*, the union's proposal was expressly directed, not at proscribing or determining the *assignment* of particular duties to positions, but at the definition and clarification of the terms in *positions descriptions*. The council held that nothing in the order renders the mere definition and clarification of general terms in job descriptions, as proposed by the union, outside the agency's obligation to negotiate under section 11(b) of the order.

The council has also held that a proposal that would limit agency discretion in assigning journeyman-level work to apprentices is related to the job content of apprentices and hence is a "discretionary" subject of bargaining under the "staffing pattern" provisions of 11(b).[58] Further, in the *VA Hospital, Montgomery, Alabama*[59] case, the council held that a proposal that would have required management to meet certain conditions before it could increase the frequency with which officer-of-the-day (O.D.) duties were assigned to physicians in the bargaining unit was outside the obligation to bargain under 11(b). Under the proposal, if unit staffing should fall below the authorized level for 30 days or more, management would be required to search all available avenues to locate nonunit physicians to assign to tours of O.D. duty before unit physicians could be assigned to additional tours as officer of the day. The agency indicated that, to carry out the proposal's mandate, the hospital director would have to take such actions as: assign supervisory and managerial physicians to tours of

O.D. duty; hire additional numbers of full or part-time physicians for assignment to such tours of duty; and/or secure non-VA physicians to staff such tours of duty under a contractual arrangement. The council found that these unspecified "procedures available to the director" are matters pertaining to the numbers and/or types of positions or employees assigned to tours of O.D. duty. By requiring their use, the proposal would impose limiting conditions on management's authority to establish staffing patterns for its organization and the accomplishment of its work.

In the more recent *Immigration and Naturalization Service*[60] case, the council ruled that a proposal to restrict the use of border patrol agents on alien bus movements when detention guards are readily available was outside the agency's obligation to bargain under 11(b). The council found that the proposal would prevent the agency from assigning duties unless certain conditions exist (namely, the unavailability of detention guards) and hence plainly imposed limitations on which types of positions or employees will actually perform the duties involved. Therefore, the council concluded that the proposal, which would constrict the agency's assignment of specific duties to particular types of positions or employees, is excepted from the agency's obligation to bargain under 11(b). However, the council noted that the decision does not preclude negotiation by the parties on the policies and procedures to be applied by the agency in the selection of individual employees (within a given job classification) for assignment to particular shifts or tours of duty, including overtime.

The council has considered several other proposals that similarly would have restricted the assignment of specific duties to particular positions or employees. In the *Wright-Patterson Air Force Base*[61] case, the council considered a proposal that would have conditioned the assignment of duties by the agency on the "scope of the classification assigned" to the respective unit employees, as defined in "appropriate classification standards." The council found that the proposal was excepted from the obligation to bargain under 11(b) because it would limit the agency in the assignment of duties to unit employees unless such duties fell within the scope of job grading standards. In so finding, the council relied upon its earlier decision in *Immigration and Naturalization Service*.

Finally in the *GSA* case, the council held that the following proposal was excepted from the obligation to negotiate under 11(b).

The Employer agrees that jurisdictional boundaries between and among crafts for the purpose of establishing a claim to the work is recognized as an appropriate subject for discussion with the consideration of the views of the union.

The council found that the purpose of the proposal, as expressly stated, is to establish "a claim to the work" on the basis of "jurisdictional boundaries between and among crafts." As the council said:

Implicit within this purpose and essential to its attainment is restriction of agency discretion in the assignment of duties to unit employees through the establishment of such claims to the work. Therefore, the proposal here is closely akin to the proposals in *Wright-Patterson* and *Immigration and Naturalization Service* in that its expressed purpose is to seek to establish limitations on management's assignment of duties. In our opinion, to require the agency to bargain on a proposal, the purpose of which is ultimately to establish restrictions on management's discretion to determine job content, would be effectively to require the agency to negotiate on job content, itself.[62]

However, in this case, the council set aside the agency's determination that the proposal was nonnegotiable because the local parties had agreed to the proposal and the agency had acted to disapprove the provision during its subsequent review of the agreement under section 15 of the order. The council pointed out that since the agency, through its local bargaining representative, had negotiated and reached agreement on the proposal in dispute, as permitted under section 11(b), the agency cannot thereafter change its position during the section 15 review process.

Decision under Section 12(b)

Most of the council's significant decisions under section 12(b) have involved the interpretation and application of 12(b), 12(b)(4), and 12(b)(5).

Section 12(b)(2) provides that management officials retain the right, in accordance with applicable laws and regulations, "to hire, promote, transfer, assign, and retain employees in positions within the agency, and to suspend, demote, discharge, or take other disciplinary action against employees."

In the *VA Hospital, Lebanon, Pa.*[63] case, the union proposal would require the hospital director to request employment of non-VA physicians to perform weekend and holiday officer-of-the-day duties. The council held that the hospital director's actions in requesting the employment of additional physicians constituted an integral part of the agency's hiring process and that the union's proposal interfered with management's reserved right "to hire" under section 12(b)(2) of the order.

On the other hand, in the *VA Research Hospital, Chicago*[64] case, the council ruled that 12(b)(2) did not preclude negotiation concerning a proposal that would require that, upon request of the union, a management official who had not participated in the selection of an employee for promotion would review the promotion decision and render a final decision thereon. The council pointed out that there is no implication that the reservation of decision-making and action authority in 12(b) is intended to bar negotiation of procedures, to the extent consonant with law and regulations, which management will observe in reaching the decision or taking the action involved, provided that such procedures do not have the effect of negating the authority reserved. Here, the union's proposal would establish procedures whereby higher level management review of a selection for promotion may be obtained before the promotion is consummated. The council noted that the proposal does not require management to negotiate a promotion selection or to secure union consent to the decision; nor does it appear that the procedure proposed would unreasonably delay or impede promotion selections so as to, in effect, deny the right to promote reserved to management by section 12(b)(2). Likewise, in the *Kirk Army Hospital*[65] case, the council held negotiable a proposal that would establish a procedure whereby, under particular circumstances (i.e., a personal relationship between the selecting supervisor and any referred candidates), the promotion selection would be made at the next higher management level.

However, a second union proposal in this case, which would prescribe the order in which employees who had voluntarily accepted a lower grade position in lieu of separation in a reduction in force would be repromoted (with some minor exceptions), was held nonnegotiable. The council found that the proposal would deprive management of the discretion, guaranteed by 12(b)(2), to select the individual once a decision had been made to fill the position by promotion.

In the *VA Hospital, Montgomery, Alabama*[66] case, the council ruled that section 12(b)(2) does not bar negotiations on the following proposal:

The employer agrees to appoint a physician of the Unit to Professional Standards Board, when the Board is considering physicians of the Unit for recommendation for promotion.

It is agreed that the Unit physician will be selected from a list recommended by the Union. The recommended physician must meet the criteria established for Board members. If the Administrator determines that the recommended physician(s) does not meet this criteria, he will then appoint another physician from the bargaining unit who he deems qualified.

The council distinguished this case from *VA Hospital, Lebanon, Pa.* on the grounds that in *VA-Lebanon* the proposal would have preempted the hospital director's discretion about whether to request the employment of additional physicians; here the proposal merely would provide for the selection, by management, of a representative nominated by the union to serve on Professional Standards Boards considering unit members for recommendation for promotion. Before the recommendations of such boards can become final, they are subject to the hospital director's approval or, if he disapproves, to further consideration and final decision at a higher level of the agency. Therefore, the council concluded that the proposal neither would limit the discretion of Professional Standards Boards considering whether to recommend the promotion of any particular candidate, nor would it require management to negotiate a promotion selection or secure union consent to the decision. Instead, it found that the proposal concerns only procedures management will observe in reaching the decision, which would assure the union an essentially noncontrolling, participatory role on boards making recommendations with respect to the promotion of unit employees. The council noted that there is no showing that the proposal would directly interfere with the ultimate decision and action authority reserved to management and it does not appear that the proposal would have the indirect effect of interfering with such reserved authority by causing unreasonable delay in the decision.

In the *Long Beach Naval Shipyard*[67] case, the agency headquarters, pursuant to the section 15 review process under the order, disapproved a legally agreed provision—which would prohibit management from temporarily assigning, detailing, or promoting employees to positions for which they could not qualify to occupy on a permanent basis. The council noted that the impact of the provision would be that "in the event no employees are qualified to occupy the positions on a permanent basis, management would be unable to assign the duties "with procedures for handling details or even for guaranteeing that 'qualified' employees are assigned or detailed before 'unqualified' employees, if there were time available to determine such qualification." The council held that the provision would so constrict management's discretion in the exercise of the right to assign personnel retained under 12(b)(2) as to effectively deny that right. Hence, the agency's position was upheld. Thus, the agency authority to disapprove provisions on 12(b) grounds during the section 15 review process contrasts sharply with an attempt by the agency in the *GSA*[68] case to disapprove a provision in the section 15 review process on the grounds that the provision was contrary to 11(b).

Section 12(b)(4) provides that management officials retain the right, in accordance with applicable laws and regulations, "to maintain the efficiency of the Government operations entrusted to them."

The leading case concerning the meaning of this provision is the *Little Rock*[69] case. In that case, the union proposal was intended to prevent the activity from assigning "swing-shift" personnel in such a way to avoid the payment of overtime. The council overruled the agency's determination that the proposals violated section 12(b)(4) of the order because the agency position equating reduced premium-pay costs with efficient and economical operations improperly ignored the total complex of factors encompassed within the concept of "efficiency and economy." (The council had concluded that the term "efficiency" in section 12(b)(4) embraces the concept of "economy" as well.) It pointed out that, in general, agency determinations about negotiability made in relation to the concept of efficiency and economy in section 12(b)(4) of the order require consideration and balancing of all the factors involved, including the well-being of employees, rather than an arbitrary determination based only on the anticipation of increased costs. Other factors such as the potential for improved performance, increased productivity, responsiveness to direction, reduced turnover, fewer grievances, contribution of money-saving ideas, improved health and safety, and the like, are valid considerations. Thus, the council held that section 12(b)(4) may not properly be invoked to deny negotiations unless there is a substantial demonstration by the agency that increased costs or reduced effectiveness in operations are inescapable and significant and are not offset by compensating benefits.

In the *Charleston Naval Supply Center*[70] case referred to previously, the agency contended that the union proposal to affirm Monday through Friday as the basic workweek for unit employees (with certain specified exceptions) was contrary to 12(b)(4). The agency had asserted that in common industrial parlance "efficiency of operations" is synonymous with "cost or economy of operations"; and, therefore, since the union's proposal would require the payment of avoidable overtime, that is, would increase costs, it would, by that fact alone, impinge on the 12(b)(4) right reserved to management. Based upon its decision in the *Little Rock* case, the council rejected this contention. Applying the test set out in that case, the council concluded that the agency did not indicate the amount of additional cost the proposal's adoption would involve or any other impact such adoption would have on the efficiency or effectiveness of the agency operations, nor that offsetting factors, such as those described above, would not balance out the additional cost. The union, on the other hand, did offer certain claims about benefits to employees and operations that might result from the proposal's adoption, as well as an estimate of the relative cost impact, which was inconsiderable. In these circumstances, the council found that there was insufficient showing by the agency to sustain its determination that the proposal is not negotiable under section 12(b)(4).

Finally, in the *Animal and Plant Health Inspection Service*[71] case referred to earlier, the agency contended that the proposal relating to the establishment of a basic workweek and limitations upon the starting time of that workweek for meat and poultry inspectors employed by the agency was nonnegotiable because it would conflict with the agency's right under 12(b)(4) of the order. The council found without merit the agency's argument that the proposal would result in overtime expenses, which would conflict with the agency's right to maintain efficient agency operations under section 12(b)(4). The council relied upon the reasoning in its earlier decisions in the *Little Rock* and *Charleston* cases. The council also held that the requirements under section 12(b)(4) were not rendered inapplicable, as claimed by the agency, merely by reason of the source of funds involved (the payment of overtime costs by industry rather than by government), or the type of service rendered (the direct servicing of a regulated industry rather than a government facility). The council then found that, as the agency had failed to demonstrate that the proposal would result in increased costs not offset by compensating factors, the proposal was not properly determined by the agency to be proscribed under section 12(b)(4).

Upon review, the federal district court agreed with the council that the proposal did not violate the literal language of section 12(b)(4). Nevertheless, in its remand of the case, the court directed that the council reconsider, as a matter of policy, the negotiability of the basic workweek and starting times of the inspectors, in view of the congressional intent to minimize the burden of inspection costs on the industry, and the economic impact of negotiability particularly on small operators as exemplified by increased overtime costs that would be required under the subsequent agreement of the parties. On remand, the council concluded generally that some additional overtime costs reimbursable by the industry would probably result from the union proposal, and that, although the additional overtime costs would appear to be relatively limited in amount, the industry would be adversely affected to that extent by adoption of the proposal. However, even fully weighing such economic impact and the congressional intent to minimize the burden of inspection costs on the industry in the balance, as directed by the court, the council concluded that such circumstances did not render the union's proposal nonnegotiable under section 12(b)(4) of the order.[72]

Section 12(b)(5) provides that agency management shall retain the right, in accordance with applicable laws and regulations, "to determine the methods, means and personnel by which such [government] operations are to be conducted."

In the *Yuma Border Patrol*[73] case, the council found that a union proposal dealing with the maintenance of "drag roads," which are used as a means of surveillance to detect persons illegally entering the United States, was negotiable. The council concluded that the proposal specified only *what* health and safety standards shall be operative, that is, "regular" maintenance of the drag roads, so they are "reasonably" level and free of "excessive" airborne particles. Since the proposal did *not* specify in any manner *how* these standards are to be achieved by the agency, it did not conflict with the agency's right to determine the methods and means by which its operations are to be conducted.

In the *Tidewater*[74] case, the council was presented with a negotiability dispute over union proposals relating to "work assignments" and "contracting out." Specifically, the "work-assignment" proposal would limit agency discretion to assign supervisors, military personnel, and other nonbargaining-unit personnel to perform work historically performed by bargaining-unit employees. The "contracting-out" proposal would limit agency discretion to contract out or transfer out work normally performed by personnel in the bargaining unit. The council sustained the agency's determination that the proposals here involved contravene management's reserved right under section 12(b)(5) of the Executive Order. However, the council emphasized that this decision does not foreclose all bargaining on matters relating to "work assignment," "contracting out," and "transfer out." The council noted that proposals to establish procedures that management would observe leading to the exercise of the retained management rights under 12(b)(5) would be negotiable to the extent they do not interfere with the exercise of the rights themselves. Moreover, proposals to establish appropriate arrangements for unit employees adversely affected by the impact of decisions to contract out, transfer out, or reassign work normally or historically performed by bargaining-unit personnel would be negotiable.

Relying on this decision, the council issued decisions in several other cases involving similar proposals and held each to be nonnegotiable.[75] However, one of these cases, the *Philadelphia Naval Shipyard*[76] case, also involved the negotiability of a proposal that would, in effect, prevent the agency from making overtime assignments of work normally performed by employees in the collective-bargaining unit to nonunit personnel where the *sole purpose* of doing so is to deny overtime work to unit employees. The council concluded that this proposal was clearly distinguishable in scope and effect from the work assignment proposal in the *Tidewater* case. Here, the union's proposal would only affect assignment of overtime and, if agreed to, would not restrict management in any way in otherwise assigning to nonunit employees work usually performed by unit employees during nonovertime periods. Further, under the union's proposal, assignment to nonunit personnel of work normally assigned to employees in the unit could be made even in situations involving overtime for any purpose determined by management to be valid, *except* "for the sole purpose of eliminating the need for such [unit] employees on overtime." Therefore, the agency contention that the proposal violates management's reserved right under section 12(b)(5) was found to be without merit because the proposal, in effect, was solely concerned with the assignment of overtime.

The decision in *Tidewater* was also relied upon in the *Philadelphia Cafeteria Association*[77] case. The union proposal provided that if the cafeteria association (which at the time directly operated the cafeteria at the activity) elected to contract out such operations, the contractor would be required for six months to maintain existing personnel and assume the bargaining agreement between the association and the union. The council held that the union's proposal would render it more difficult, if not impossible, to locate an acceptable contractor and would thereby constrain the management in its selection of the personnel to conduct the cafeteria operations and hence violated management's rights under section 12(b)(5).

Finally, in the *Animal and Plant Health Inspection Service*[78] case, which involved a proposal concerning the particular days of the week that will constitute the basic workweek for unit employees with limitations upon the starting time for that workweek, the council set aside the agency's determination of nonnegotiability under 12(b)(5). The council explained that the proposal neither addressed, nor sought to limit, management's right to choose the methods and means by which agency operations were to be conducted, and did not constrict management in its selection of personnel for overtime work, which work was at the crux of the dispute between the parties. (On review, the federal district court agreed with the council's conclusion that the union's proposal was not violative of section 12(b)(5).)

The Scope Question and Its Effect on Collective Bargaining

There is a considerable difference of opinion among "the experts" as to the effect of the scope of bargaining on the process and the results of bargaining in the federal sector.

A mediator with the Federal Mediation and Conciliation Service has listed some of the important implications that the scope and noneconomic content of bargaining in the federal sector has concerning bargaining behavior:

1. There is less flexibility in trade-off options for the parties. Management cannot "buy out" demands that limit management flexibility by offering increased economic benefits.
2. Narrow scope and noneconomic content of bargaining pushes unions to bargain more about matters falling within the realm of management rights.
3. Parties get "hung up" on contract language.
4. Unions have no incentive to "depoliticize" the bargaining process by ceasing to lobby for their interests in Congress.[79]

One student of the program, Dr. Phillip Ross of Cornell University, has said that labor relations under E.O. 11491 are "unstable" because the scope of bargaining is not as broad as the traditional scope in the private sector and that this imbalance will lead to legislation.[80]

The federal-employee unions have taken the position that the scope of bargaining must be broadened in testimony before the council on the need for changes in the order and in testimony before the congressional commitees in arguing the need for a statute to replace the Executive Order.

The director of the Federal Mediation and Conciliation Service, in advocating "the adoption of Federal Legislation bringing true collective bargaining," had taken the position "that there is precious little collective bargaining in the Federal sector." He went on to say:

And so long as unions are restricted from bargaining on all of the vital economic issues—wages, pensions, medical care, vacations, holidays, insurance ... and many aspects of a multitude of noneconomic issues—seniority, job transfers, discipline, promotion, union security ... there can be no fulfillment of our national policy in the Government's own house.[81]

On the other hand, the chairman of the Federal Service Impasses Panel has noted:

Legislation in and of itself is no panacea. It is not the framework for collective bargaining that is important, but rather the nature of that framework. Sticky problems such as the status of legislated wages and fringe benefits, the overall scope of bargaining, and the need for faster decisionmaking may remain regardless of which branch of Government establishes the labor-relations ground rules ... collective bargaining in the Federal sector will continue to mature, whether under Executive orders or statutes. We may disagree as to whether the pace is fast enough, but the direction is clear and encouraging.[82]

An assessment of the federal-sector scope of bargaining by the U.S. Civil Service Commission is that criticism of the relative narrowness of the scope of bargaining under E.O. 11491 is, at best, premature. The director of the Office of Labor-Management Relations in the commission, has pointed out that negotiation of collective-bargaining agreements is at an all-time high. Agreements cover 2,581 units—almost three-fourths of the total (not counting nonappropriated-fund activities). All told, 1,017,000 employees—88 percent of all employees in bargaining units—are covered by agreements. The commission's review of these agreements indicates they are becoming far more substantive, with many new provisions, as well as many provisions of existing regulations now incorporated in agreements, and all increasingly being enforced under binding arbitration clauses.

A comparison of agreements negotiated during the 12 months, which ended in May 1975, with those negotiated earlier, highlights the growing pattern of union involvement in important areas. In Table 7-1 the commission reports examples of topics negotiated with increasing frequency over the past three years.[83]

Available evidence indicates the provisions that have been negotiated in agreements are regarded as important to their welfare by the majority of employees covered. In a study by the Civil Service Commission of eight agency activities selected to represent a cross section of labor-management relations experience in the federal service, employees were asked whether they considered most of the provisions of their labor agreements important to them. Fifty-seven percent said yes, 8 percent said no, and 35 percent were undecided.[84]

In considering the scope of bargaining under the Executive Order, it should

Table 7-1
Negotiated Topics—Federal Sector

| Topic | Number of Agreements | | | Increase |
	April 1974	December 1974	May 1975	
Union representation on promotion panels	197	320	433	+236
Union representation on joint promotion committees	112	149	197	+85
Union representation on joint incentive-awards committees	367	437	556	+189
Union representation on joint safety committees	886	896	1,015	+129
Leave to hold union office	727	823	920	+193
Union office space	1,179	1,296	1,437	+258
Union access to telephones	299	369	457	+158
Excused time for union training	359	495	664	+305
Environmental pay	335	390	477	+142
Safety clothing	696	784	899	+203
Safety equipment	744	882	1,014	+270
Binding arbitration of grievances	1,283	1,515	1,780	+497

be recognized that this is not the only form by which employees and their representatives participate in establishing the terms of their employment. Union-management relationships in the federal service extend well beyond the formalized labor-management relations structure. They exist within the context of total governmental mechanisms for personnel matters and employee involvement. Recent laws have established permanent vehicles for direct union involvement in white-collar and blue-collar pay setting and fringe-benefits areas. These include the Prevailing Rate Advisory Committee, the Federal Employees' Pay Council, and the Health Benefits and Life Insurance Advisory Committees. In addition, Executive Order 11612 provides for employee organization representation on the Federal Advisory Council on Occupational Safety and Health, established to advise the secretary of Labor in carrying out a federal safety program under the Occupational Safety and Health Act of 1970.[85] In addition, the Civil Service Commission has long acknowledged the need for employee input through their representatives, and regularly and extensively has consulted unions in the development of government-wide personnel policies.

In this total context, it can be said that many aspects of "personnel policies, practices, and matters affecting working conditions" are being dealt with bilaterally in one form or another, even though they may not fall within the "scope of bargaining" under the Executive Order.

Finally, in assessing the impact of scope of bargaining on the process of bargaining, it must be remembered that the changes that will result from the 1975 amendments to E.O. 11491, particularly those facilitating the consolidation of units and further restricting the assertion of agency regulations as bars to negotiation, have not yet made their impact on the bargaining scene.

Summary and Conclusions

In summary, there is no question that the scope of bargaining in the conventional sense is narrower in the federal service than it is in the private sector largely because economic matters (i.e., pay and fringe benefits), which are traditionally negotiated in the private sector, are established by statute. Thus, a major distinction of federal labor relations is that union negotiations with management in the executive departments and agencies are subsidiary and supplemental to the major employee benefits and protections that have been granted and are periodically improved through the legislative process, with traditional participation by the labor organizations. However, within this legal framework, we have seen that many substantive matters of significance to employees are open to bargaining and that, as the program has evolved, the scope of these matters has expanded. As a result, the numbers, scope, and variety of content of negotiated agreements have constantly increased since 1962. Important new changes with the potential for greatly enlarging the scope of bargaining are just now, with the issuance of implementing regulations by the council, emerging to exert their influence on the bargaining scene.

However, a number of bills have been introduced in the 94th Congress, notably H.R. 4800[86] (the Henderson Bill), H.R. 13[87] (the Nix Bill), and H.R. 1837[88] (the Ford Bill), which would further alter the picture for federal agencies and unions. Some of these bills would have drastic effects on the scope of bargaining in the federal sector. Under one or more of the bills, there would be no provision for reservation of management rights; agencies would be prohibited from issuing regulations restricting the scope of bargaining; and present laws governing establishment of pay practices and fringe benefits would be superseded. Some matters, such as use of official time, dues withholding, and the agency shop, would be granted to the unions without bargaining.

I am willing to accept the estimate that legislation somewhere in the near future is likely and there is a better than even chance that the scope of bargaining will be further increased thereby. Those responsible for developing that legislation bear a heavy responsibility to assure that it enables federal managers effectively to carry out the missions of government, and that it maintains the continuity of public services while affording opportunity for a broad range of collective bargaining within a balanced system reflecting employee needs and public expectations.

Notes

1. Government Organizations and Employees, 5 U.S.C. (1970), 80 Stat. 378.

2. Act of August 24, 1912 (Lloyd-LaFollette Act), 37 Stat. 555, *as amended* 5 U.S.C. § § 7101-02 (1970).

3. Act of January 16, 1883 (Pendleton Act), 5 U.S.C. § 632 (1964).

4. Government Organizations and Employees, 5 U.S.C. § 302 (1970), 80 Stat. 379.

5. The President's Task Force on Employee-Management Relations in the Federal Service, *A Policy for Employee-Management Cooperation in the Federal Service* (1961), at 17.

6. Study Committee Report and Recommendations, August 1969, *Labor-Management Relations in the Federal Service* (1975), at 63.

7. *Id.* at 70-71.

8. *Id.* at 71-74.

9. *IAM Local Lodge 2424 and Aberdeen Proving Ground, Aberdeen, Maryland*, FLRC No. 70A-9 (March 9, 1971), Report No. 5.

10. *United Federation of College Teachers Local 1460 and U.S. Merchant Marine Academy* FLRC No. 71A-15 (November 20, 1972), Report No. 30,

National Federation of Federal Employees, Local 779 and Department of the Air Force, Sheppard Air Force Base, Texas, FLRC No. 71A-60 (April 3, 1973), Report No. 36.

11. Report and Recommendations of the Federal Labor Relations Council on the Amendment of Executive Order 11491, as Amended, *Labor-Management Relations in the Federal Service* (1975), at 38.

12. *Id.* at 34-37.

13. *Id.* at 42-44.

14. 40 Fed. Reg. 5743 and 7391 (1975).

15. 5 C.F.R. § 2413.2 (1976).

16. *See* section 11(c) of Executive Order 11491, *as amended.*

17. *See, e.g., IAM-AW and Department of the Navy*, FLRC No. 71A-6 (February 12, 1971), Report No. 4; *NFFE Local 476 and Department of the Army*, FLRC No. 71A-50 (January 21, 1972), Report No. 18.

18. Section 2411.27 of the council's rules, 5 C.F.R. 2411.27 (1973), provides:"Subject to the requirements of this part, the Council shall issue its decision sustaining or setting aside in whole or in part, or remanding the agency head's determination."

19. Report and Recommendations on the Amendment of Executive Order 11491, *Labor-Management Relations in the Federal Service* (1975), at 71.

20. *International Association of Machinists and Aerospace Workers and U.S. Kirk Army Hospital*, Aberdeen, Md., FLRC No. 70A-11 (March 9, 1971), Report No. 5.

21. *Federal Employees Metal Trades Council of Charleston and Charleston Naval Shipyard, Charleston, South Carolina*, FLRC No. 72A-27 (May 25, 1973), Report No. 40.

22. *Association of Civilian Technicians, Inc., and State of New York National Guard*, FLRC No. 72A-47 (December 27, 1973), Report No. 47.

23. *Lodge 2424, IAM-AW and Kirk Army Hospital and Aberdeen Research and Development Center, Aberdeen, Md.*, FLRC No. 72A-18 (September 17, 1973), Report No. 44.

24. *United Federation of College Teachers Local 1460 and U.S. Merchant Marine Academy*, FLRC No. 71A-15 (November 20, 1972), Report No. 30.

25. *Local Union No. 2219, International Brotherhood of Electrical Workers, AFL-CIO and Department of the Army, Corps of Engineers, Little Rock District, Little Rock, Arkansas*, FLRC No. 71A-46 (November 20, 1972), Report No. 30.

26. *American Federation of Government Employees, National Joint Council of Food Inspection Locals and Office of the Administrator, Animal and Plant Health Inspection Service, U.S. Dept. of Agriculture*, FLRC No. 73A-36 (December 27, 1973), Report No. 47.

27. *NAGE Local R3-84 and Washington, D.C., Air National Guard*, FLRC No. 72A-23 (April 26, 1973), Report No. 37.

28. *National Federation of Federal Employees Local 1636 and Adjutant General of New Mexico*, FLRC No. 73A-23 (October 18, 1973), Report No. 45.

29. *See, e.g., AFGE Local 2197 and Rocky Mountain Arsenal, Denver, Colorado*, FLRC No. 70A-5 (April 29, 1971), Report No. 7.

30. *See* n. 24 *supra*.

31. *Tidewater Virginia Federal Employees Metal Trades Council and Naval Public Works Center, Norfolk, Virginia*, FLRC No. 71A-56 (June 29, 1973), Report No. 41.

32. *Local Lodge 2424, IAM-AW and Aberdeen Proving Ground Command*, FLRC No. 72A-37 (May 22, 1973), Report No. 39; and *American Federation of Government Employees Local 1966 and Veterans Administration Hospital, Lebanon, Pennsylvania*, FLRC No. 72A-41 (December 12, 1973), Report No. 46.

33. *Veterans Administration Independent Service Employees Union and Veterans Administration Research Hospital, Chicago, Illinois*, FLRC No. 71A-31 (November 22, 1972), Report No. 31.

34. *See* n. 22 *supra*.

35. *NFFE Local 1636 and New Mexico National Guard*, FLRC No. 73A-13 (September 17, 1973), Report No. 44.

36. *National Federation of Federal Employees, Local 779 and Department of the Air Force, Sheppard Air Force Base, Texas*, FLRC No. 71A-60 (April 3, 1973), Report No. 36.

37. *American Federation of Government Employees, Local 1668 and Elmendorf Air Force Base (Wildwood Air Force Station), Alaska*, FLRC No. 72A-10 (May 15, 1973), Report No. 38; *National Federation of Federal Employees, Local 476 and Joint Tactical Communications Office, Ft. Monmouth, New Jersey*, FLRC No. 72A-42 (August 8, 1973), Report No. 43; and *United Federation of College Teachers Local 1460 and U.S. Merchant Marine Academy*, FLRC No. 71A-15 (November 20, 1972), Report No. 30.

38. *IAM Local Lodge 2424 and Aberdeen Proving Ground, Aberdeen, Maryland*, FLRC No. 70A-9 (March 9, 1971), Report No. 5; *Seattle Center Controller's Union and Federal Aviation Administration*, FLRC No. 71A-57 (May 9, 1973), Report No. 37; and *National Federation of Federal Employees, Local 779 and Department of the Air Force, Sheppard Air Force Base, Texas*, FLRC No. 71A-60 (April 3, 1973), Report No. 36.

39. *IAM Local Lodge 2424 and Aberdeen Proving Ground, Aberdeen, Maryland*, FLRC No. 70A-9 (March 9, 1971), Report No. 5.

40. *See* n. 24 *supra*.

41. *See* n. 36 *supra*.

42. *Federal Employees Metal Trades Council of Charleston and Charleston Naval Shipyard, Charleston, South Carolina*, FLRC No. 73A-1 (January 31, 1974), Report No. 48.

43. *Philadelphia Metal Trades Council and Philadelphia Naval Shipyard*, FLRC No. 72A-16 (April 3, 1973), Report No. 36.

44. *See* n. 33 at 3 *supra.*

45. *Id. See also* n. 31 at 11 *supra.*

46. *Id. See also* n. 31 at 11-12 *supra.*

47. *Seattle Center Controller's Union and Federal Aviation Administration*, FLRC No. 71A-57 (May 9, 1973), Report No. 37.

48. *International Association of Fire Fighters, Local F-111, and Griffiss Air Force Base, Rome, N.Y.*, FLRC No. 71A-30 (April 19, 1973), Report No. 36.

49. *Federal Employees Metal Trades Council of Charleston and Charleston Naval Shipyard, Charleston, South Carolina*, FLRC No. 72A-46 (February 27, 1973), Report No. 47.

50. *AFGE Council of Locals 1497 and 2165 and Region 3, General Services Administration, Baltimore, Maryland*, FLRC No. 74A-48 (June 26, 1975), Report No. 75.

51. *AFGE Local 1940 and Plum Island Animal Disease Laboratory, Dept. of Agriculture, Greenport, N.Y.*, FLRC No. 71A-11 (July 9, 1971), Report No. 11.

52. *Id.* at 3-4. *See also American Federation of Government Employees, National Joint Council of Food Inspection Locals and Office of the Administrator, Animal and Plant Health Inspection Service, U.S. Department of Agriculture*, FLRC No. 73A-36 (June 10, 1975), Report No. 73, at 15-16.

53. *Federal Employees Metal Trades Council of Charleston and U.S. Naval Supply Center, Charleston, South Carolina*, FLRC No. 71A-52 (November 24, 1972), Report No. 31.

54. *Federal Employees Metal Trades Council of Charleston AFL-CIO and Charleston Naval Shipyard, Charleston, South Carolina*, FLRC No. 72A-35 (June 29, 1973), Report No. 41.

55. *American Federation of Government Employees, National Joint Council of Food Inspection Locals and Office of the Administrator, Animal and Plant Health Inspection Service, U.S. Department of Agriculture*, FLRC No. 73A-36 (June 10, 1975), Report No. 73.

56. *See* n. 48 *supra.*

57. *Local Lodge 830, International Association of Machinists and Aerospace Workers and Louisville Naval Ordnance Station, Department of the Navy*, FLRC No. 73A-21 (January 31, 1974), Report No. 48.

58. *See* n. 49 *supra.*

59. *American Federation of Government Employees Local 997 and Veter-*

ans Administration Hospital, Montgomery, Alabama, FLRC No. 73A-22 (January 31, 1974), Report No. 48.

60. *AFGE (National Border Patrol Council and National Council of Immigration and Naturalization Service Locals) and Immigration and Naturalization Service*, FLRC No. 73A-25 (September 30, 1974), Report No. 57.

61. *Local Lodge 2333, International Association of Machinists and Aerospace Workers, and Wright-Patterson Air Force Base, Ohio*, FLRC No. 74A-2 (December 5, 1974), Report No. 60.

62. *See* n. 50 *supra*, at 4.

63. *American Federation of Government Employees Local 1966 and Veterans Administration Hospital, Lebanon, Pennsylvania*, FLRC No. 72A-41 (December 12, 1973), Report No. 46.

64. *See* n. 33 *supra*.

65. *See* n. 23 *supra*.

66. *See* n. 59 *supra*.

67. *Local 174 International Federation of Professional and Technical Engineers, AFL-CIO, CLC and Long Beach Naval Shipyard, Long Beach, California*, FLRC No. 73A-16 (July 31, 1974), Report No. 55.

68. *See* n. 50 *supra*.

69. *Local Union No. 2219, International Brotherhood of Electrical Workers, AFL-CIO and Department of the Army, Corps of Engineers, Little Rock District, Little Rock, Ark.*, FLRC No. 71A-46 (November 20, 1972), Report No. 30.

70. *See* n. 53 *supra*.

71. *See* n. 26 *supra*.

72. *See* n. 52 *supra*.

73. *AFGE Local 2595 and Immigration and Naturalization Service, U.S. Border Patrol, Yuma Sector (Yuma, Arizona)*, FLRC No. 70A-10 (April 15, 1971), Report No. 6.

74. *See* n. 31 *supra*.

75. *Local 3, American Federation of Technical Engineers, AFL-CIO and Philadelphia Naval Shipyard, Philadelphia, Pennsylvania*, FLRC No. 71A-48 (June 29, 1973), Report No. 41; *Local 174, American Federation of Technical Engineers, AFL-CIO and Supships, USN, 11th Naval District, San Diego, California*, FLRC No. 71A-49 (June 29, 1973), Report No. 41; *Federal Employees Metal Trades Council of Charleston, AFL-CIO and Charleston Naval Shipyard, Charleston, South Carolina*, FLRC NO. 72A-33 (June 29, 1973), Report No. 41; *Federal Employees Metal Trades Council of Charleston, AFL-CIO and Charleston Naval Shipyard, Charleston, South Carolina*, FLRC No. 72A-35 (June 29, 1973), Report No. 41; and *Philadelphia Metal Trades Council, AFL-CIO and Philadelphia Naval Shipyard, Philadelphia, Pennsylvania* FLRC

No. 72A-40 (June 29, 1973), Report No. 41. *See also Pattern Markers League of North America, AFL-CIO and Naval Ship Research and Development Center, Bethesda, Maryland*, FLRC No. 73A-28 (August 17, 1973), Report No. 43.

76. *Philadelphia Metal Trades Council, AFL-CIO and Philadelphia Naval Shipyard, Philadelphia, Pennsylvania*, FLRC No. 72A-40 (June 29, 1973), Report No. 41.

77. *Philadelphia Metal Trades Council and Philadelphia Naval Shipyard Employees' Cafeteria Association*, FLRC No. 73A-5 (August 10, 1973), Report No. 43.

78. *See* n. 26 *supra*.

79. Nancy Fibish, "A Mediator's View of Federal Sector Labor Relations," *Public Personnel Administration* [¶ 3109] (1974).

80. All Government Employee Relations Report A-2 (1975).

81. Address by William J. Usery, Jr., Sixth Annual Utah Federal Employees' Banquet, Salt Lake City, Utah, May 16, 1975.

82. Address by Jacob Seidenberg, Federal Bar Association-American Arbitration Association Seminar on Employee Relations in the Federal Government, Mayflower Hotel, Washington, D.C., May 29, 1975.

83. Address by Anthony F. Ingrassia, Conference on Bargaining in the Federal Sector, Los Angeles, California, June 13, 1975.

84. Office of Labor-Management Relations, U.S. Civil Service Commission, *Elements of Success in Federal Labor-Management Relations* (1974).

85. Robert E. Hampton, Chairman, U.S. Civil Service Commission, *Statement for the Record Submitted to the House Committee on Manpower and Civil Service*, May 21, 1974, Attachment 10 at 16-17.

86. H.R. 4800, 94th Cong., 1st Sess. (1975).

87. H.R. 13, 94th Cong., 1st Sess. (1975).

88. H.R. 1837, 94th Cong., 1st Sess. (1975).

8

The Scope of Bargaining in the Public Sector in Wisconsin

James L. Stern

From a statutory point of view, the scope of bargaining for different occupational categories of Wisconsin public employees is not uniform. State employees are covered by separate legislation and have encountered problems unique to that group. Police, fire fighters, and deputy sheriffs, although covered by the general municipal-bargaining statute, are bound by statutory-impasse procedures that differ from those applicable to other municipal employees. Furthermore, scope of bargaining questions for these employees involve the interrelationship of the bargaining law with the older statutes establishing the rights and powers of police and fire commissions. Teachers, in turn, have been covered historically by school statutes that have had to be harmonized with the general municipal-bargaining law, which also applies to them.

In this chapter the problems of state employees are considered first, next the problems of municipal employees generally are reviewed, and then attention is focused upon the special problems of public-safety employees and teachers. Finally, there is a concluding section dealing with the trends in the scope of bargaining and prospects for change in the future.

State Employees

Legislative Developments

State employees were granted statutory bargaining rights in 1966,[1] seven years after the first bargaining law for municipal employees had been enacted.[2] Some departments and agencies of the state had been bargaining informally with various employee groups prior to passage of the 1966 statute, and its enactment represented an attempt by the state to coordinate its own labor-relations policies as well as an attempt by the American Federation of State County and Municipal Employees union (AFSCME) and other unions to obtain legal backing for their organizational efforts.

The 1966 statute covering state civil-service employees limited the scope of bargaining to "the following conditions of employment for which the appointing

The author wishes to thank the chairman of the Wisconsin Employment Relations Commission (WERC), Commissioner Morris Slavney, WERC staff members Marvin Schurke and George Fleischli, and attorneys Herbert Wiedemann, Jean Setterholm, and John Coughlin for their helpful comments.

officer has discretionary authority" and listed in the statute such matters as application of seniority rights, scheduling of vacations, use of sick leave, grievance procedures, and other similar matters.[3] Specifically excluded from coverage were:

statutory and rule provided prerogatives of promotion, layoff, position classification, *compensation and fringe benefits*, examinations, discipline, merit salary determination policy and other actions provided for by law and rules governing civil servicee.[4] (underlining added)

This initial, extremely narrow scope of bargaining was found to be unsatisfactory within a few years and attempts were made to broaden it.

The unions wanted to expand the scope of bargaining to make it similar to the scope in the private sector. Public-management representatives favored the inclusion of salary and fringe benefits within the scope of bargaining because, under the then-existing system, such management-rights type issues as rescheduling of employees took on undue importance since unions were not free to bargain about compensation. The governor therefore created a blue-ribbon committee for the purpose of holding hearings and making recommendations for the revision of the State Employment Labor Relations Act (SELRA). The first two recommendations in the committee report were that the scope of bargaining be broadened to include economic issues and that representatives of the legislature be integrated into the bargaining process.[5]

These committee recommendations were accepted by the legislature and, along with other changes, were incorporated into the amended statute passed by the 1971 legislature.[6] Although wages and fringes were made mandatory subjects of bargaining, certain features of the civil-service merit system (initial appointment procedures, promotions, and the job-evaluation system including position classification) continued to be excluded from the scope of bargaining. The legislation also called for the establishment of a Joint Committee on Employment Relations (JOCER) to be composed of the legislators holding the eight most influential legislative positions (Senate and Assembly co-chairmen of the Joint Committee on Finance, Senate and Assembly majority and minority leaders, and speaker of the Assembly and president pro-tempore of the Senate).

This rather unique and relatively new arrangement under which powerful representatives of the legislative branch are involved with the executive branch in bargaining decisions raises interesting questions about the scope of bargaining. The representatives of the legislature serve in a capacity analogous to policy committee members of the board of directors of a private firm. Economic offers are cleared with them initially and their assent is obtained to those last-minute economic concessions needed to resolve the final bargaining crisis. The monetary package that JOCER has agreed to is reduced to bill form and simultaneously introduced in the Assembly and Senate.

Department of Administration representatives now serve as negotiators in meetings with the representatives of employees in statewide broad-occupation-type bargaining units statutorily created, as opposed to the original procedure under which representatives of individual state agencies had this responsibility and dealt with units established at the departmental level. In effect, the negotiators represent the governor and the Joint Committee represents the legislature, thereby involving the full decision-making power of the state in the bargaining process and presumably eliminating the end-run problem. These arrangements, however, have certain consequences for scope-of-bargaining decisions that, as of the summer of 1975, were still unclear.

Fringe-Benefit Problems

No court decisions or Wisconsin Employment Relations Commission orders concerning the scope of bargaining had been issued by mid-1975, but an attorney general ruling about insurance and pension problems may eventually lead to court decisions and/or new legislation. In response to inquiries from the Department of Administration, the attorney general ruled that:[7]

(1) The legislature would not commit an unfair labor practice if it unilaterally increased pension benefits and costs to state employees in bargaining units provided however that this was done by legislation passed by the Senate and Assembly and signed by the governor and provided that the new statute clearly called for such changes. The attorney general noted that the SELRA did not give state employees "a property right in collective bargaining which subsequently cannot be abolished" and that subsequent legislation could specifically repeal rights granted in previous legislation.

(2) The state would commit an unfair-labor practice if it did not bargain collectively about the removal of employees from the state retirement system or the cessation of all contributions. The attorney general based this ruling on that portion of the SELRA which describes the procedure by which changes in fringe benefits agreed upon in bargaining will be made effective subsequently through legislative action.

(3) The Group Insurance Board would commit an unfair-labor practice if it unilaterally increased benefits and costs to state employees in collective-bargaining units. The attorney general noted here that the board was a part of the executive branch of government and was given powers under legislation passed prior to the passage of the SELRA. Harmonization of the earlier statute with the subsequent one would deny the board the right to change insurance provisions and costs as such provisions and costs were subsequently brought within the scope of bargaining by the legislature, and such legislative actions cannot be overturned by an administrative agency of the executive branch.

The effect of this ruling on the Group Insurance Board is clear. It no longer will be the autonomous agency determining when new health and medical insurance coverages will be added and how much will be paid for such new benefits. Instead, the board is likely to become an arm of the Department of

Administration and will assist it in negotiations with the unions about changes in insurance benefits. Although the legislature could reverse itself and enact new legislation excluding insurance from the scope of bargaining, there is no sign as yet of such a move.

The status of pensions, however, is much more murky than that of insurance. Initial negotiations for improved pension benefits were underway as of this writing (July 30, 1975) but, so far as was publicly known, no agreement was near on this issue. In the interim the Senate passed a bill (S.B. 174, 1975) providing for a three-year moratorium on pension bargaining and the creation of a blue-ribbon committee to study the problem. The Assembly Labor Committee was sitting on the bill, however, for the time being. It may well be that, as in New York and elsewhere, the Wisconsin legislature will eventually exclude pensions from the scope of bargaining.

At this moment, however, at least for public consumption, both the union and the executive branch of government favor the inclusion of pensions within the scope of bargaining. The governor reportedly fears that separation of the pension from other economic items will complicate the formulation of the state budget and may lead to the passage of legislation with heavy cost implications subsequent to the conclusion of bargaining and the passage of the budget. The budget bill adopted into law on July 30, 1975 requires that demands relating to retirement and health insurance shall be submitted to the employer at least one year prior to commencement of negotiations. This line of thinking runs contrary to that of the groups in New York and elsewhere, which believe that inclusion of pensions within the scope of bargaining increases pension costs inordinately and causes unwarranted fiscal problems for the state.

Bargaining and the Civil Service System

As was stated earlier, the present legislation covering state employees excludes bargaining on such matters as appointments, promotions, position classification, and other aspects of the job-evaluation system. This exclusion rankles the leaders of the Wisconsin State Employees Union (WSEU), AFSCME, particularly because the legislation governing municipal employees contains no such restriction. As a result, the WSEU leadership caused a bill to be introduced into the 1975 legislature (A.B. 539) repealing the existing management-rights language in SELRA and substituting for it new language based on the language presently in the MERA.

If this bill passes in its present or some amended form, it is anticipated that problems of promotion and placement of employees in classifications will be subject to the grievance and arbitration procedure as is typical in the private sector. If the management rights language of the Municipal Employment Relations Act (MERA) is adopted in the SELRA, then the scope of bargaining rules and practices that are being built up in the municipal sector may well be duplicated in the state sector. Since the dichotomy followed in determining scope of bargaining in the municipal sector is considered in some detail subsequently, further discussion of these developments is omitted at this point.

Subcontracting

One further example of the desire of the WSEU to expand the scope of bargaining is its support of a bill about subcontracting. The bill would require that the employer notify the union before making arrangements to subcontract work and also requires that the wages and fringes paid to employees of the subcontractor be equal to those of state employees who otherwise would have performed the work.

Although the WSEU may raise this topic at the bargaining table, despite the strong management-rights clause and the absence of language about subcontracting, its attempts to gain its end through new legislation can be interpreted as evidence that it does not believe it would succeed in an attempt to persuade the state to voluntarily expand the scope of bargaining beyond its present legal scope (narrowly defined). Alternatively, one can view the proposed bill as a union technique designed to make it easier for the union to gain its ends through bargaining. Under this theory, some bargaining compromise will be reached and the pending bill will not be acted upon.

Faculty Bargaining

The SELRA defines employees as those individuals in the classified service of the state with the usual exceptions for managerial personnel and others. Faculty, other academic staff and graduate-student teaching assistants are not a part of the classified service and therefore are excluded from coverage under SELRA. Despite this, however, several interesting scope-of-bargaining problems have arisen among these groups.

The Madison campus administration of the University of Wisconsin negotiated a "structure" agreement with the Teaching Assistant's Association (TAA), which provided that the TAA would be recognized as the bargaining agent for the teaching assistants if it won a majority vote in a WERC-supervised election. The TAA won a majority and, after several weeks on strike, negotiated a contract covering about 1,500 teaching assistants. One important bargaining issue was whether the TAA, students, and individual teaching assistants would share with the faculty and administration the responsibility for determining educational policy including such matters as course content.

The TAA maintained that the subject was within the scope of bargaining and that the granting of the demand would improve the education of the students. The faculty denied both claims and argued that it should not share the responsibility for the decision with the students and teaching assistants although maximum input from them to the faculty was desirable. The faculty position prevailed and this attempt to expand the scope of bargaining to include the determination of educational policy failed. In the absence of statutory guidelines and an administrative agency to determine whether such a demand was within the scope of bargaining, the parties determined the issue by the private-sector test-of-strength method.

Interesting and opposing views about the scope of faculty bargaining are found in two bills currently before the Wisconsin legislature. A.B. 511, supported primarily by The Association of University of Wisconsin Faculty members (TAUWF) on what were formerly teacher-college and state-college campuses, provides for bargaining on wages, hours, and working conditions. A.B. 900 supported by the Board of Regents limits the scope of bargaining to the general salary increase and fringe benefits and excludes those matters traditionally handled on the Madison campus through the long-established system of university governance.

Bargaining about some items is seen by TAUWF as an advance but bargaining about the same items is seen by the Madison faculty as a step backwards. For example, an early TAUWF proposal specifically listed the selection of textbooks as an item that TAUWF thought should be within the scope of bargaining, probably because textbook selection in the past had been determined primarily by administrators rather than by the individual faculty member teaching the course. On the Madison campus, the individual faculty member selects the texts for his courses and believes that bargaining about this decision would deprive him of his academic freedom. In this instance we find some employees favoring a narrow scope of bargaining to maintain prerogatives they have exercised as individuals over the years while others who have not had this prerogative argue that it should be included within the scope of bargaining in order to obtain it.

Municipal Employees Generally

Legislative History

Although the 1959 Wisconsin statute, giving municipal employees the right to join unions and negotiate wages, hours, and working conditions with their employers is usually cited as the first state statute of this type, it is seldom mentioned that the initial law was essentially only a declaration of rights and contained no provisions for administration. In 1961 the law was amended to give the Wisconsin Employment Relations Board, subsequently renamed Commission

(WERC), the power to conduct representation elections, mediate disputes, arbitrate grievances, and administer the fact-finding procedure and select the ad hoc fact finders.

Ten years later the MERA was extensively amended.[8] Among other things it permitted negotiation of an agency shop (called a "fair-share agreement") and defined and excluded supervisors. Also, the unit-determination rules were changed to give the WERC greater powers to prevent what was considered excess fragmentation. Insofar as the scope of bargaining is concerned, the major changes made by the 1971 legislature were to state specifically that there was a duty to bargain in good faith and in disputes involving fire fighters and law-enforcement personnel, to replace the fact-finding procedures with binding arbitration.

Although most parties bargained in good faith in the 1961-71 period and indeed assumed that such conduct was required by the statute, the WERC ruled in the late sixties that the failure of a city to bargain in good faith was not subject to restraint as a prohibited practice (the Wisconsin euphemism for an unfair-labor practice).[9] The definition of collective bargaining adopted in the 1971 revision of the statute was more specific than the language of either the Labor Management Relations Act (LMRA) or the Wisconsin Peace Act governing private sector intrastate labor relations. Section 111.70(1)(d) of the 1971 MERA stated that:

(d) "Collective bargaining" means the performance of the mutual obligation of a municipal employer, through its officers and agents, and the representatives of its employees, to meet and confer at reasonable times, in good faith, with respect to wages, hours and conditions of employment with the intention of reaching an agreement, or to resolve questions arising under such an agreement. The duty to bargain, however, does not compel either party to agree to a proposal or require making of a concession. Collective bargaining includes the reduction of any agreement reached to a written and signed document. The employer shall not be required to bargain on subjects reserved to management and direction of the governmental unit except insofar as the manner of exercise of such functions affects the wages, hours and conditions of employment of the employees. In creating this subchapter the legislature recognizes that the public employer must exercise its powers and responsibilities to act for the government and good order of the municipality, its commercial benefit and the health, safety and welfare of the public to assure orderly operations and functions within its jurisdiction, subject to those rights secured to public employees by the constitutions of this state and of the United States and by this subchapter.

Subsequent to passage of the 1971 amendment to the MERA making bargaining mandatory, several decisions of interest were made. The essential question raised in these decisions was whether the bargaining law took precedence over city ordinances. In one instance, a county had an ordinance prohibiting retroactive pay increases and refused to bargain about retroactivity. A union prohibited-practice-complaint on this point was upheld by the WERC, which ruled that retroactivity fell within the wages, hours, and working conditions definition of scope in the bargaining statute.[10]

Another issue involving a conflict between a city ordinance and the scope of bargaining in the state statutes was "residency." This problem led to several declaratory rulings by the WERC applying in one instance to employees of a sewerage commission, in another to fire fighters, and in a third to police.[11] In all instances the WERC has ruled that the employer must bargain about residency on the ground that it is a condition of employment within the scope of the MERA.

Other Declaratory Rulings

In addition to the cases arising out of attempts by employers to exclude those conditions of employment covered by ordinances from the scope of bargaining, there were cases similar to those found in the private sector involving attempts by employers to exercise management rights unilaterally without prior bargaining.

In one instance a school board decided to subcontract to a private firm the food-service program in the school cafeteria. Until that time, cafeteria workers had been employees of the school board and were represented by a union in a collective-bargaining unit including custodial, maintenance, and cafeteria employees. The school board informed the union of its decision to take this step but refused to bargain about the matter on the ground that it did not have a duty to bargain about the decision to subcontract, although it acknowledged that it would have an obligation to bargain about the impact of the decision. The WERC ruled, however, that the school board had the obligation to bargain about the decision as well as its impact.[12]

In another case involving fire fighters, a village argued that it did not have a duty to bargain about premium pay for individuals assigned as dispatchers.[13] The employer argued that the bargaining statute reserved to management the powers and responsibilities to act for government and to assure orderly operations. The WERC ruled that the subject was within the scope of bargaining and that the village had a duty to bargain about it. The WERC noted in this decision and several others, however, that

such duty to bargain does not compel the Municipal Employer to agree to any proposal by Petitioner concerning such premium rate, nor does it require the Municipal Employer to make a concession with respect thereto.[14]

In practice, the parties are bargaining about such matters as residency, retroactivity, subcontracting, and premium pay. Municipal ordinances attempting to restrict the scope of bargaining have usually fallen before the power of the

MERA where the WERC has decided that the issue involved wages, hours, or conditions of employment. Special problems have arisen, however, among fire fighters, police, and teachers because of the existence of special state statutes regulating employment of these groups and also, in the case of the teachers, because of their interest in participating in educational policy decisions, and it is to these problems that we turn next.

Public-Safety Employees

Special Legislation

Police, deputy sheriffs, and traffic-patrol officers were not granted full collective-bargaining rights until passage of the 1971 amendments to the MERA. They were specifically excluded from the definition of covered employee by the original 1959 statute and in the 1961 amendments were only given the limited right to petition the employer for changes in wages, hours, and working conditions and to submit impasses about these matters to fact finding. Fire fighters, however, were not differentiated from other municipal employees under the 1959 law or the 1961 amendments.

The 1971 amendments to the MERA changed the situation in several respects. One 1971 amendment eliminated the former exclusion of law-enforcement personnel from the definition of employee and thereby brought them fully under the provisions of the MERA. As mentioned previously, another 1971 amendment, applicable to all municipal employees, provided that there was a duty to bargain, which, if violated, was subject to a prohibited-practice charge. In addition, the MERA was changed, effective in 1972, to provide for the replacement of fact finding by binding arbitration of interest disputes for public-safety employees only, that is, for police, deputy sheriffs, traffic-patrol officers, and fire fighters.[15]

Public-safety employees are considered separately for two reasons insofar as scope of bargaining is concerned. First, there is the question of the degree to which the powers of the police and fire commission (and police and fire chiefs) under section 62.13 of the State Statutes restricts the scope of bargaining under the MERA. Second, there is the question of whether ad hoc arbitrators may enlarge or restrict the scope of bargaining through their arbitral decisions.

WERC Decisions

The primacy of the MERA over the authority of the police and fire commissions under section 62.13 was enunciated by the WERC in the fall of 1973.[16] Essentially, it found that the subsequent statute took precedence over the earlier statute and that harmonization of the statutes required that the earlier statute setting forth the powers of the police and fire commissions must give way before the powers extended to arbitrators under the MERA.[17] The issue involved was whether a union demand for inclusion of discharge, suspension, and discipline in the grievance procedure ending in arbitration was outside the scope of mandatory bargaining because it took these statutorily protected powers from the police and fire commission and gave them to an arbitrator.

Other police matters the WERC has considered to be a part of wages, hours, and conditions of employment have been subject to prohibited-practice rulings. For example, in one case the employer acted unilaterally on promotion procedures and claimed that its managements rights under section 62.13 would be violated if it were forced to bargain about the subject. In line with its earlier decision on the relationship of the two statutes, the WERC ruled that such matters fell within the scope of bargaining defined in the MERA and ruled against the city.[18] In the same case, the WERC ruled that a demand to bargain about promotions to jobs outside of the bargaining unit was not a mandatory subject of bargaining because individuals holding such out-of-unit jobs were supervisory, managerial, or confidential employees who are not municipal employees under the MERA. The examiner also had occasion to declare that exemption of police from arrest and prosecution for offenses such as traffic violations for which nonemployees would be cited is an illegal subject of bargaining and that demands to substitute other forms of discipline for such offenses are not permissible.

In a case involving fire fighters, a city claimed that it did not have to bargain about the decision to lay off personnel because of its right to dismiss employees under section 62.13. In this instance, the WERC ruled that there was both a duty to bargain about the decision to lay off and about the impact of any layoff that takes place.[19] Insofar as minimum manning is concerned, another issue in the same case, the WERC ruled that the determination of the number of employees on duty at one time does not "directly and intimately affect"[20] the wages, hours, and working conditions and that therefore the employer did not have a duty to bargain about the decision. Implicitly, however, if not explicitly, the employer would have a duty to bargain about the impact of any manning schedule it adopts. Further exploration of the distinction between the duty to bargain about decisions in contrast to the more limited duty to bargain about the impact of the decisions is considered in the remarks about the scope of teacher bargaining because it is in that context that the WERC elaborated on the difference.

Arbitrator Decisions

In the WERC decisions in which it has said there was a duty to bargain about such matters as residency, retroactivity, subcontracting, discipline, layoff, and promotions, the WERC has enunciated the usual doctrine that such a duty does not imply the duty to agree to union demands on these subjects. Public-safety employees have the right, however, to take disputes about such matters to binding arbitration and by this process possibly can force a city to agree to demands it otherwise would oppose.

For example, in one interest arbitration, the size of the wage increase and whether employees could live outside of city limits were at issue. Under the "final-offer" selection procedure the arbitrator ruled for the union, primarily because he favored its position on wages, and thereby set aside the residency requirement that had formerly existed.[21] In another "final-offer" interest arbitration with multiple issues the arbitrator ruled for the union because he believed its economic package to be the more reasonable and as a consequence granted a demand, which in his words "would prohibit the Employer from establishing any new work rule, regulation or condition, or modifying any existing rule regulation or condition without first negotiating and reaching agreement thereon with the Association."[22]

So far neither the WERC nor the courts have been asked to make decisions relating to the question of whether the arbitrator has exceeded his authority insofar as the scope of bargaining is concerned. In the meantime, such issues as one or two officers in a squad car and whether or not fire fighters should be given educational incentive-pay programs have been referred to arbitrators.[23] Despite the broad scope covered by arbitral awards, there has not been an attempt by management to restrict them either through court action, appeals to the WERC, or the introduction of legislation on this point. If binding arbitration is extended to teachers, however, as is proposed in a bill pending before the legislature (A.B. 605, 1975), attention may be directed to this question because of the importance that school boards have given in the early seventies to attempts to clarify the scope of bargaining.

Teachers

School boards and educational administrators, like police and fire commissions and police and fire chiefs, found that the MERA prevailed over the previously enacted statutes upon which they had customarily relied. The basic WERC decision on this point was made in a case involving nonrenewal of a teacher contract under the Wisconsin school statutes. In that instance the Supreme Court of Wisconsin overruled the contention of a school board that it could refuse to renew teacher contracts under the school statutes without regard to the MERA. The court ruled that in the harmonization of the statutes, the MERA as the most recent one should prevail.[24]

Although this decision clearly established the primacy of the MERA, the interpretation of the MERA insofar as the scope of teacher bargaining was concerned, did not emerge until the WERC issued two declaratory rulings on this subject in the fall of 1974.[25] In its memorandum accompanying the declaratory ruling concerning the scope of bargaining the WERC stated:

We hold that matters, not concerning basic educational policy, which primarily affect wages, hours and conditions of employment, are subject to mandatory bargaining. We further hold that matters, which do concern basic educational policy, but by their impact secondarily affect wages, hours and conditions of employment, are subject to mandatory bargaining as to said impact.[26]

The WERC also noted that school boards were permitted to discuss educational policies with teachers and suggested that such discussions might promote the resolution of disputes.

In these two declaratory rulings the WERC established three categories of bargaining subjects and placed a list of specific items in each category. Category one decisions, which primarily affect wages, hours, and conditions of employment, must be bargained. These include such items as school calendar, number and timing of in-service days, discontinuation of requirement that teachers perform certain clerical functions, pay of department chairmen (an in-unit position), procedures used to evaluate teachers, access to teacher files and rules about the use of materials in the files, right of representation prior to discipline, use of the just-cause standard in suspension, discipline and discharge, teacher-layoff procedures, and relief of teacher responsibility in dealing with problem children.

The more conventional private-sector issues of wage and fringe matters of various sorts were not at issue because school boards were not challenging the duty to bargain about such items. Reflection about the above laundry list of items on which a school board has a duty to bargain because they primarily affect wages, hours, and working conditions suggests that most of these items have little importance in the field of educational policy, although it can be argued, contrary to the view of the WERC, that determination of the school calendar is a matter of educational policy.

In any event, the more controversial items are those in the second category established by the WERC—basic educational-policy decisions that secondarily affect wages, hours, and working conditions. The WERC stated that the impact of these decisions are mandatory subjects of bargaining but that the decisions themselves are not. Included in this category are items such as class size, remedial-reading programs, and summer programs. Under this ruling the school board can determine class size, whether to offer remedial-reading and summer programs of one kind or another, and need bargain only about the effect of the decision as distinguished from the decision itself.

If school boards were to follow this distinction insofar as class size is concerned, for example, it would set the class size and then bargain about premium pay for teachers with large classes. In actual practice, however, this has been sufficiently cumbersome that some school boards have chosen instead to bargain about class size directly. Absolute rigid restrictions on maximum size of class are not commonly found in contracts although many contain language establishing class-size standards and principles to which school boards will adhere when feasible.

The third category established by the WERC includes items not subject to mandatory bargaining. These are management functions that do not significantly involve wages, hours, and working conditions of teachers, such as selection and qualifications of individuals who would evaluate teachers and who would counsel teachers having professional difficulties, and the hiring of clerical aides. Insofar as clerical aides are concerned, the WERC ruled in effect that the school board must bargain with the teachers about whether the teachers could be required to perform certain clerical functions, but that the school board need not bargain about how such clerical functions would be performed if not done by the teachers. In actual practice, in some of the larger districts of the state, the teachers have sought successfully to represent paraprofessionals who in turn may have been assigned the clerical work that teachers successfully eliminated from their job requirements.

In essence the WERC rulings have interpreted the language of the MERA to provide for a broad scope of bargaining. The language, quoted previously has been relied upon almost literally by the WERC. It states that municipal employers must bargain about policy decisions that have an effect on wages, hours, and conditions of employment. It may not be broader than the language of the LMRA but it is more specific about the problem arising from the need to harmonize the rights of municipal management and those of its employees. Adjustments have had to be made in the traditional employment-relations policies of city councils, mayors, school boards, and police and fire commissions because of the advent of collective bargaining but the initial resentment against the process may be receding somewhat as the ground rules become clear.

In the field of teacher bargaining, as of the summer of 1975, educational-policy decisions and the impact of bargaining upon them is not attracting very much attention. Continued inflation and a depressed market for teachers have led teachers to concentrate on job-security items and compensation. Crucial demands at present seem to be focused on layoff-procedure language and protection of real wages. These traditional private-sector issues are not regarded by anyone as attempts to expand the scope of bargaining and, therefore, for the moment at least, scope-of-bargaining problems of teachers are not leading to impasses and attempts to obtain WERC declaratory rulings and court decisions.

The problem may become more important again in the future, however, because of pending legislation, court appeals of the WERC declaratory rulings, and new school-board positions that may be taken because of the declaratory rulings. The pending legislation referred to previously (A.B. 605, 1975) provides for arbitration of impasses reached in negotiating agreements. If an impasse arises, which includes the question of class size among the items at impasse, a school board may ask the WERC to rule that such item cannot be submitted to an arbitrator because it is not a mandatory subject of bargaining. This problem may be further complicated by the fact that the school board in question may have bargained about class size prior to the issuance of the WERC rulings but now argues that it need bargain only about the impact of class-size decisions. Finally, it should be noted that it is possible for either the circuit or supreme court to issue rulings that change the present WERC interpretation of the statute.

An Overall View of Scope-of-Bargaining Problems in Wisconsin

State Employees

Conceptually, the most intriguing scope-of-bargaining problem is the one faced by the state in its attempt to reduce the scope of bargaining with state civil-service employees. The management team, that is, the bargainers and the policy group with which these management bargainers consult, represents the governor and the legislature. In effect, management brings to the bargaining area those representatives who can determine legislatively the rules of the game. What the legislature has created it can amend and even terminate if it so desires. If the unions and the management cannot agree upon the size of pension-benefit increases, the management bargainers can either put their own position into effect legislatively, or, as is more likely, could exclude pensions from the scope of bargaining and then make changes of the type they had sought in bargaining.

Union reaction to this problem has not yet been officially enunciated. One possibility is that the unions might seek a constitutional amendment that would preclude legislative changes in the scope of bargaining. This objective might turn out to be unattainable politically and unions might turn instead to economic conflict. Unions in Europe, which are faced with a similar problem because most European government representatives who control the bargaining policy also guide the legislative process, rely upon demonstrations and strikes to persuade government either to agree to their demands or alternatively to agree to give up their sovereign powers over the issues in dispute and permit them to be resolved by arbitration. American unions may also decide to follow this approach.

It is not clear whether the scope of bargaining of state employees will expand or contract in the coming years—it may well do both, expanding in some areas and contracting in others. Pensions may be excluded from bargaining in the future but promotions and job-classification problems may be placed within the scope of bargaining. If faculty are granted bargaining rights, it is anticipated that this will lead to further problems about the scope of bargaining. Here, we may have the unusual situation in which some employees fight to exclude some issues from the scope of bargaining because traditionally these employees, under the banner of academic freedom, have had unilateral control in these areas. However, other employees who have had little to say about these same issues may wish to include them within the scope of bargaining.

Municipal Employees

Blue-collar and clerical municipal employees have engendered very few scope-of-bargaining problems in the last few years. For the most part, their situation is analogous to that of private-sector employees and employers have been willing to bargain about most of the conventional private-sector items with the exceptions of residency and retroactivity. These particular problems have been solved—that is, they are clearly bargainable—and arguments about the scope of bargaining are rare in the usual AFSCME-represented blue-collar and clerical-bargaining situations.

Public-safety employees have achieved their goal of bringing personnel practices of the police and fire chief into the bargaining arena and have sufficient scope to digest at present that it is doubtful whether they will be looking to expand it in the near future. For the most part, efforts are confined to attempts to make sure that the present scope of bargaining is not reduced. Fire fighters and police, for example, have introduced a bill (A.B. 321, 1975) that amends the police and fire statutes (Section 62.13) specifically to provide that provisions of a collective-bargaining agreement supersede the general civil-service law concerning police and fire fighters when the two are in conflict.

Over the years teachers in many districts have bargained about a variety of matters in the educational-policy area. In some instances, the bargaining has been informal and the results have not been reduced to contract language. In other instances, specific contract language provides for teacher input into educational-policy decisions. The requests for declaratory rulings by school boards in 1973 (discussed previously in some detail) are seen by the teacher unions as attempts to limit the scope of bargaining. Further attempts by some boards are seen by teachers in demands of boards to remove some items from the collective-bargaining contract and put them in the school-board manual.

At the same time as school boards attempt to limit the scope of bargaining, teacher unions are forced by market conditions to concentrate on job security and bread-and-butter items. Therefore, it seems likely that scope of bargaining by teachers will not expand greatly in the near future and even may be slightly reduced if the present management drive is successful.

So far as municipal-employee unions are concerned in Wisconsin, it appears that the 1971 amendments to the MERA have given them a broad scope of bargaining with which they are relatively content. Management attempts to reduce it seem to be confined primarily to teacher bargaining and to be somewhat minor. Union attention is focused more upon attempts to obtain the right to strike or to binding arbitration along the lines of the system used by Canadian federal employees. On the whole, therefore, it appears that the scope of bargaining of municipal employees will not change greatly in the coming years. The action insofar as scope of bargaining is concerned can be looked for among state employees presently covered by a separate statute, and among faculty who are, at this writing, not covered by any bargaining statute.

Notes

1. Ch. 612, L. 1966, State Employment Labor Relations Act (SELRA), Sections 111.80 to 111.94, effective January 1, 1967.

2. Ch. 509, L. 1959, Section 111.70, Wisconsin Statutes.

3. Section 111.91(1), SELRA, 1966.

4. Section 111.91(2), SELRA, 1966.

5. See "Report of Governor's Advisory Committee on State Employment Relations," December, 1970 (mimeo, Dept. of Administration, State of Wisconsin, Madison, WI), pp. 7-12.

6. Assembly Bill 475, L. 1971 effective April 30, 1972.

7. April 18, 1975 letter from Bronson C. LaFollette, attorney general to Anthony S. Earl, secretary, Department of Administration, identified as OAG 10-75.

8. Chs. 124, 246, and 247, L. 1971, Municipal Employment Relations Act (MERA) Sections 111.70-111.77 as amended, effective November 11, 1971 and April 11, 1972. (Chs. 247 providing for arbitration of public-safety employee disputes was enacted separately and became effective on the second date.)

9. City of New Berlin, WERC Decision No. 7293, 3/66; affirmed by Wisconsin Supreme Court in Madison School, 37 Wis. 2nd 483, 12/67.

10. Racine County Deputy Sheriffs' Association vs. Racine County, WERC Decision No. 10917-A, June 22, 1972, affirmed Racine County Circuit Court, File No. 72-493-CI & 72-630-CI, September 11, 1973.

11. WERC decision 11228-A, Milwaukee Sewerage Commission, 10/72; WERC decision 11406-A, City of Brookfield, 7.73, affirmed Waukesha County Ci. Ct. 7/21/74: WERC decision 12186-B, City of Clintonville, 7/74.

12. Local 152 Service Employees, SEIU, vs. Unified School District #1 of Racine County, WERC decision No. 12055-V, 10/74.

13. Firefighter Local 808, IAFF vs. Village of Shorewood, WI, WERC decision #11716, March 26, 1973.

14. Ibid.

15. Section 111.70(4) (jm) as added by Ch. 246, L. 1971 provided for

binding conventional arbitration for city of Milwaukee police only. All other public-safety employees in Wisconsin in municipalities of over 5,000 population were covered by section 111.77 as enacted by Ch. 247, L. 1971. Subsequently, when the law was further amended by Ch. 64, L. 1973, Milwaukee fire fighters were exempted from coverage and thereby reverted to coverage under fact finding and the lower population limit was dropped to 2,500. Section 111.77 provides for "final-offer (package) arbitration" unless the parties agree to proceed by conventional arbitration.

16. City of Sun Praire, WERC Decision No. 11703-A, September, 1973.

17. The theory set forth had been advanced previously in a case involving teacher statutes and had been affirmed by the Wisconsin Supreme Court.

18. City of Green Bay, WERC Decision No. 13252-B, and 12402-B, January, 1975.

19. City of Brookfield, WERC Decision No. 11489-B & 11500-B, April, 1975.

20. Ibid., p. 16.

21. City of Manitowoc, MIA-81.

22. City of Wauwatosa, MIA-41.

23. Adams County, MIA-66 and City of Cudahy, MIA-142.

24. Muskego-Norway School District No. 9 v. WERC, affirmed 35 Wis 2d 540, 1970.

25. City of Beloit, WERC Decision No. 11831-C, 9/74 and Oak Creek-Franklin Joint City School District No. 1, WERC Decision No. 11827-D, 9/74.

26. Memorandum Accompanying WERC Declaratory Ruling in City of Beloit, Decision 11831-C, 9/74, p. 18.

9

Themes and Issues—An Afterword

Bernard Ingster

In an unanticipated way, the report in Chapter 6 on the scope of public-sector bargaining in Texas—the only state discussed in the Taylor Conference, upon which this book is based, that statutorily declares public-employee collective bargaining to be against public policy—serves well to symbolize the national maturation of public-sector collective bargaining during the past 15 years.

Until 1973 Texas denied all public employees the right to organize for purposes of collective bargaining, but in that year the legislature determined that:

... collective bargaining is deemed to be a fair and practical method for determining wages and other conditions of employment for the employees who comprise the paid fire and police departments of the cities, towns, and other political subdivisions within this state. (Sec. 2[b] [1] of the Fire and Police Employee Relations Act)

The reason given by the legislature for extending collective bargaining only to these two groups of employees is:

A denial to such employees of the right to organize and bargain collectively would lead to strife and unrest, with consequent injury to the health, safety, and welfare of the public. (Sec. 2[b] [1])

Having crossed the line of granting recognition and exclusive representation rights to police and fire-employee associations, the legislature rapidly moved in the same act to define the scope of bargaining for these employees to include "wages, hours, and other terms and conditions of employment" and to bar strikes in the event of impasse in negotiations. (Arbitration is encouraged, but judicial determination of unsettled issues is required if arbitration is not selected by the parties.)

Thus, even Texas, without a comprehensive public-employee collective-bargaining statute similar to those of Michigan, New Jersey, New York, Pennsylvania, and Wisconsin—the other states whose experiences were described in this book—appears to be moving in a limited sense toward emerging, commonly shared patterns of experience and judgments about the issue of the scope of public-sector bargaining. In the latter named five states, the results of allowing public employees to engage in collective bargaining reveal, to a surprising extent, greater similarities than differences in the subject matters that are bargained.

This is noteworthy since the statutes involved are different in certain very significant characteristics. These range from the New York Taylor law, which has no management-rights provision and which prohibits strikes, through the Pennsylvania Act, which has an extensive, carefully stated description of the employer's exclusively retained rights and which grants a limited right to strike. Even the scope of bargaining in the federal sector, based upon a unique definition of collective bargaining and its supporting administrative practices, includes a range of issues and rulings that have readily identifiable counterparts in the brief bargaining history of many state-level governmental jurisdictions.

This chapter summarizes the patterns of experiences as they were described in the individual chapters in this volume. It is an attempt to state some of the major themes of current understandings about the scope of public-sector bargaining as well as to state several of the persisting issues about which no strong consensus has yet developed.

Influence of Differing Bargaining Units on Scope of Bargaining

Prior to the advent of public-employee collective-bargaining, civil-service legislation provided job benefits and protection to classified public employees on an "employer unit-wide" basis. Collective bargaining has introduced a somewhat greater attention to occupational and functional grouping of employees, and these separate groups, reflected in certified bargaining units, have differed—both statutorily and in the contracts they negotiate—in the subjects that have been bargained.

Separate public-sector contracts commonly have been written for clerical and blue-collar positions; law-enforcement personnel; fire fighters; basic-education teachers (through twelfth year of high school); higher education teachers; and a variety of employees in nonprofessional, technical positions as well as those in specialized professional functions such as social-service workers, nurses, and physicians.

In general, organized police and fire personnel have agreements that encompass a somewhat greater range of issues than do the contracts of employees in clerical and blue-collar units. These latter groups have tended not to press scope-of-bargaining claims beyond the conventional economic issues of private-sector bargaining.

Teachers and other professional employee groups have concluded agreements that address issues that both encroach upon or are included within the role of policy making of the employer. (The scope of bargaining is much broader than that found in police and fire negotiations.) Such participation in policy development by professionals is not, however, attributable to their involvement in collective bargaining.

As a characteristic of their performance of professional functions, teachers, nurses, physicians, and social workers have traditionally been involved to some extent in the development of policies relating to the service they provide. An administrator of professional functions, to successfully give leadership to professional employees, tends to attempt to build consensus support for a change in a rule or practice that directly affects the kind of quality of professional services offered. In the absence of such efforts, conflicts that are particularly bitter and long continuing tend to break out between the professionals and the administrators, and, most frequently, the issue is resolved to the advantage of the professionals. A professional practitioner frequently attempts to contribute significantly to the subject matter of the profession followed. Thus, inclusion in professional decision making is not thought to be unusual.

If the private-sector experience had been adopted completely in the public sector, the scope-of-bargaining questions would, of course, be readily resolved within the context of the longer National Labor Relations Act (NLRA) history. Yet in addition to the differences relating to the special interests of professionals during collective bargaining, public-sector bargaining units even of clerical and blue-collar employees face unique scope-of-bargaining difficulties. These arise because of existing and potential conflicts between a variety of statutes governing public-personnel relations and the efforts of the parties to conclude a bilateral collective-bargaining agreement.

Legal Framework of Public-Sector Bargaining

Of the enabling legislation (and presidential Executive Orders) in the seven public jurisdictions discussed in this volume, only the federal sector removes the traditional subject matter of collective bargaining—compensation and benefits— from bilateral negotiations and offers a limited area of bargaining around conditions of employment. Setting aside temporarily in this analysis both the federal practices and the special state-level legislation providing for police and fire-personnel bargaining, three strategies for structuring the scope of public-sector collective bargaining are discernible.

The New York law, except for one amendment, does not limit the scope of negotiations. In denying public employees the right to strike, and in attempting to provide for legislative review of bargaining impasses, the framers of the New York legislation sought to give meaningful participation in collective bargaining to public employees by granting the right to discuss—and negotiate, if possible —all subjects of interest to the parties. In 1969 the State Public Employee Relations Board (PERB) was given authority to determine improper practices.

The broad scope of bargaining permitted by the Taylor law has not created a large number of problems. Very few of the improper practices charges filed annually with PERB involve scope-of-negotiations questions. The issue is being settled at the bargaining table. In the eight years under the law, there has been no successful attempt—or particularly strong interest on the part of any constituency—to limit the scope of bargaining.

Despite scope-of-bargaining language in the Michigan statute that is similar to that of section 8(d) of the NLRA—the Michigan public employers must bargain in good faith with respect to "wages, hours, and other terms and conditions of employment"—the actual Michigan experience is not unlike that of New York.

Although it is too early to know, it is likely that the New Jersey experience will be comparable with that of New York and Michigan. New Jersey's Public Employment Relations Commission (PERC) will probably be an active locus of decision making on scope-of-bargaining questions.

A second strategy is evident in Pennsylvania. Here the framers of the legislation granted a limited right to strike—circumscribed by possible injunctive relief to the employer through the courts—but attempted to define carefully the inherent managerial prerogatives of the employer to prevent bargaining of these matters. There have been relatively few challenges to the scope limitations by unions either before the Pennsylvania Labor Relations Board or in the courts. Generally, the public-employee unions have succeeded in having their interests met at the bargaining table. In practice, despite the differences in the bargaining law, the outcomes of bargaining in Pennsylvania, as viewed from the perspective of scope of bargaining, have not been substantially different from the results in any of the other states. The greatest impact of the statutory differences has been in the carrying of negotiability of subjects into half of the legal strikes in Pennsylvania.

A third strategy for influencing the scope of public-sector bargaining was fashioned in Wisconsin. Here an initially unsatisfactory law, with extremely narrow limits for mandatory bargaining, was revised in 1971 to broaden the scope of bargaining while, at the same time, granting direct executive and legislative intervention into the bargaining process. With the employer's negotiators being designated by the governor's office, and by having eight of the most influential legislative positions represented in a committee that gives assent to economic offers, it is hoped that the interests of the public both in policy and economic matters can be protected.

The Wisconsin model—the particular effectiveness of which has not yet been clearly determined—does provide, in theory, the opportunity for the governor and the legislature unilaterally to deal with matters that are not mutually agreed upon during bargaining. For example, if the employer has a position on pensions that is not acceptable to the unions, the employer could, through unilateral legislative enactment, achieve a desired economic objective. Actually, however, the outcomes of bargaining in Wisconsin are very similar to those found in other states with comprehensive public-employee bargaining laws. In each case, the scope of bargaining has, in fact, been somewhat broader than is the case in private-sector bargaining.

An additional influence on the limits of bargaining exists in the statutes and regulations that may deal with the same subject matter that is being discussed in collective bargaining. No predominant pattern is clear, but it does appear as though conflicts between a bargained agreement and an existing statute are being resolved in favor of the negotiated settlement. Even in Pennsylvania, where the act specifically grants precedence to the laws of the state and home-rule communities, the burden is shifting somewhat to the employer to demonstrate that there is a clear legal prohibition to the implementation to a provision of a labor contract.

Civil-service statutes have also been superseded when the subjects of collective bargaining concern seniority, promotions, position classification, and layoff procedures. As in the private sector, many of these issues are able to be grieved to binding arbitration.

One additional "enlarging" factor in the scope of public-sector bargaining has been the growing acceptance from the private sector of the concept of mandatory bargaining on the *impacts* of management-policy decisions upon wages, hours, and conditions of employment. (In Pennsylvania, there is a requirement that the employer discuss the impacts of excluded subjects of bargaining as they affect employees' wages and conditions of employment.)

Although the distinctions between the substantial elements of a policy design and the impacts of that decision are real and can be described, even highly skilled negotiators on both sides of the bargaining table have difficulty walking this tightrope. At the minimum, the opportunity for enlarging the scope of issues to be bargained is achievable through a union's challenge of the "line" drawn by management. The potentials for facing impasse resolution by boards, courts, or arbitrators might result in a less-restrictive "management-rights" declaration by an employer than would otherwise be the case.

Public-sector collective bargaining has not yet clearly chosen a position on the private-sector experience governing mandatory, permissive, and prohibited subjects of bargaining. New York now is closest to the private-sector practice, and PERB uses three tests for mandatory subjects of bargaining. The subject:

1. Must be a term and condition of employment
2. Must be within the discretion of the employer
3. May not go to the mission of the employer

Michigan has adopted a different "balance-the-conflicting-demands" principle to deal with conflict over mandatory subjects of bargaining. Interestingly, to arrive at this principle the Michigan board considered concepts that were similar to some of the original New York Taylor Commission views on the scope of bargaining. MERC felt that since public employees had been denied the right to strike, there was no source of economic force that could push a public employer into the acceptance of union demands that infringed upon management functions. The only Michigan Employment Relations Commission (MERC) standard in this regard is that management should not be "unduly restrained"; all bargaining was seen to have some limiting effect on the freedom of an employer.

Some interesting anomolies exist in public-sector labor contracts on this issue. Agency-shop provisions exist in contracts where the subject is clearly illegal under a state law, and school-district employers have incorporated voluntarily into contracts provisions that are excluded from bargaining. There are some "citizen suits" developing in such cases, however, and these discrepant practices may not proliferate in the future.

On one subject—subcontracting—public employers and public unions are behaving like their counterparts in the private sector. The employers are pressing for a unilateral right to determine when a subcontracting relationship is appropriate, and the unions are pressing for prior notification, discussions, and negotiation about the matter. Public employers have not yet generally offered in their arguments on the matter all of the sophisticated private-sector employer viewpoints, and it is not yet clear that in the long term the private-sector experience will prevail.

Impasse-Resolution Practices

The public sector has witnessed a greater variety of experimentation with impasse-resolution procedures than has been the case in the private sector, and it is through the development of some of these techniques in the public sector that a greater use may then be made by private employers and unions.

Initially, public employers were extraordinarily hesitant about accepting grievance arbitration. (Their arguments about losing management prerogatives were not unlike those offered by private employers many years ago.) For some, these fears are easing. However, they probably contributed to a widespread public-sector preference for mediation and fact-finding processes, certainly less "threatening" means for attempting to resolve differences.

In New York the legislative hearing was to be the final stage for impasse considerations if all voluntary means proved fruitless.

Wisconsin has final offer arbitration containing multiple issues. Thus, if an arbitrator accepts an economic package, he or she may thereby also impose a new work practice. Complex issues, particularly during police and fire-fighters negotiations, frequently have been going to the arbitrators.

In Michigan the final-offer selection process is used during police and fire-fighter bargaining only with regard to economic issues. Conventional binding arbitration on noneconomic issues is retained, and some Michigan arbitrators have determined policies in some very novel areas.

In Pennsylvania unresolved police and fire-personnel disputes go to binding arbitration on all issues. These matters could—and do—include questions of scope of bargaining and unfair practices. There is no administrative agency to treat such matters for these employees. Act 111 of 1968 provides that there can be no appeals to the courts after an arbitration award, but there has been extensive litigation because employers have forced suits by the unions for implementation of the awards.

The relationship between the impasse procedures selected in a public jurisdiction and the breadth of scope of bargaining permitted is ambiguous. For example, the traditional determination of rules and work practices for police and fire fighters has been altered by the use of compulsory binding arbitration. The anxieties of public employers about losing their control of managerial functions have not been reduced by their experiences with some of the results of police and fire arbitrations. However, with the exception of New York State, there are no clear movements to attempt to fashion alternative procedures for adjudicating disputes about such matters as negotiability of subjects for these employees—procedures that might include an employee-relations-board determination for example. The problem for the public employer appears to be less acute with regard to other employee groups—such as clerical and blue-collar personnel and teachers. Perhaps the difference rests in the generally more restrictive use to which binding arbitration is put during the negotiations of contracts for this latter group of employees.

Special Interests of Public-Sector Employees

It is probably in the variety of special interests advanced in negotiations by public employees that some of the complex differences between public- and private-sector collective bargaining are displayed.

Public-safety employees have achieved strength in their bargaining relationships by gaining rights to participate in determining manning requirements and in the control of the nature of their assignments, two subjects that would most rarely be mandatory subjects for private-sector bargaining.

Public-school-district teachers frequently have contractually required joint study committees that review matters that would be regarded as exclusive management functions in other types of organizations. These employees have been most active in testing the limits of scope of bargaining.

Teachers are engaging in mandatory bargaining on subjects such as curriculum, classroom schedules, class size, selection of textbooks, planning of facilities, length of workday and year, and student disciplinary procedures.

As was noted earlier in this chapter, however, many of these subjects were not "exclusively determined" by school administrators before collective-bargaining rights were granted. Teacher committees were commonly used in curriculum development and textbook selection. "Good" architectural planning for new educational facilities required careful involvement of teachers in discussions with building designers to ensure that the latter understood the programs that would be offered in the new buildings. Thus, in many situations, the collective-bargaining agreement merely formally incorporated already existing, desirable forms of professional participation in management decision making.

Similarly, in higher education, faculties have retained in collective bargaining many traditional roles of governance that they exercised prior to bargaining. In a significant number of institutions, the faculties have increased their impact in setting salaries, defining work loads, and participating in tenure-granting procedures.

There has been one unusual condition in higher education, however. In some aspects of the teaching, research, and service roles of a faculty member, the unions have been pressed by their memberships to exclude from a collective, representational relationship those personal conditions of employment that are considered to be matters of academic freedom. For example, for these faculty members, personal selection of textbooks and teaching materials is not to become a matter of joint consideration with management. When such personal freedoms have not existed prior to bargaining, the union's negotiators are sent to the table to win such traditional academic privileges.

Finally, social workers tend to seek mandatory bargaining on client loads and client services, and their disputes with management on these issues have led to extensive litigation and have been important elements in strikes by these employees.

An Issue of Continuing Controversy

Not all of the raging dispute in public-sector collective bargaining has been between employers and unions. There has been profound disagreement among scholars and labor-relations professionals who are advocates of public-employee bargaining as to the differences between the nature of employment in the public and private sectors and the differences in the purposes and character of public- and private-sector employers.

The differing positions on these matters condition viewpoints about two fundamentally important questions associated with the granting of collective-bargaining rights to public employees. One of these—What shall be the scope of bargaining?—has been initially examined through the experiences of the seven jurisdictions studied in this volume. The second—Shall public employees be granted the right to strike?—influences and is influenced by the first question. The second question continues to ignite controversy. The essential evidence for forming a definitive judgment is still being collected.

Just one week prior to his death on December 15, 1972, Dr. George W. Taylor contributed his last writing to the Twenty-Fifth Anniversary Volume of the Industrial Relations Research Association, *The Next Twenty-Five Years of*

Industrial Relations. In Dr. Taylor's paper, entitled "Collective Bargaining in the Public Sector," he restated his persistently held positions that a public employer has a significantly different mission from that of a private employer and that the taxation and budget-making processes of government cannot be viewed as merely a different form of the sales and profit objectives in the private sector. He also continued to argue for the development of alternatives to the strike, and he cited once more the limiting effect on the scope of bargaining of providing a right for public-employee strikes. Dr. Taylor was not convinced that compulsory arbitration was the way out.

The public-sector experience, as revealed in the preceding chapters, appears to be yet too brief to help us decide upon this matter.

Pennsylvania does not plan to extend the right to strike to police or fire fighters, nor does it plan to curtail the right as it now exists for all other public employees. These decisions were made with the state having had experiences of an exceptionally large number of public-schoolteacher strikes and sanitation worker strikes of long duration that generated extensive hostility within the communities affected.

Michigan is considering legalizing public-schoolteacher strikes of limited duration, in effect recognizing a de facto condition of illegal teacher strikes.

New York holds firm to its view that the Taylor law strike prohibitions have served well both the public interest and public-employee interest.

In Conclusion

Within just a decade and even with relatively few opportunities for assessment, there is substantial evidence that collective bargaining in the public sector has taken solid hold as a new form of public-employee personnel relations. Neither the fears nor the promises of the early advocates and opponents of the process appear to have been decisively realized. Civil-service systems have been permanently altered. Public employers have expanded somewhat the opportunities for employee participation in the decisions of government. Informal personnel practices have been codified and published. The scope of collective bargaining is reflecting essentially the range of interests and concerns of employee groups that existed—and were given recognition—prior to the establishment of public-employee bargaining laws.

List of Contributors

John T. Dunlop
Lamont University Professor
Harvard University

Henry B. Frazier III
Executive Director
U.S. Federal Labor Relations Council

Ernest Gross
Extension Specialist, Chairman of the
    Public Education Department, and
    Director, Public Sector Collective
    Negotiations Project
Institute of Management and Labor Relations
University Extension Division
Rutgers—The State University of New Jersey

Robert D. Helsby, Chairman
New York State Public Employment Relations Board

James W. Klingler
Research Assistant
Temple University

Charles J. Morris, J.D.
Columbia University
Professor of Law
Southern Methodist University

Charles M. Rehmus
Professor of Political Science
The University of Michigan
Co-director, Institute of Labor and
    Industrial Relations
The University of Michigan—Wayne
    State University

Milton L. Rock
Managing Partner
Hay Associates

James L. Stern
Professor of Economics and Industrial
    Relations
University of Wisconsin

About the Editors

Walter J. Gershenfeld is a professor of industrial relations and Director of the Center for Labor and Human Resource Studies at Temple University. He has completed a study on productivity bargaining for the National Commission on Productivity and Quality of Work Life and was a contributor of a chapter on compulsory arbitration in Jamaica in *Compulsory Arbitration* (Lexington Books, D.C. Heath and Company). Dr. Gershenfeld is part of a team studying the contribution of the late Dr. George Taylor to the field of industrial relations. He is also a member of the National Academy of Arbitrators.

J. Joseph Loewenberg is a professor of industrial relations at Temple University. Among his research and demonstration projects for the U.S. Department of Labor was one on the use of neutrals to improve public-sector relations. He is the author of *Final-Offer Arbitration* (Lexington Books, D.C. Heath and Company) and senior editor of *Compulsory Arbitration* (Lexington Books, D.C. Heath and Company). Dr. Loewenberg is a member of the labor arbitration panels of the American Arbitration Association and the Federal Mediation and Conciliation Service.

Bernard Ingster is Director of Special Governmental/Educational Services for Hay Associates. He consults extensively with institutions of higher learning, particularly in the public sector, on improvements in human resource management practices. He is labor-relations policy advisor to the Commonwealth of Pennsylvania in collective bargaining with the faculties of the fourteen state-owned colleges and university. Dr. Ingster has written for personnel management handbooks and is regularly published by the *Journal of the College and University Personnel Association*.